ANTIQUITY AND THE MEANINGS OF TIME

A PHILOSOPHY OF ANCIENT AND MODERN LITERATURE

DUNCAN F. KENNEDY

I.B.TAURIS

LONDON · NEW YORK

In memory of

Rev. Thomas Henry Kennedy
1916 – 1970

A life metaphysical

NEW DIRECTIONS IN CLASSICS

Editors

Duncan F. Kennedy (Emeritus Professor of Latin Literature and the Theory of Criticism, University of Bristol) and Charles Martindale (Professor of Latin, University of Bristol)

Published in association with the Institute of Greece, Rome and the Classical Tradition, University of Bristol.

In the last generation Classics has changed almost beyond recognition. The subject as taught thirty years ago involved enormous concentration on just two periods: fifth-century Athens and late Republican Rome. There was no reception, virtually no study of women or popular culture, and little attention given to late antiquity. Today, Classics at its best again has an unusually broad interdisciplinary scope, and reaches out to the arts and humanities generally as well as beyond. It is just such a 'New Classics' that this exciting series seeks to promote – an open-minded Classics committed to debate and dialogue, with a leading role in the humanities; a Classics neither antiquarian nor crudely presentist; a Classics of the present, but also of the future. *New Directions in Classics* aims to do something fresh, and showcase the work of writers who are setting new agendas, working at the frontiers of the subject. It aims for a wide readership among all those, both within the academy and outside, who want to engage seriously with ideas.

TITLES IN THE SERIES

The Modernity of Ancient Sculpture: Greek Sculpture and Modern Art from Winckelmann to Picasso – Elizabeth Prettejohn

A Spectacle of Destruction: Pompeii and Herculaneum in Popular Imagination – Joanna Paul

Empire without End: Postcolonialism and the Ancient World – Phiroze Vasunia

Thucydides and the Idea of History – Neville Morley

The Reception of Virgil: Landscape, Memory and History – Juan Christian Pellicer

The Classical Tradition: Transmitting Antiquity and its Culture – Timothy Saunders

Antiquity and the Meanings of Time: A Philosophy of Ancient and Modern Literature – Duncan F. Kennedy

Published in 2013 by I.B.Tauris & Co Ltd
6 Salem Road, London W2 4BU
175 Fifth Avenue, New York NY 10010
www.ibtauris.com

Cover illustration: Oedipus answering the questions of the sphinx in Thebes, cup, 5th century BC. Apic/Getty Images.

New Directions in Classics Series: 1

ISBN: 978 1 84511 815 0 (hb)
ISBN: 978 1 84511 816 7 (pb)
eISBN: 978 0 85773 369 6
ePDF: 978 0 85772 216 4

A full CIP record for this book is available from the British Library
A full CIP record is available from the Library of Congress

Library of Congress Catalogue Card Number: available

Society and contemporary culture seem forever fascinated by the topic of time. In modern fiction, Ian McEwan (*The Child in Time*) and Martin Amis (*Time's Arrow*) have led the way in exploring the human condition in relation to past, present and future. In cinema, several cultural texts (*Memento, Minority Report, The Hours*) have similarly reflected a preoccupation with temporality and human experience. And in the sphere of politics, debates about the 'end of history', prompted by Francis Fukuyama, indicate that how we live is deeply determined by our relationship not only to place but also to the passing of time. But what did the ancients think about time? Is our interest in chronology a relatively recent phenomenon? Or does it go further back? In his major new work, Duncan F. Kennedy indicates that our own fascination with time-reckoning is by no means unique. Discussing a number of key texts (such as Homer's *Odyssey*; Sophocles' *Oedipus Rex*; Virgil's *Aeneid*; and Augustine's *Confessions*) and imaginatively setting these side-by-side with modern works (such as George Orwell's *Nineteen Eighty-Four*; the short stories of Jorge Luis Borges; and Martin Heidegger's *Being and Time*), he shows that, from era to era, and in different ways, human beings have uniformly striven to understand the unfolding of history and their relationship to it. This sophisticated cross-disciplinary book will appeal not only to classicists, but also to scholars and students in the humanities more broadly, as well as beyond.

Duncan F. Kennedy is Professor Emeritus of Latin Literature and the Theory of Criticism in the Department of Classics and Ancient History at Bristol University. In addition he is the co-editor, with Charles Martindale, of the 'New Directions in Classics' series published by I.B.Tauris. His previous books include *The Arts of Love: Five Studies in the Discourse of Roman Love Elegy* (1993) and *Rethinking Reality: Lucretius and the Textualisation of Nature* (2002).

CONTENTS

PREFACE

A n issue of abiding concern, time seems a particularly pressing one at the moment. Renewed interest in chronology and time-reckoning within specific cultural contexts; a readiness to experiment with temporality even in mainstream novels, cinema and television; the recent vogue for counterfactual history; reflections about the nature of time in physics; controversies in epistemology about relativism and in politics over 'the end of history' – all attest to current preoccupations with time. Whether events are seen as determined or as contingent deeply affects our sense of ourselves and our actions. Debates over concepts central to human experience (causation, choice, knowledge, identity, hope and desire) have often been related to human beliefs about time and the different ways we situate ourselves in relation to past, present and future. *Antiquity and the Meanings of Time* will engage with these issues, but first, a few remarks on what this book is not. It is not about ancient chronologies, which have recently received the expert attention of Denis Feeney in *Caesar's Calendar* (2007). Nor is it a history of ancient theories of time, of which the standard treatment remains Richard Sorabji's *Time, Creation and the Continuum* (1983). Nor is it a philosophical investigation of time *per se*, though the metaphysics of time cannot but come into the reckoning.

Rather, it takes as its point of departure Paul Ricoeur's influential observation in *Time and Narrative* (1984–88) that

> between the activity of narrating a story and the temporal character of human experience there exists a correlation that is not merely accidental but that presents a transcultural form of necessity. To put it another way, *time becomes human to the extent that it is articulated through a narrative mode, and narrative attains its full meaning when it becomes a condition of temporal existence.*[1]

The philosophical consideration of time, he suggests, leads to irresoluble aporias. He invokes, as many have done before him and many will again, Augustine's agonised reflection as he contemplates time in the *Confessions* (11.14.17): 'What is time?... We surely know what we mean when we speak of it. We also know what is meant when we hear someone else talking about it. What then is time? Provided that no one asks me, I know. If I want to explain it to an enquirer, I do not know.' That is not to rule out, even if we could, the question of the nature of time;[2] however, what we should not expect to come upon is a definitive answer. Aristotle looks outward towards the physical world to define time not as movement but as having 'something to do with movement' (though conceding also that 'it is impossible for there to be time if there is no mind – except that there might still be whatever it is that time is' [*Physics* 4.14]). By contrast, Plotinus insists that we turn inward (looking outward only to the eternity that time for him mimics), and Augustine develops this internalisation of time in his notion of the stretching out of consciousness (*distentio animi*). Ricoeur terms these approaches to time respectively the 'cosmological' and the 'psychological'.

The psychological conception of time can, he argues, legitimately be *added* to the cosmological conception but cannot *replace* it, and neither conception can absorb the other into a unified account of the nature of time.[3] 'A constant thesis of this book,' he remarks, 'will be that speculation on time is an *inconclusive* rumination to which narrative activity alone can respond.'[4] We may never be able to say, finally, what time *is*, but we can, through the various stories we tell, gain purchase on our experience of time. He asserts that 'what is ultimately at stake in the case of the structural identity of the narrative function, is the temporal character of human experience. The world unfolded by every narrative work is always a temporal world.' He then states what is the mantra of his work: 'time becomes human time to the extent that it is organized after the manner of a narrative; narrative, in turn, is meaningful to the extent that it portrays the features of temporal experience.'[5]

Although Ricoeur is the starting point for this book, it is not a book about Ricoeur nor a systematic critique of his ideas;[6] in that sense it is *after* Ricoeur. Nor is it a book exclusively about narrative, although the analysis of narrative will be a prominent concern. Genevieve Lloyd has suggested that Ricoeur's distinction between philosophy and literature in *Time and Narrative* is too rigid, and that philosophy also fashions its own sorts of 'fictions' through which we extend our understanding of what is problematic in the human experience of time.[7] She also points to the 'changes in the angle of intellectual vision' that philosophical writings have provided on the relations between time and consciousness. Gary Saul Morson has put it well:

> Intellectual models – whether pertaining to the natural or the social world, to history or psychology, to ethics or politics – implicitly or explicitly depend on a specific sense of time. Some of our schools of thought seek to transcend time, others to reveal the temporality of all things, but in one way or another our interest in time is chronic.[8]

So, *Antiquity and the Meanings of Time* will seek to address the questions raised by temporality in discourse more generally, and in particular the ways in which time is configured in acts of interpretation, including my own. The relationship between time and texts is a fiendishly complex one which I hope the chapters that follow will help to disentangle a little. The chapters each address specific issues which are adumbrated in the introductions, but arcs of argument bridge them. The issues raised are often ones of very long standing, but the texts from what we call 'antiquity' – a term that will come under scrutiny in the final chapter – continue to address these questions in fresh and unforeseen ways. Each chapter takes as its focus the analysis of a 'classical' text – Augustine's *Confessions*, Virgil's *Aeneid*, Sophocles's *Oedipus the King*, Livy's monumental history of Rome, and Lucretius's poetic exposition of Epicurean philosophy – but then brings in texts of other times and other provenances to tease out some of the interpretative issues raised in the course of reading them.

We hear a lot these days about research-led teaching, but this book is, unashamedly, the result of teaching-led research. For ten years at the University of Bristol, I co-taught a final-year undergraduate unit entitled 'Time, Temporality and Texts' which rejoiced in a wonderfully flexible syllabus that brought a welcome element of the unexpected into the learning experience we shared. Each cohort of students introduced me in their seminar presentations to books and movies I was unfamiliar with, and which wrestled with intriguing configurations of temporality; they kept me thinking with their enthusiasm, curiosity and insights, and with questions to which I knew I was responding inadequately. I was fortunate to have over that period three intellectually agile colleagues as co-teachers – Genevieve Liveley, Joanna Paul and Ika Willis – whose commitment to the pleasures and challenges of reading have made this the most enjoyable experience of my academic career. They will recognise here much that they have made me familiar with, but I hope they will find a thing or two to surprise them yet. When the time came to condense this into a book, I received help, guidance and encouragement, without which it would never have been completed, from Alessandro Barchiesi, Simon Goldhill, Stephen Hinds, Charles Martindale, Ellen O'Gorman and Alex Wright at I.B.Tauris – whose patience I have abused for long enough. The research and writing of the book was to a significant extent made possible by the award of a two-year Major Research Fellowship by the Leverhulme Trust, which is owed the greatest respect and gratitude by many for its continuing commitment, against the grain, to funding research projects that are open-ended and embrace a future that is, as yet, unknown.

1

DOES AUGUSTINE PUT HIS FINGER ON TIME?

I n *Time and Narrative*, Ricoeur's recourse to Augustine's *Confessions* is primarily as a philosophy of time, and it is remarkable, given his theme of time *and* narrative, how little attention he devotes to Augustine the narrator. I want to shift the perspective by considering Augustine in the first place as the narrator of his restless search for knowledge of God and of his own self from which his reflections on time emerge – reflections that focus on himself as author, reader and interpreter of texts. Why do issues of textuality – acts of reading, of writing, of language use and interpretation – loom so large in considerations of the human experience of time, and not only in Ricoeur? In the first section of the chapter, I explore the temporal dynamics involved in the narrative of the famous scene of the 'conversion' in the garden at Milan, and in particular the moment when Augustine responds to the prompt to 'pick up and read' the codex containing the writings of Paul. In the second section, I seek to relate Augustine's narrative and the temporalities it constructs to his philosophy of time, with particular attention to the way he manipulates tenses and the trope of apostrophe to construct a distinction between the flux of experiential time and a discursive time which seeks to look beyond that flux. The figures of the author and the reader are central to Augustine's thinking, and in the final section I explore how the *Confessions* can help us to think about how the temporal aspects of authorship and authorial intention, and how the interpretation of texts in and over time have been bound up with theological thinking – though not always in ways Augustine himself may have intended. The title of the chapter may sound flippant, but I trust the point of it will emerge in due course.

PICKING UP AND READING

Augustine's *Confessions* pose a considerable challenge to the modern reader. Often treated nowadays as autobiography (the first nine books draw on some events in his life, and in chronological order), the work does not sit comfortably in that category,[1] especially when it turns to reflect on memory in Book 10 and then to interpret the opening of Genesis in Books 11–13. Shortly before narrating his conversion, he addresses his 'Lord, my helper and redeemer' and says (8.6.13): 'I will now tell the story, and confess to your name [*narrabo et confitebor nomini tuo*] of the way in which you delivered me from the chain of sexual desire, by which I was tightly bound, and from the slavery of worldly affairs.'[2] However, although confession and narration are linked here, they are not identical. The act of narration is not addressed to God, who is all-knowing. When Augustine turns from the books he has written on himself and on the subject of memory (1–10), he addresses God and says (11.1.1): 'Lord, eternity is yours, so you cannot be ignorant of what I tell you. Your vision of occurrences in time is not temporally conditioned. Why then do I set before you an ordered account of so many things [*cur ergo tibi tot rerum **narrationes** digero*]?' Augustine's God isn't a reader and doesn't narrate – existing outside time, he doesn't need to.[3] A few lines later he draws attention to the limitations of human narration: 'See, the long story I have told to the best of my ability [*ecce **narravi** tibi multa, quae potui*].' Augustine exists in time, but is trying to make sense of a relationship with a being who exists outside time, and to understand himself in a way that, he believes, that being knows him. 'May I know you, who know me. May I "know as also I am known" (1 Cor. 13: 12)' are the words with which he introduces Book 10, in which he turns from the narration of the events of his life to explore the theme of memory, a key concern of any narration of the self. As Garry Wills puts it,

> More than any other writer – more than Bergson, even, or Proust – memory is the key to Augustine's thinking because he thought it the key to his identity. He knows who he is only because memory connects events in his life over time. Without memory he is a series of disjunct happenings – like an amnesiac he has no name, no connections with other human beings, and no clues to the existence and action of God. Memory creates the self.[4]

The *Confessions* reflect Augustine's 'inward turn' in search of the truth.[5] For whom, then, does he narrate? This is the question he posed to himself in 2.3.5 (*cui narro haec?*): 'Not to you, my God. But before you I declare this to my race, to the human race, though only a tiny part can light on this composition of mine.' If narrative is a constative act, to use the terminology associated with J.L. Austin's speech act theory,[6] designed to set out a state of affairs for Augustine and his human audience to the best of his ability, confession is a performative one, that seeks to bring about a state of affairs, his relationship to God. Each of these modes manipulates grammatical tense in distinctive ways, and that will be one of our concerns in what follows.

First, the role of narrative. If God is all-knowing, and thus only God's 'version' of Augustine's life could be the definitive one,[7] the readers of Augustine's text are beings in time and differ in what they regard as the climax of that narrative. In the words of Augustine's commentator, James O'Donnell, 'Bks 7, 8, and 9 each present crucial and essential scenes.'[8] Thus for Henry Chadwick, Augustine's encounter with Platonism and his attempts to achieve a union with God in Book 7 are a mystical experience 'through which he was confronted by the antithesis between his own impermanence and the eternal changelessness of the God who is';[9] but it is also the case for Chadwick that 'the vision of Ostia and the last hours of Monica form a climax in emotional intensity, and Book 9 is a turning point in the *Confessions*.'[10] However, Augustine's narration of his 'conversion' in the garden in Milan with which Book 8 concludes marks a pivotal distinction in this first-person narrative between a past and a present self, for this is a structuring division which the *Confessions* seeks to move beyond.[11] 'Conversion' has recently been seen as something of a misnomer, though it has become so deeply embedded in discourse about the *Confessions* that it is now difficult to uproot – though, as we shall see, the temporal perspective of the *Confessions* also gives it some rationale. Augustine did not 'convert' to Christianity in the garden (his encounter with the Neoplatonists of Milan had dissolved his intellectual objections to Christianity); rather he made the resolve to give up sex and to be baptised.[12]

The garden scene is actually the third of three interrelated stories of renunciation of the world in Book 8 of the *Confessions*. Earlier, his Neoplatonist confidant Simplicianus had recounted to Augustine the story of his friend Marius Victorinus, who, though a Christian believer in private, was reluctant to be baptised for fear that his pagan admirers would turn against him. Then Augustine's fellow-countryman Ponticianus tells him and his friend Alypius the story of two imperial agents who gave up their positions to become hermits after coming upon Athanasius's Life of the hermit Antony (8.6.14–15).[13] Scholarship dates the scene in the garden in Milan to 386 AD, and Augustine's account in the *Confessions* to about 397 or shortly thereafter, though notably Augustine himself does not use the public chronologies that were available to him. The *Confessions* is only incidentally an account of his 'public' life and does not seek to be interpreted in accordance with the limits such modes of ordering bring with them. As Donald J. Wilcox has put it, 'Writing of his private life, Augustine chose the dating system most appropriate to that subject: his own age. Furthermore he used his age to direct the reader away from a simple numerical chronology and towards the deeper realities Augustine saw in time.'[14] Or, as that other great North African philosopher of texts, meaning and time, Jacques Derrida, would put it: dates, timetables, property registers, place names are all 'codes that we cast like nets over time and space – in order to reduce or master differences, to arrest them, determine them.'[15]

An important aspect of those 'deeper realities' Wilcox refers to lies in the narrative form Augustine has adopted. From a narratological perspective, first-person narratives characteristically have what is termed a deictic past tense in relation to the moment of utterance or writing of the first-person narrator which constitutes the present of the teller of the story: the narrator 'points to' a moment in the experience of his or her earlier self ('deictic' is derived from the Greek verb *deiknumi*, 'to show'). Some recent experiments in first-person narrative, particularly in fiction, have sought to manipulate or even suppress aspects of this teller function, such as a determinable teller figure or moment of speaking, adopting what has been called the 'reflector' mode. This focuses on the experiences of the 'I' figure 'without evaluating them from the perspective of a teller who retrospectively views his or her former life and ensures narrative closure.'[16] The first nine books of the *Confessions* emphatically adopt the 'teller' mode, and in a manner that makes great demands upon the reader. James O'Donnell remarks,

> We are presented throughout the text with a character we want to call 'Augustine', but we are at the same time in the presence of an author (whom we want to call 'Augustine') who tells us repeatedly that his own view of his own past is only valid if another authority, his God, intervenes to guarantee the truth of what he says.[17]

In what follows, I shall jettison the ambiguous 'Augustine' in favour of a useful, if cumbersomely expressed, distinction between the narrated self and the narrating self who looks back on the narrated self. Each has his own temporality, his own experience of past, present and future. This junction of temporalities, which can be felt throughout the narrative portion of the *Confessions*, comes to dominate the narration in Book 8, and provides the framework for Augustine's subsequent meditations on time in Book 11. The narrating self, in the light of subsequent events, discovers significance in details and actions that have limited or no significance at the time for the narrated self; that significance was in some sense already there, had his earlier self but known it. Thus at the very beginning of Book 8, the narrating self addresses God and says, 'You put into my heart, and it seemed good in my sight that I should visit Simplicianus' (8.1.1), who tells him the story of the conversion of Victorinus. The narrating self, with the benefit of hindsight in the aftermath of conversion, sees God's providence (etymologically 'foresight') in what his narrated self experiences largely as a personal impulse.[18] The temporality of the narrated self's point of view is richly contextualised, and in this instance given a strong orientation towards a desired future that for the narrating self is now an achieved state: 'As soon as your servant Simplicianus told me this story about Victorinus, I was ardent to follow his example. He had indeed told it to me with this object in view' (8.5.10). The narrative weaves together these temporal contextualisations and re-contextualisations.

The disjunction between narrating and narrated self and the associated contrasts of perceived significance are particularly emphatic in the introduction to the second story of conversion in *Confessions* 8, that of the imperial agents, which Ponticianus will go on to relate (8.6.14):

> One day when Nebridius was absent for a reason I cannot recall, Alypius and I received a surprise visit at home from a man named Ponticianus, a compatriot in that he was an African, holding high office at the court. He wanted something or other from us. By chance he noticed a book on top of a gaming table which lay before us. He picked it up, opened it, and discovered, much to his astonishment, that it was the apostle Paul. He had expected it to be one of the books used for the profession [that of teacher of rhetoric] which was wearing me out. But then he smiled and looked at me in a spirit of congratulation. He was amazed that he had discovered this book and this book alone open before my eyes. He was a Christian and a baptized believer.

Some elements here ('a reason I cannot recall'; 'he wanted something or other from us') clearly mark out the temporality of the narrating self. In that retrospective view, details that may at the time have been important for the narrated self and for Alypius and have motivated their behaviour at that point fade into insignificance in contrast with others that have, in terms of what eventuated, come to take on a significance that they did not at the time have for his narrated self. For that earlier self, the visit of Ponticianus is a 'surprise' (the Latin uses the demonstrative *ecce* plus the present tense *venit* – 'look, Ponticianus arrives' – thus drawing the reader into the point of view of the narrated self); Ponticianus noticed the book of the apostle Paul 'by chance'. Its position on the gaming table may even serve symbolically to heighten the sense of the contingency of these events for the actors within the narrative, while from the narrator's perspective providing (i.e. 'looking forward to') a piquant juxtaposition of the narrated self's gaming past and his Pauline future.[19] Ponticianus's action of picking up the book and opening it – the very same codex that will play such a climactic role in the garden at Milan – foreshadows (for the narrating self and for readers already familiar with the outcome) what the narrated self will do with the book there. Ponticianus acts as a half-way house between the narrated and the narrating selves. While his astonishment and amazement signals that he shares the narrated self's sense of the surprise at seemingly 'chance' events, his smile suggests that he, a baptised Christian, shares some of the narrating self's sense that these are part of a pattern – a story – in which their causation will eventually (i.e. 'in the outcome') become clear.

As readers of Augustine's account of his conversion, we are drawn into the complex of temporalities the narrative constructs. The point of view of the narrated self is past in relation to the point of view of the narrating self. From the reader's perspective, the present time is taken to be that of the narrating self's utterance – and the narrating self's utterance is always the text's 'present' (no matter when, chronologically, the moment of reading takes place, late antiquity or the twenty-first century). Recall how O'Donnell remarked that 'We are *presented* with a character...but we are at the same time *in the presence* of an author...' Thus, in representing (making present once more) the conversion scene in *Confessions* 8, the narrating self *describes* how his earlier self, in spiritual turmoil, *went* into the garden of his lodging in Milan in the company of his friend Alypius 'where no one could interfere with the burning struggle with myself in which I was engaged, until the matter could be settled' (*donec exiret*, 8.8.19). The subjunctive mood in *donec exiret* takes us into the narrated self's point of view, determined to see a resolution to the issue, but not knowing the 'outcome' (*ex-ire*, 'come out'). Addressing God, the narrating self comments of his earlier self, 'You knew, but I did not, what the outcome would be.' The narrating self is now aware of that outcome, and so – in relation to his narrated self – has some slight intimation of God's superior knowledge.

The narrated self fervently desires conversion, but feels trapped in the agony of hesitation. As he is pulled spiritually to and fro, eight paragraphs of narrated time elapse (8.8.20–8.11.27) since the narrating self brought Alypius and the narrated self into the garden in Milan. The reader is kept waiting upon the outcome too. A ratio is established in which the narrated self stands in relation to God as the reader does to the author of this text. Alypius has not been mentioned in the meanwhile, but at length a further reference to him in 8.11.27 signals retrospectively his presence throughout, a counterpart to the reader's suspense, as well as a marker of the shift from description of inner turmoil to that of external action: 'Alypius stood quite still at my side, and waited in silence for the outcome (*exitum*) of my unprecedented state of agitation.' Within the narrative, Alypius acts as an external observer of what could be seen or heard, but not, from his inevitably restricted human viewpoint, of what was going on 'inside' the narrated self during those moments, which is known to God and, in a more restricted way, to the narrating self. Following the conversion, Alypius needs to be told what has happened, just as the narrated self has to find out what had been going on in Alypius's mind (8.12.29). However, although the conversion is an event internal to the narrated self, Alypius's presence acts as testimony to its historicity.[20]

In a storm of tears, Augustine gets up from beside Alypius and throws himself down 'somehow under a certain figtree' (*ego sub quadam fici arbore stravi me nescio quomodo*), and as his tears flow profusely, he addresses God repeatedly '(though not in these words, yet in this sense): "How long, O Lord? How long, Lord, will you be angry to the uttermost? Do not be mindful of our old iniquities."' The vagueness ('somehow', *nescio quomodo*) indicates a lack of interest on the part of the narrating self in that detail, a feature to which we shall return.[21] The *presence* of the narrating self is signalled also in the phrase 'though not in these words', as he frames his earlier self's cry in a combination of the words of Psalm 6:4 and 78:8. At first sight, this may seem a careless attitude to 'how it actually happened', but for the author of the *Confessions* the truth of the matter, insofar as it can be humanly ascertained, lies in the combination of the points of view of the narrated and narrating self. The narrating self, at this stage the bishop of Hippo and deeply engaged in explicating the Psalms,[22] uses biblical language and reference in a way that his narrated self ten years earlier may not have. It is in re-present-ation, the superimposition of one 'present' upon another, that humankind can fashion the truth. Augustine writes at 10.1.1, '"Behold, you have loved the truth" (Ps. 51:8), for he who "does the truth comes to the light"

(John 3:21). This I desire to do, in my heart before you in confession, but before many witnesses with my pen.' (*ecce enim* **veritatem** *dilexisti, quoniam qui* **facit eam** *venit in lucem. volo* **eam facere** *in corde meo coram te in confessione, in stilo autem meo coram multis testibus*). The truth is something he wishes to *make* (*facere*), and his desire for the truth of his conversion lies in the narration he makes, in the complex of temporalities it presents. The truth he fashions requires witnesses: the readers of the *Confessions* reprise the role of Alypius in the garden.

He presents his earlier self as tossing forth wretched cries (*iactabam voces miserabiles*): 'How long, how long is it to be?' An unidentified voice responds, 'Tomorrow, tomorrow', and the narrated self responds, 'Why not now? Why not an end to my impure life in this very hour?' The rhythmic repetitions in the interchanges of these conflicting voices, represented as oriented to the point of view of the narrated self, and internal to him, abruptly give way to something else, seemingly external: 'suddenly I heard a voice from the nearby house chanting as if it might be a boy or a girl (I do not know which), saying and repeating over and over again "Pick up and read, pick up and read [*tolle, lege*]."' The Latin word translated by 'suddenly' here, *ecce*, is a demonstrative interjection that graphically presents the narrated self as drawing attention to something apparently external that attracts his attention at that very moment; what Chadwick translates by a past tense ('I heard') is in the Latin a present (*audio*, 'I hear'), which aligns us with the present of the narrated self and invites us to share his temporal experience. O'Donnell notes that *ecce* is a favourite word in the *Confessions*, occurring no fewer than 115 times. He describes it as 'a spoken punctuation mark, adding emphasis', an observation to which we shall return shortly; in addition, he draws attention to the fact that in Book 8 this use of *ecce* and the one of Ponticianus's 'surprise' visit (8.6.14) are 'the only ones not in direct discourse' (i.e. related to the voice of the narrating self), thus further binding together those two scenes.[23]

The narrated self is depicted as initially striving to understand the command to 'pick up and read' in terms of its worldly associations, as he tries, unsuccessfully, to remember a children's game in which such a chant is used.[24] 'As if it might be a boy or a girl (I do not know which)' aligns us, in the temporality of the narrated self, with an access of confusion and hesitation that casts doubt on such attempts to understand: 'I checked the flood of tears and stood up. I interpreted it solely as a divine command to me to open the book and read the first chapter I might find.' In the Latin, the past tenses used in checking his tears and standing up (*repressoque impetu lacrimarum surrexi*) are combined with the present participle *interpretans*, suggesting that the realisation that it was a divine command is

> exactly simultaneous with and causative to stopping the tears and getting up. Thus A[ugustine]'s own first reaction as he lived through it was to think it material; his mature reaction then and ten years later was to be agnostic about the event, but to interpret it unambiguously as a divine command.[25]

With the passage of time, the narrating self feels no need to revise this earlier judgement of his narrated self.

The narrated self returns to Alypius, where he had left 'the book of the apostle', 'seized it, opened it and in silence read the first passage on which my eyes lit'. His actions are reminiscent of the practice known as the *sortes biblicae*, opening a book of scripture, supposedly under divine direction, reading the first words that meet the eye and applying them to one's circumstances.[26] In this case, the passage on which his eyes light comes from Paul's Epistle to the Romans 13:13–14: 'Not in riots and drunken parties, nor in eroticism and indecencies, not in strife and in rivalry, but put on the Lord Jesus Christ and make no provision for the flesh in its lusts.' This proves sufficient for the narrated self: 'I neither wished nor needed to read further. At once with the last words of this sentence [*statim quippe cum fine huiusce sententiae*], it was as if a light of relief from all anxiety flooded into my heart. All the shadows of doubt were dispelled.' *Statim*, 'on the spot' or 'immediately', reduces the duration of this event towards zero. Eric Jager encapsulates the remarkable temporal characterisation of this scene of reading: 'all has happened as though "in no time". The flash of readerly understanding, which changes Augustine's life in the twinkling of an eye, points not only backward and forward in time but also beyond time into eternity', and he notes that there 'is no verb, no linguistic marker of temporal process, in the phrase that describes the act of reading itself'.[27] A person performing the *sortes* experiences a sense of the most acute contingency: the book is opened apparently at random, but the words the eye lights upon may seem to have a peculiar significance in respect of circumstance, hope or aspiration. As an avid reader of the apostle's works, it is possible that the narrated self had read these verses before and even pondered their applicability to his own circumstances, though a detail we will discuss in a moment suggests that he may not have been familiar with this text.[28] As O'Donnell remarks, 'the effect of the garden scene is lost unless the verse strikes A[ugustine] as apt by sheer happenstance.'[29] In the performance of the *sortes*, the sense of randomness and chance in opening the book is seen as a function of the narrated self's restricted point of view and imperfect understanding in contrast with those of the author of the larger story of which it is part. As Henry Chadwick puts it, 'Augustine did not believe in "chance", which he thought merely a word for describing an event when we cannot discern the cause.'[30]

The *sortes* scene has not been exhausted yet. The narrating self continues immediately (8.12.30), 'Then I inserted my finger or some other mark in the book and closed it' (*tum interiecto aut digito aut nescio quo alio signo codicem clausi*). The curiously imprecise alternatives 'my finger or some other mark' may indicate the narrating self's retrospective lack of interest in this detail, but his reference to the finger may have an importance to which he has not drawn explicit attention. He continues (my emphasis),

> With a face now at peace I told everything to Alypius. What had been going on in his mind, which I did not know, he disclosed in this way. *He asked to see the text I had been reading. I showed him* [*petit videre quid legissem. ostendi*], and he noticed a passage following that which I had read. *I did not know how the text went on* [*ignorabam quid sequeretur*]; but the continuation was "Receive the person who is weak in faith" (Rom. 14:1). Alypius applied this to himself, and he made that known to me.

Alypius had never suffered the sexual addiction that plagued Augustine, but he had problems in committing himself to Christianity, which are resolved in this moment.[31] For Alypius, the experience is similar to that of the *sortes*, and for the narrated self, who was unaware of how the text went on, this seems like a confirmation or an aftershock of that first experience. Alypius asks to see the text the narrated self has been reading. How does he show the text to him? Presumably by pointing to it with the finger he has used to bookmark the page of the codex; and that raises the possibility that when he performs the *sortes* he similarly uses his finger to point to the passage 'on which my eyes lit'.

This scene may well have been the source of some anxiety to the narrating self. Earlier in the *Confessions* (4.3.5), he reports a discussion he has with an eminent physician called Vindicianus, which has induced him to question his belief in astrology (a feature of the Manicheanism he then espoused but later came to reject):

> I asked him why it was that many of their forecasts turned out to be correct. He replied that the best answer he could give was the power apparent in lots, a power everywhere diffused in the nature of things. So when one happens to consult the pages of a poet whose verses and intentions are concerned with a quite different subject [*de paginis poetae cuiuspiam longe aliud canentis atque intendentis*], in a wonderful way a verse often emerges appropriate to the decision under discussion. He used to say that it was no wonder if from the human soul, by some higher instinct that does not know what goes on within itself [*nesciente quid in se fieret*], some utterance emerges not by art but by 'chance' [*non arte sed sorte*] which is in sympathy with the affairs or actions of the inquirer.

At the time when the Bishop of Hippo was composing the *Confessions*, he still maintained an uneasy toleration of the *sortes*, so long as the book consulted was the Scriptures and the consultation was for a religious not a secular end.[32] His comments here suggest that the significance of a text for a reader may be quite different from what its author intended (cf. *intendentis*), and that the reader never wholly knows what is going on within himself (*nesciente quid in se fieret*).

The process of reading presented here is comparable to the *sortes* (cf. *non arte sed sorte*), though once more there is no explicit discussion of how one's attention is drawn to the passage in question or what physical activity it entails. That it involves pointing may be elided here and in the conversion scene because it is an action that Augustine elsewhere is dismissive of. In his dialogue *The Teacher* (*De magistro*), 10.34, he asks his interlocutor to suppose that we hear the word 'head' for the first time, and it is pointed out to us:

Aiming with the finger can only signify what the finger is aimed at, and it's aimed not at the sign but at the bodily part called the head. Consequently, by aiming the finger I can't know either the thing (which I knew already) or the sign (at which the finger isn't aimed).

I don't much care about aiming with the finger, because it seems to me to be a sign of the pointing-out itself rather than of any things that are pointed out. It's like the exclamation 'look!' [*sicut adverbium quod 'ecce' dicimus*] – we typically also aim the finger along with this exclamation, in case one sign of the pointing-out isn't enough.[33]

This dismissiveness is associated with his epistemology and theory of language. Early on in the *Confessions* (1.6.8), Augustine has been fascinated by the attempts of his infant self to communicate his desires. In an effort to convey his meaning to adults, who 'were external to me and had no means of entering my soul,' he says, 'I threw my limbs about and uttered sounds [*iactabam membra et voces*], signs resembling my wishes, the small number of signs of which I was capable but such signs as lay in my power to use.' Though they do not go into the possible significance of the resemblance, commentators on the conversion scene in the *Confessions* point out that a phrase used to convey the anguished cries of the narrated self, *iactabam voces miserabiles*, recalls the actions of the infant, inviting comparison between the frustrated infant trying to communicate with adults and the soul seeking conversion appealing to God. The infant, the baby incapable of speech (*infans*), learns how to talk not simply through the formal teaching of words, Augustine suggests, but by the gestures of those teaching them, 'the natural vocabulary of all races [*tamquam verbis naturalibus omnium gentium*]... made with the face and the inclination of the eyes and the movement of other parts of the body' (1.8.13). For Augustine, when the eyes 'light upon' something, as they do with the text of Paul in the conversion scene, they actually reach out and touch it.[34]

In Plato's dialogue on language, *Cratylus* (422d–e), it is suggested that, if communication took place solely through pointing, misunderstanding would be avoided.[35] Augustine is justified in *The Teacher* in seeing what philosophers call 'ostensive definition' as an inadequate theory of meaning,[36] but throws the baby out with the bathwater in being so dismissive of pointing. In a superb analysis of the complexity – and peculiarly human capacity – of pointing, Raymond Tallis explores how the gesture brings together what he describes as the producer, the consumer and the pointee:

> Identifying the act as one of pointing should not be too difficult, if only because there are relatively few reasons for holding up one arm and making it and the index finger stick out in what we call the "indicative" mode or mood. Pointing postures are assumed only for the sake of pointing; they rarely happen accidentally or as part of other actions.

The gesture, seemingly so instinctive, so 'natural' as Augustine puts it, so easy to recognise, is in fact a rather demanding one, Tallis suggests:

> What is so difficult about it? Quite simply this: in order to locate the pointee, the consumer has to adopt the position of the producer. Clearly we do this mentally, not bodily, though when pointing fails and we cannot see what the other person is pointing out, we might come close to her and look along her arm as if along a telescope... Normally, though, the consumer has to cast herself in her imagination out of her own body and mentally look along the line drawn in space by the arm and index finger extending from the producer's body. The consumer, that is to say, has to put herself in the producer's body. This is a rather remarkable thing to do: it amounts to an, admittedly minor and temporary, but nonetheless real, abdication from the sense that one is at the centre of those things that are lit up in one's sensory field; that one is the centre of the experienced universe.[37]

The importance of this cannot be underestimated. Tallis argues that

> this voluntary displacement of the human subject from the material centre of his world is a first step in the growth of an important intuition: that one is part of something greater than one's self and greater than the parish uncovered by one's sense experience; that one is part of an explicit community of subjects; and, ultimately, that one is an atom or unit of a society.

It signals an awareness of the minds of others, and that their perspective or so-called viewpoint on the world is different from one's own. This helps us to grasp the importance of the presence of Alypius in the conversion scene. He does not know what is going on, and needs to be told; he does not know which bit of the text the narrated self has been reading, and has to have it pointed out to him. Tallis remarks that the 'point of pointing something out to another is to amend a perceived deficit in their knowledge, or experience, or awareness'.[38] The narrated self points to the passage in the text that has struck him so forcefully, and Alypius in turn points to something the narrated self explicitly remarks that he had not noticed. It is crucial to the act of pointing that it is deliberate: 'pointing does not have meaning by accident; nor is the meaning it has usually accidental... That which is meant – the pointee that is pointed to – is *meant to be meant*.'[39] It is, precisely, *intentional*: you stretch out in its direction (Latin *in-tendere*). The producer seeks to do something with the mind of the consumer. To point to is to point out, and the producer seeks to solicit the *attention* of the consumer, to get the consumer to adopt the viewpoint of the producer and in turn to 'stretch towards' (Latin *ad-tendere*) the pointee and the meant meaning associated by the producer with it.

However, we need also to consider the narrated self's performance of the *sortes* in this light. When Alypius asks what has happened, the narrated self points to the text, an action that is easily encompassed in Tallis's dynamic of producer, consumer and pointee. But, in the case of the narrated self's own moment of enlightenment just previously, who is the producer and who the consumer in this act? Although the narrated self rushes back to where Alypius is sitting to get the book, this performance of the *sortes* is presented as a solitary act that, for the moment, excludes Alypius and is not meant for him: 'I seized it, opened it and in silence read the first passage on which my eyes lit.' Whether he directed his index finger to the passage in Romans, or even if his eyes just lit upon it, how does this relate to the dynamics of pointing that Tallis discusses? The narrated self's attention is drawn to the passage, but by whom? It corrects a deficit of knowledge or awareness, to be sure, but the point about the *sortes* is precisely that the act of pointing is not entirely deliberate, at least on the narrated self's part, even though the meant meaning becomes immediately clear to him. One answer would be to say that the narrated self's self is not entirely present to itself, a division in microcosm of the one we posited in relation to the narrating self and the narrated self. The act of pointing then signifies a particular instant or moment (what in Latin is called *punctum temporis*, a 'point in time', from the verb *pungere*, 'point') of realisation, of *becoming* one's self. Who is doing the pointing and who means the meant meaning are both rendered problematic in the pointing enacted in the performance of the *sortes*. Another answer would be to say that the 'hand' of God is implicated in this particular act, the human hand with its 'index' finger (created in God's image) its proxy in the temporal world, pointing to a truth that escapes the flux of time.

Whatever one's feelings about this theological gloss, the performance of the *sortes* can serve to crystallise a number of important entailments of the act of pointing which Tallis discusses precisely in such a way as to distance himself from the theological. Pointing gives rise to what Tallis calls 'indexical awareness': human beings are explicitly related to the objects within their sensory field, and the act of pointing shows us as aware of those objects as arrayed in relation to the self – near or far, here or there, left or right, and so on. This awareness is reflexive, centred on the embodied subject – designated as 'I' – aware of those objects that confront it within its field: 'Pointing makes the relationship between the embodied subject – present to itself among the objects that are present to it – more explicit'; Tallis describes this indexical awareness as 'the ground floor of distinctively human consciousness'.[40] The action is never (normally) a solitary or solipsistic one, and though it often draws attention to an object within a shared visual field, Tallis notes that the producer and the consumer do not have to share such a field:

> When you are pointing to an object that I cannot see, and which is actually beyond the horizon of my visual field, you are affirming the existence of a world lying outside of what I can sense. You are affirming possibility beyond actuality by pointing to a particular possibility that I cannot see … what is actual for one person is proposed as a possibility for another.[41]

Pointing highlights not only what is revealed but also what is concealed. The 'beyond' has two dimensions, the spatial and the temporal: 'When you point to something you can currently see and I cannot, the pointee is located not only in a spatial beyond but, so far as I am concerned, in a temporal beyond. You are pointing to a future experience I might have if I follow your instructions to attend.'[42] For the consumer, the temporal beyond may be 'not-yet', but it could also be 'no longer'. From the perspective of the producer, what is pointed to is present and in the present: 'the tense of pointing is *now*'[43] – the tense we call the *present indicative*.

This brings us to language, which can have a directly 'deictic' function of pointing things out, as do exclamations such as 'look!' or *ecce* (as Augustine himself remarked);[44] or so-called demonstratives such as *this* and *that*. Verbs are said to have an 'indicative' mood, and tenses, which point to the no longer, the now and the not-yet. Thus language is at the heart of what Tallis calls 'deindexicalized awareness', the capacity to draw attention to and point out (rather than at) what lies beyond the immediate sensory field; words can 'open up the sense of the there and then, the general elsewhere and the no-when'.[45] Verbs also have a subjunctive/optative mode, the mood that points not to actuality but to potentiality or desire. 'Pointing,' he remarks, 'stands on the borderline between enhanced indexical awareness and deindexicalized awareness, where that of which I am aware is no longer related to my body or, indeed, my existence.'[46] Tallis draws our attention to Raphael's Vatican fresco *School of Athens*, in which Aristotle gestures to the ground and the world of sensible experience while Plato's index finger points vertically up to the heavens, the realm of pure intelligence. He explicitly distances himself from the theological by referring to deindexicalised awareness as the 'everyday transcendent', explaining that the transcendent, 'which is the most salient condition of our being able to point, is rooted in the intuition of the hidden, in the presence or reality of that which is unobserved, absent, beyond'.[47]

The object thus pointed out may be in the world, past, present or future, actual or potential, or, as in the conversion scene, in a text. Characteristically in the latter case, as we point to what interests us, we use the present tense: 'here, Augustine *says*'.[48] The historical moment of the inscription of the words of a text gives way to a temporality of writing and reading with its own 'now' as it becomes the object of attention, indeed an object with the capacity for a repeated attention that forever situates itself in some or other reader's here-and-now. The pointing finger plays its part here too. The age that rejoices in the name 'digital' has an extended index finger in the 'point and click' symbol used in various graphical user interfaces. Books that profess a relationship to knowledge usually have an 'index' through which their authors point you to what you are interested in. But the pointing finger can be an indication of a much deeper process of engagement and self-realisation associated with the reading of texts. In his study of the symbols that readers have written in the margins of the manuscripts and books they have owned, William H. Sherman devotes a chapter to those representations of small pointing hands, often highly elaborated, which draw attention to something in the text that has caught the reader's interest.[49] In the absence of an accepted technical name, Sherman has advocated the term 'manicule' ('little hand').[50]

The use of such manicules goes back at least to the twelfth century AD and they were frequently deployed (in styles that were as distinctive as handwriting) by humanists such as Petrarch, Boccaccio and Bembo. 'The practice seems to die out as we move through the eighteenth century and into the nineteenth century,' Sherman notes with regret.[51] From this very period, there is a striking reference not simply to the readerly practice of annotation, but to the way in which such marks can form a record, or be seen as evidence, of moments in which a sense of self is established. In Chapter 7 of Pushkin's *Eugene Onegin* (published in 1830), Tatiana visits the hero's country estate, deserted by him after he has killed his friend Lensky in a duel. She is drawn to its study, and weeps as she opens and avidly reads the volumes therein, encountering a 'different world' (7.21) and pondering the nature of the man, distant emotionally as well as physically, whom she loves (7.23):[52]

There were preserved on many pages
The trenchant marks of fingernails,
With them the watchful girl engages
As if she were deciphering spells.
Tatiana saw with trepidation
What thought it was or observation
Had struck Onegin, what they meant,
To which he'd given mute consent.
And in the margins she encountered
His pencil marks by certain lines.
Throughout, his soul was by such signs,

Without his knowing it, expounded,
Whether by cross, by succinct word,
Or question mark, as they occurred.

The practice of marking one's books with a fingernail was a familiar one at the time.[53] The index finger points not only to a specific portion of text but also draws attention to the 'now' of the reader reading it; a mark made there signifies the moment of the reader's realisation of meaning – of the text or the self. For Tatiana, such traces of Onegin's body left on his books are residues of his presence and somehow hint at 'the true persona/To sigh for whom it is her lot,/By fate united to this stranger' (7.24) – though ultimately the man she so desires to know, and to whom she feels bonded across distances of time, space and circumstance by 'fate', remains an enigma to her.

The index finger, and the hand more generally, articulate the human relationship to time. As well as the finger that points to a moment of realisation, the hand grasps in a gesture that seeks to *maintain* (from the Latin *manus*, hand, and *tenere*, hold, which also gives us the French for 'now', *maintenant*) that intimation of presence and eternity over time, the act of *comprehension* (from *comprehendere*, grasp) which we express in our *concepts* (from *cum* plus *capio*, take hold of). These terms relate strongly to the issue of knowledge, but in the case of Augustine's account of his gestures in the garden in Milan, the issue is not, or only incidentally is, that of information transfer: the words his narrated self reads as he performs the *sortes* do not tell him much that he doesn't already know, nor does his narrating self write the *Confessions* to tell us the life and times of some rake from North Africa. Rather, like Tatiana, Augustine is not looking for information so much as seeking presence – between God and himself and between himself and the reader. What is crucial for this is the *representation*, here and now, of the person in question being presented with the gift of presence. And how did we grasp this? By reading the *Confessions*, which point our attention towards, and so make us (no less than Alypius) again and anew witnesses of, the scene in the garden and the truth realised there.

TIME AND TEXTUALITY

What is so compelling about the *Confessions* is not simply the story Augustine has to tell, but the unremitting determination he brings to the analysis of representing his experience. As time passes, the 'same' event doesn't seem quite the same; subsequent events cast earlier ones in a new light, as the narrating self is acutely aware. The action of Ponticianus in picking up the book on the gaming table, opening it and discovering to his surprise that it is by the apostle Paul takes on a fresh significance in the performance of the *sortes* with the very same book in the garden. Through the interplay of the temporalities of narrated and narrating selves, the later event reveals a 'lack' in the earlier, which the later is seen to complement. Thus the first story of conversion in Book 8, that of Marius Victorinus, which so fired the narrated self at the time when he heard it, takes on an added significance in the light of his conversion, when it forms part of a sequence of such stories that all have their outcome in conversion. The narrated self's conversion might in turn take on a further significance if its representation likewise impels another figure in the future – as it does almost immediately with the conversion of Alypius, when the narrated self tells him what has happened and shows him the passage he has been reading – and may do so again in the future for readers of the *Confessions* when they open the book and find themselves in it. Narrative poses questions of the relationship of time and knowledge for both author and reader.

The narrating self is in a position to realise the significance of or see a pattern in – to *know* – things that the narrated self does not. The mode of understanding here is the typological interpretation familiar in particular from (though not restricted to) exegesis of the Bible: thus Jonah swallowed by the whale and ejected after three days is the 'type' which finds its 'anti-type' in Christ's later death and resurrection.[54] From the point of view of the narrating self or of the reader who knows the outcome and sees the pattern, the earlier event 'foreshadows' the later. But for Augustine, in both narrated and narrating selves, the recognition of such types is not just a literary effect. It is, crucially, part of his lived experience and his worldview, and is not simply experienced in retrospect. Recall the smile of Ponticianus as he notices the book on the gaming table, which is a smile of anticipation: he recognises the syndrome of conversion and is confident that he *already* knows what the outcome will be. From the temporal perspective of Ponticianus as he picks up the book, we should perhaps speak of the anticipation of retrospection, as he imagines the moment when he can look back on the process as completed and fulfilled. Augustine attempts to theorise this temporality in *Confessions* 11.18.24:

> Whatever may be the way in which the hidden presentiment of the future is known, nothing can be seen if it does not exist. Now that which already exists is not future but present. When therefore people speak of knowing the future, what is seen is not events which do not yet exist (that is, they really are future), but perhaps their causes or signs which already exist. In this way, to those who see them they are not future but present, and that is the basis on which the future can be conceived in the mind and made the subject of prediction.

Knowledge and time are closely associated here. An insight into the meaning of an event and its place in an anticipated pattern brings the future into the experience of the present. Ponticianus seems sure of himself, and his confidence is vindicated in the outcome, but things do not always turn out as anticipated. The passage of time seems to be associated with greater knowledge, though what at any moment we assume to be the case is subject to change.

So, that greater knowledge is itself only ever going to be partial for a human being living in time: the moment of narration will itself be superseded, and the significance of the events narrated will again be subject to revision, the act of looking back once more, with the benefit of further hindsight. One might see this as a sort of retrospective causation. What happened to Paul on the road to Damascus is widely held to 'influence' Augustine's account of his own conversion – forward causation – but it has also been suggested that what happened to Paul does not become his 'conversion' until Augustine configures his own experience in terms of it.[55] The process does not end even with the death of the author.[56] Subsequent narrations (including the one you are reading now) may discover further significance (which if taken as true seems in retrospect to have been always there), but are themselves going to be imperfect, in the sense of uncompleted, always liable to change. For Augustine, the full significance of any event can only be known to God, who is outside time: 'You are always the same, and you always know unchangeably the things which are not always the same' (8.3.6). This offers Augustine an intimation, no more, of what it is to be free of the experience of being in time, free from the fragmentation of the self that the very telling of his own story makes so anxiously obvious, an intimation of what it is like for the self to be fully *present* to itself. Augustine thus remains acutely aware that there is a difference between the self as known in autobiography, who is a being in time, and the self known to God, who is not.[57]

To narrate is therefore not enough for Augustine. He must reflect on that act, and this is what he does in the final four books of the *Confessions*. 'May I know you, who know me. May I "know as also I am known" (1 Cor. 13:12)' is the wish with which he introduces Book 10, in which he explores the question of memory, through which he has access to the past, and which plays such an important part in giving him whatever imperfect sense of himself he has. His memory is a 'treasury' in which all the representations, images and concepts his senses have given him are held on deposit (*commendatum*), awaiting withdrawal (10.8.13). It is a 'vast hall' in which his narrated and narrating selves bump into one another: 'There…I meet myself [*mihi et ipse occurro*] and recall what I am, what I have done, and when and where and how I was affected when I did it' (10.8.14). The memory is not simply orientated towards the past, for it is there that the patterns are stored which can be mapped forwards and allow insights into the future (recall the figure of Ponticianus once more). However, his memory is also 'a vast and infinite profundity…I myself cannot grasp the totality of what I am' (10.8.15). Augustine exists in time, but is trying to make sense of a relationship with a being who exists outside it. Time, then, is inescapably part of his attempt to know himself and know God, but famously, it is something that bewilders him (11.14.17):

> What is time? Who can explain this easily and briefly? Who can comprehend this even in thought so as to articulate the answer in words? Yet what do we speak of, in our familiar everyday conversation, more than of time? We surely know what we mean when we speak of it. We

also know what is meant when we hear someone else talking about it. What then is time? Provided that no one asks me, I know. If I want to explain it to an inquirer, I do not know.

If the experience of time seems relatively straightforward, reflection engenders perplexity. Although Augustine knows and echoes the Neoplatonist Plotinus's analysis of eternity and time (*Enneads* 3.71.1– 13),[58] Augustine does not follow the Platonic approach of trying to understand time as 'a moving image of eternity' (*eikō… kinēton tina aiōnos, Timaeus* 37d). In *Confessions* 11, 'it is rather the total contrast between God's transcendence of time and man's anguished experience of dispersion and fragmentation in time that he wishes to emphasize.'[59] Ultimately, human beings may not be able to understand time: 'in order to accomplish this, they would have to understand what time is not, namely eternity. As matters stand, the sequence of words by which they make their enquiry into time is the mirror image of their mode of existence as creatures living in time.'[60]

Augustine makes this clear in the words he addresses to God in 11.1.1: 'Lord, eternity is yours, so you cannot be ignorant of what I tell you. Your vision of occurrences in time is not temporally conditioned. Why then do I set before you an ordered account of so many things [*cur ergo tibi tot rerum **narrationes** digero*]? It is certainly not through me that you know them.' Augustine's account of himself in *Confessions* 1–9 has itself been arranged in and over time, a *narration*; given that he cannot 'know' his own life, there must be a degree of narrativity and fictiveness (though not necessarily fiction) in giving an account of it. It is precisely through words that he will try to understand time, and, more generally in Books 11–13, a main reference point is the analysis of another narration, the opening chapters of Genesis which recount God's creation of heaven and earth. From studying his own life and fashioning a narrative through which he hopes to *make* truth (cf. *veritatem…facere*, 10.1.1), he becomes a student of a text with which he is intimately familiar, and of which God could be said to be, in some sense, the ultimate 'author'.[61] But Augustine is exercised by the difference between human words and the 'Word' of God. The difficulties of communication, from human to human no less than from human to God, weigh him down with a sense of the inadequacy of words.[62] In commenting on the creation of heaven and earth, he remarks (11.5.7–6.8):

> Therefore you spoke and they were made, and by your word you made them (Ps. 32:9, 6). But how did you speak? Surely not in the way a voice came out of the cloud saying: 'This is my beloved Son' (Matt. 17:5). The voice is past and done with; it began and is ended. The syllables sounded and have passed away, the second after the first, the third after the second, and so on in order until, after all the others, the last one came, and after the last silence followed.

His study of the Neoplatonists emphasised for him how language marks the separation of the human from the divine. Henry Chadwick remarks, 'Our use of words in which meaning is conveyed by one sound after another, never in a simultaneous present, is for Plotinus, as for Augustine, a symptom of the fallen condition of humanity.'[63]

This seems a dilemma without solution. But if words can point up the passing of time by the sequentiality of their ordering and by their use to construct narrative form, they can also be orchestrated, as in the conversion scene, to create a different effect, a sense of *presence* – though if one tries to *describe* that effect, one tumbles back into words and images that cannot fully 'capture' that sense. Thus Jager's description of the *sortes* as happening 'in no time' offers a description of presence in terms of what it is not. James O'Donnell draws attention to the rhetorical contrast between the opening of Book 11 and what has come before:

> The speaking voice and that of which it speaks become now unequivocally *present*. That present-ness foreshadows eternity, but for fallen creation that present-ness can only be found by reaching into the 'future' – every attempt in Bk. 10 to reach the present ends by slipping into memory – the past – again. Here A[ugustine] leaves memory to live in the present.[64]

As we have seen, readers tend to align themselves with the temporal perspective of the authorial voice of a text. When I was paraphrasing the 'voice' of the narrating self in *Confessions* 8 earlier in this chapter, I 'spoke' of how Augustine '*describes* how his earlier self, in spiritual turmoil, *went* into the garden of his lodging in Milan...' Augustine explicitly contrasts the *narrationes* of the earlier books with what the later books offer. If narrative expresses the human experience of time, then the more those elements of one's discourse that contribute to the sense of its narrativity can be suppressed – if the gap between narrated self and narrating self is closed, for example by restricting one's use in reference to oneself of verbs in past or future tenses – the more one is drawn into the 'present' of its speaking 'voice'. O'Donnell puts it thus:

> Where before the reader could remain a voyeur looking curiously, side by side with A., at A.'s past, now the reader is urged to share A.'s exploration of the nature of God, and of himself – but not in the sense that the reader is expected to go away and re-create certain actions and emotions after reading the text: the reading of the text is itself the participation.[65]

But this is the effect not simply of the orchestration of verb tenses, crucial though they are. It is his apostrophes, his second-person addresses to God, that are crucial in bringing this effect about. With the help of Jonathan Culler's classic essay on the trope, let us explore Augustine's use of apostrophe, a trope that is intimately associated with the notion of the text's 'voice' and the inward turn the *Confessions* stages, and with the attempt to bridge the gap between what exists inside time and outside time.

Apostrophe asserts a relationship between 'I' and 'you', which can be with something inanimate (as famously in Romantic poetry; Culler's example is 'O rose thou art sick'), or, as in the case of Augustine, with something transcendent. The *Confessions* repeatedly presents itself as addressing God, as though in his presence, and makes explicit use of the metaphor of speech. Thus at the beginning of Book 10: 'May I know you, who know me. May I "know as also I am known" ... This is my hope, and that is why I speak ... This I desire to do, in my heart before you (*coram te*) in confession, but before many witnesses (*coram multis testibus*) with my pen.' While the address is directed primarily to God and only secondarily to the readers of the written text, the preposition *coram* ('in the presence of') is used exclusively with animate objects in Latin,[66] and so the parallelism of phraseology momentarily brings God and the reader of the text together as if they were similar, with the explicit metaphor of speech working to summon up in each case the presence of what might otherwise be thought to be absent. More precisely, apostrophe constitutes the other as a subject with whom one might hope to establish a responsive relationship – 'May I know you, who know me. May I "know as also I am known".' Recall[67] the figure of Augustine crying out in the garden, seeking the conversion he craved. The narrated self has withdrawn from company; in his distress, he has retreated out of earshot, seemingly, of Alypius, when he apostrophises God: 'How long, O Lord?' A paraphrase such as 'I wondered how long it would be until what I wanted came to pass' serves to point up what the trope can bring. The phrase *iactabam voces miserabiles* which introduces that apostrophe suggests the violent expulsion of the words. As an outburst, apostrophe signifies an investment of emotion, indicative of a desire to overcome absence by presence, and accordingly has an optative or imperative aspect. It is thus often orientated towards the future, as Culler suggests: 'to apostrophize is to will a state of affairs.'[68]

Although apostrophe is directed to the object of address, when a third party, a witness of some sort, is involved (as the readers of the *Confessions* explicitly are in 10.1.1), the effect is to dramatise the speaking subject and constitute an image of himself, to cut a particular figure depending on the content of the apostrophe. Thus a speaking subject who invokes God is one to whom God might respond and so is constituted as a religious subject; to cite Culler once more, 'invocation is a figure of vocation.'[69] In the conversion narrative, the apostrophe is presented as an event: Alypius may not be privy to the outburst (perhaps it was shame at cutting such a figure by such outbursts when he fell short of such a vocation that was behind the narrated self's withdrawal), but we the readers are, and it helps us to characterise the narrated self as a desiring subject and as one with a willed trajectory, albeit one at that point uncertain how or when he would achieve his goal. The apostrophes of the narrating self partake of these qualities, but another level is brought into play. The ability to sustain this apostrophic discourse establishes the *narrator's* presence through an image of voicing, and is thus related to the temporality not of narrated action but of writing; it is one of the devices by which the text establishes its 'now'. This 'now' is not a date in time, but such voicing establishes a discursive event whenever the text is read. Culler draws attention to a paradoxical feature of apostrophe, that a figure 'which seems to establish relations between the self and the other can in fact be read as an act of radical interiorization and solipsism'.[70] The narrating self's apostrophes seek to make God into a 'you' that can be addressed; but if the addressee (the rose of the poet or in Augustine's case a transcendent God) cannot be reduced to a 'you', then the object of the apostrophe is only addressed in terms of those activities that it provokes in the addressing subject: the questions, the doubts, the hopes, the aspirations and so on. The 'you' addressed is a projection of the concerns of that voice, and apostrophe *dramatises* its shifts (i.e. offers a representation as though they were happening before our eyes).[71]

Culler continues, 'This internalization is important because it works against narrative and its accompaniments: sequentiality, causality, time, teleological meaning.'[72] In Books 1–9 of the *Confessions*, events in Augustine's life are organised into just such a narrative sequence and pattern. They demand to be temporally located. Their causes and their consequences are probed, and, as we have seen, their very temporal location in relation to the act of narration makes any knowledge of them problematically incomplete. The past, and the events associated with it, are represented as absent in narration, and the narrative, even as it re-presents moments of teleological fulfilment and presence, such as the conversion, is marked no less by absence and loss: Book 9 significantly closes with the death of Augustine's mother Monica. The temporal sequence it represents is irreversible. Culler shows how

> [a]postrophes displace this irreversible structure by removing the opposition between presence and absence from empirical time and locating it in a discursive time. The temporal movement from A to B, internalised by apostrophe, becomes a reversible alternation between A' and B': a play of presence and absence governed not by time but by poetic power.[73]

The shift of speaking voice in *Confessions* 11–13 emphasises how the text, rather than narrating events, itself *becomes* the event, located in a temporal order that is freed from the constraints of empirical time as experienced by the narrated self, and is now subject to the control of the narrating self. Augustine's concerns in these books resist being organised into events to be narrated. Instead they are incorporated into the text as components of the event the text stages, as Culler suggests: 'Apostrophe is not the representation of an event; if it works, it produces a fictive, discursive event.'[74] It is within this temporality of discourse, of reading and writing, that Augustine pursues his theoretical analysis of time. And it coincides with a shift in what he is doing in the *Confessions*, from a narrator narrating the experience of his earlier self to that of a reader of a narrative, the account of creation in the opening chapters of Genesis.

Language provides the focus for Augustine's analysis of the problematics of time in his analysis of Genesis in *Confessions* 11. When God 'says' let there be light, it is clear that he is not using language in any human sense, for words are enunciated over time, and for Augustine, when God created the heavens and the earth, he created time as well (we will be returning to this in greater detail in Chapter 5 below). Time is an existential problem for Augustine, but it is a philosophical problem as well. What, then, *is* time? 'We surely know what we mean when we speak of it' he says in 11.14.17, but it is not that easy. We learnt when children, and teach our children in turn, that there are three times, past, present and future (11.17.22), but past events have passed away, and future events do not yet exist. Can it be the case that only present time exists? How, then, can people tell stories of the past, as Augustine narrated his own past in *Confessions* 1–9, or make predictions about the future?

Augustine is here taking up problems with time that Aristotle had raised in his discussion in Book 4 of his *Physics*, particularly a paradox relating to time's existence.[75] How can one say that the past 'exists' when it is not now present? How can one say that the future 'exists' when it is not yet present? Even what we have come to call the 'present' may not be immune. For Aristotle, 'time has parts, and some of them have existed, while others will exist, but none of them currently exist' (*Physics* 4.10, 218a3ff.). Aristotle's flirtation with this radical scepticism is associated with his repeated use of what he calls the 'now'. But what is a 'now'? Rather like a spatial point, it has no dimension, but marks a boundary between past and future.[76] Time, then, 'is defined as the quantifiable stretch that there is between any two such instants',[77] but whenever we try to identify a present moment, it is already in the past, and only recognised retrospectively. However, Aristotle suggests that, although time is not the motions of the heavens, as previous thinkers had believed (*Physics* 4.10, 218a33–b1),[78] we become aware of time through motion and change, and that time is related to the quantification – what he repeatedly refers to as the 'number' or measure – of motion and change. Time is 'a number of change with respect to the before and the after. Time is not change, then, but it is that feature of change that makes number applicable to it' (*Physics* 4.11, 219b1–3).[79] But would time exist with no one to measure it? 'It might be wondered whether or not there would be time if there were not mind: if the existence of anything to do the numbering is ruled out, the existence of anything numerable is also ruled out' (*Physics* 4.14, 223a21–23).[80] In saying that 'if nothing else except mind…is such that it can number, it is impossible for there to be time if there is no mind – except that there might still be whatever it is that time is' (*Physics* 4.14, 223a26–27), Aristotle somewhat tortuously tries to draw a distinction between time experienced in the mind or soul (what we might translate as human or phenomenological time), and time that exists independently of human observation (cosmological or universal time).

Augustine has suggested at the outset of his argument that he is enquiring into the existence and nature of time itself, but quickly concedes that, posed in these terms, any answer or definition can prove very elusive ('So indeed we cannot truly say that time exists except in the sense that it tends towards non-existence,' 11.14.17). It is the *experience* of time that counters the radically sceptical denial of the existence of time. Augustine thus adopts Aristotle's suggestion that time is to be understood as an experience of the soul, and suggests that the past and the future are aspects – the past as memory, the future as anticipation – of the soul's attention which constitutes the 'present' (11.17.22–23). This leads to Augustine's theory of the three-fold present (11.20.26):

> What is by now evident and clear is that neither future nor past exists, and it is inexact language to speak of three times – past, present, and future. Perhaps it would be exact to say: there are three times, a present of things past, a present of things present, a present of things to come. In the soul there are these three aspects of time, and I do not see them anywhere else. The present considering the past is the memory [*memoria*], the present considering the present is immediate awareness [*contuitus*], the present considering the future is expectation [*expectatio*].

It is this psychological view of time that absorbs Augustine in *Confessions* 11, and moves his argument away from the definition of time towards an analysis of the cognitive act of measuring time. The measurement of time cannot be explained solely in terms of Augustine's theory of the three-fold present; events are stretched through more than a present moment to which the mind is paying attention. He coins a term *distentio* (11.23.30) to characterise this extension in time, which, in keeping with his psychological approach to time here, he explains as *distentio animi* (11.26.33), an 'extension' or 'distension' of the mind – the term reflecting a sense of tension, or even painful stretching, in the mind that the perception of time creates.[81]

In the case of future processes in which we are involved, we measure them by anticipation, but only if we already have some experience of what we are measuring or a pattern we have already noticed so as to make prospective calculations. Memory is thus as important for measuring future processes as it is for processes which have ceased. When it comes to measuring time, Augustine's examples are, significantly, textual: the sequentiality of ordered language provides a paradigm for measuring the time of all processes where anticipation is based on past experience. First is a line of a favourite hymn in iambic metre (11.27.35–36):

'God, Creator of all things' – *Deus Creator omnium* – the line consists of eight syllables, in which short and long syllables alternate. So the four which are short (the first, third, fifth and seventh) are single in relation to the four long syllables (the second, fourth, sixth and eighth). Each of the long syllables has twice the time of the short. As I recite the words, I also observe that this is so, for it is evident to sense-perception. To the degree that the sense-perception is unambiguous, I measure the long syllable by the short one, and perceive it to be twice the length. But when one syllable sounds after another, the short first, the long after it, how shall I keep my hold on the short, and how use it to apply a measure to the long, so as to verify that the long is twice as much? The long does not begin to sound unless the short has ceased to sound. I can hardly measure the long during the presence of its sound, as measuring becomes possible only after it has ended. When it is finished, it has gone into the past. What then is it which I measure? Where is the short syllable with which I am making my measurement? Where is the long which I am measuring? Both have sounded; they have flown away; they belong to the past. They now do not exist. And I offer my measurement and declare as confidently as a practised sense-perception will allow, that the short is single, the long double – I mean in the time they occupy. I can do this only because they are past and gone. Therefore it is not the syllables which I am measuring, but something in my memory which stays fixed there.

So it is in you, my mind, that I measure periods of time.[82]

Although the example's formal metrical properties illustrate what Augustine wants to say about the measurement of time, the content is not fortuitous. This evening hymn, which praises God for the rest that 'lightens weary minds/And dissolves the causes of grief', was composed by the Bishop of Milan, Ambrose, who was Augustine's guide and mentor on the spiritual journey he has narrated, and who baptised him. It is cited on several occasions in the *Confessions*, at greatest length when Augustine recalls how it crystallised the comfort he experienced in the wake of the death of his mother Monica.[83] Citation here towards the climax of Book 11 provides resolution of the intellectual aporia he has been grappling with, and for the reader giving full attention to the text serves to recall how his reflections on time in Book 11 have juxtaposed the narrative of his spiritual journey with the contemplation of God as Creator of all things. Citation of the hymn thus not only brings a sense of closure to the theoretical difficulty at hand, but has the capacity to enact a distension of the mind across the text of the *Confessions* and the life that it narrates.

The future does not yet exist, the past now has no being and present time passes in a flash, 'yet, attention is continuous', thus giving the mind a reach into past and future. The second textual illustration develops this (11.28.38):

Suppose I am about to recite a psalm which I know. Before I begin, my expectation is directed towards the whole. But when I have begun, the verses from it which I take into the past become the object of my memory. The life of this act of mine is stretched [*distenditur vita huius actionis meae*] in two ways, into my memory because of the words I have already said and into my expectation because of those which I am about to say. But my attention is on what is present: by that the future is transferred to become the past. As the action advances further and further, the shorter the expectation and the longer the memory, until all expectation is consumed, the entire action is finished, and it has passed into the memory. What occurs in the psalm as a whole occurs in its particular pieces and its individual syllables. The same is true of a longer action in which perhaps that psalm is a part. It is also valid of the entire life of an individual person [*hoc in tota vita hominis*], where all actions are parts of a whole, and of the total history of 'the sons of men' (Ps. 30:20) where all human lives are but parts [*cuius partes sunt omnes vitae hominum*].

Augustine draws attention to the capacity of the mind to alter the scale of its stretching, down from what he calls the 'life' of the action of reading the psalm to its smallest constituent parts, the syllables of words, and up to the level of the individual human life, of which reading a psalm may be but a part, and beyond that to the history of the human race, of which human lives are but parts.

Thus Augustine's own life is a distension (*distentio est vita mea*, 11.29.39), its temporality an essential condition of its being. It is a life that can be read as a text, but also that can be read as part of a yet greater text. Within one's own life, still less within the sweep of history, the narrating self's position is hardly privileged. It can never have full access to the meaning of any event in all its intentional and consequential significance, from a God's-eye viewpoint *sub specie aeternitatis*, the perspective of eternity (11.30.41):

> Certainly if there were a mind endowed with such great knowledge and prescience that all things past and future could be known in the way I know a very familiar psalm, this mind would be utterly miraculous and amazing to the point of inducing awe. From such a mind nothing of the past would be hidden, nor anything of what remaining ages have in store, just as I have full knowledge of that psalm I sing.

However, while the human experience of time, and in particular the capacity of attention to bridge moments of time, may anticipate eternity, temporal successiveness makes this distension also an experience that Augustine has just before this characterised in terms of bodily dismemberment and evisceration, a disintegration that can only be made good by union with the divine (11.29.39):

You are my eternal Father, but I am scattered in times whose order I do not understand [*at ego in tempora dissilui quorum ordinem nescio*]. The storms of incoherent events tear to pieces my thoughts, the inmost entrails of my soul [*tumultuosis varietatibus dilaniantur cogitationes, intima viscera animae meae*], until that day when, purified and molten by the fire of your love, I flow together to merge into you.

Divine knowledge is thus of a quite different order from human knowledge (11.30.41, continued):

I know by heart what and how much of [the psalm] has passed since the beginning, and what and how much remains until the end. But far be it from you, Creator of the universe, creator of souls and bodies, far be it from you to know all future and past events in this kind of sense. You know them in a much more wonderful and much more mysterious way. A person singing or listening to a song he knows well suffers a distension or stretching in feeling and in sense-perception [*variatur affectus sensusque distenditur*] from the expectation of future sounds and the memory of past sound. With you it is otherwise. You are unchangeably eternal, that is the truly eternal Creator of minds. Just as you knew heaven and earth in the beginning without that bringing any variation [*sine variatione*] into your knowing, so you made heaven and earth in the beginning without that meaning a tension [*sine distentione*] between past and future in your activity.

Although Augustine here moves to a position that suggests that God transcends the analogy of reading a text that one knows, that analogy invests texts and the knowledge they are thought to contain, their reading and their writing, with theological assumptions which will be explored in the remainder of this chapter, and beyond.

PLAYING GOD?

Augustine's examples are not simply texts, but texts that he *knows* – the hymn of Ambrose, a psalm – so that memory and anticipation can give him a sense of the text as a whole at any one moment. His command of that text serves as an intimation of God's command of, on a sliding scale, an individual event, a single human life, or of the total history of 'the sons of men', as if these too were texts. The metaphor of the individual's life as 'a narrative that is "written" in the "books" of both personal memory and divine omniscience' is one that is widespread in both classical antiquity and biblical literature, as Eric Jager has traced.[84] The textual serves as the model for the self and consciousness, and dominates not simply the *Confessions*, but Augustine's writings more generally.[85] This makes the performance of the *sortes* by the narrated self in the garden at Milan particularly piquant. The book the narrated self opens is emphatically a codex rather than a scroll.[86] This format does not simply facilitate the performance of the *sortes* but serves as a psychological symbol ('as a container having an interior and an exterior and as enclosure that can be opened and closed') and to focus attention on the precise moment of conversion as well: 'Augustine's sudden opening of the codex – a gesture more precise and binary than the slow unrolling of a scroll – results in an inward flood of light that suggests a heart finally opened to God's word.'[87] The self is an 'open book' to God, the significance of everything within it complete and fully known, with no distinction between 'implicit' and 'explicit' meanings (the imagery of these adjectives is associated with the rolling and unrolling of a scroll).[88] If the book can serve as a psychological symbol of the soul at the level of the individual human life, at the level of 'the total history of the sons of men' it can serve as a symbol of time itself – a particular vision of time that has a beginning, a middle and an end, as in God's scripture, which moves from creation to end days.

The textual metaphor can figure God as either the reader or the author of the book concerned, but the tenor of signification of the metaphor can run both ways, and the reader and the author of a book can no less be figured as God.[89] If the anxieties about the 'authority' of the first-person narrator are particularly acute, the position of the third-person narrator, sometimes granted omniscient status by literary critics, only dubiously offers a God's-eye view. It could be argued of autobiographical narrative that the narrating self occupies a third-person function in respect of the narrated self's first-person, and Augustine is clear on the limits of the narrating self's knowledge in this respect. The term 'omniscience' tends to be invoked more readily of the narrator of fiction, where novelists are thought to stand in relation to their work as God does to his creation, than of history or biography. The assertion is made most forcefully by

Meir Sternberg: 'Within the limits of the microcosm of the universe he has himself created, the author is invariably, divinely omniscient; the common phrase "the omniscient author" forms, as a matter of fact, a self-implicative attribution, in which the modifier is logically redundant'; though the *author* may choose not to invest the *narrator* (who may be represented, for example, as unreliable) with omniscience.[90] This can be the source of some amusing play. In James Joyce's *Ulysses*, Molly Bloom, in the midst of her great stream of consciousness, suddenly apostrophises *her* creator: 'Oh Jamesy, let me up out of this.'[91] More generally, the question of the God-like author raises issues of human freedom: do the characters within the world of the narrative have any choice in their actions? In *The French Lieutenant's Woman*, John Fowles frets over the god-like powers narration seems to give him: 'When Charles left Sarah on her cliff edge, I ordered him to walk straight back to Lyme Regis. But he did not; he gratuitously turned and went down to the Dairy... The idea seemed to me to come clearly from Charles, not myself. It is not only that he has begun to gain an autonomy; I must respect it, and disrespect all my quasi-divine plans for him, if I wish him to be real.'[92] Fowles even equips the novel with two endings, and does not decide between them. He seeks to present the figure of the author as one whose creation floats free of his control. This looks like a version of process theology, which considers God as involved in and affected by temporal process, and as granting his creatures free will. Fowles reflects, 'There is only one good definition of God: the freedom that allows other freedoms to exist.'[93] For better or for worse, the analogies of God and author, and life and text, tie discussion of narration into issues of interpretation that link literary criticism and theology.

Jonathan Culler has argued that no narrator can be accounted truly omniscient, and that the term is misleadingly used of a number of phenomena which would be better kept distinct in the analysis of narrative:

> (1) the performative authoritativeness of many narrative declarations, which seem to bring into being what they describe; (2) the reporting of innermost thoughts and feelings, such as are usually inaccessible to human observers; (3) authorial narration, where the narrator flaunts

his or her godlike ability to determine how things turn out; and (4) the synoptic impersonal narration of the realist tradition.[94]

Broadly, these phenomena often distinguish fictional from non-fictional narratives, though that boundary can easily be blurred. But, from the perspective of Augustine's argument, the idea of an 'omniscient narrator' is a contradiction in terms, because God, being omniscient, has no need to narrate. Rather than God being an analogy for the author, the author is an analogy that seeks to help to explain God – but an analogy that falls short. What Augustine's narrative illustrates is the capacity of narrative, even in the first person, to create a multiplicity of perspectives which juxtapose different degrees of knowledge. Culler turns the analogy round through 180 degrees, by granting that it may help us to 'imagine the possibility of a creator, a god, a sentient being, as undetectable to us as the novelist would be to the characters who exist in the universe of the text this god created', and further on adds, 'Our habit of naturalizing the strange details and practices of narrative by making the consciousness of an individual their source, and then imagining a quasi-divine omniscient consciousness when human consciousness cannot fill that role, generates a fantasy of omniscience...'[95]

Corresponding to the literary-critical notion of the omniscient narrator is Michael Riffaterre's idea of the 'superreader' in total control of every detail of the text she reads – an idea that has never caught on theoretically, but one which floats as a kind of ghostly presence behind commentaries and intertextualist readings that look to be exhaustive, or, at least, *authoritative*.[96] One thinks here of Augustine's suggestion of his totalising knowledge of a *psalm* that he knows by heart, but if we think of the way he 'reads' his *life*, the corresponding critical model is reception theory. Within the perspective that reception theory offers, the text never gives up its full meaning, because the point of reception, the moment of reading the text, is always superseded by further points *ad infinitum* which may render a particular detail significant in ways that only that later context of reading could reveal. Augustine attests to this frisson of recognition in his discussion with Vindicianus about reading poetry (4.3.5): there is such a strong sense that the meaning is somehow *there* 'in' the text, awaiting its 'discovery', even while we may be aware on historical grounds that this reaction may be at odds with what the author thought he was putting there. The author is not the ultimate source of authority, for the meaning of the text is not circumscribed by his intention, and the text continues to accrue meaning even after his death. For Augustine, herein lies the authority of the Bible, which historically was the product of a number of human writers writing at particular moments in the past:

> Your divine scripture has more sublime authority since the death of the mortal authors through whom you provided it for us…Indeed, by the very fact of their death the solid authority of your utterances published by them is in a sublime way 'stretched out' over everything inferior. While they were alive on earth, it was not stretched out to express this supreme authority. (*Confessions* 13.15.16)

What Augustine here says of scripture goes also for those texts that are accorded, as embodying 'timeless' verities, the status of 'literature' or 'the classics'. The quest for the 'meaning' of texts so designated has theological undertones: if Virgil's *Aeneid* is a 'classic', it cannot be reduced to what its historical author intended, but expresses a vision that unfolds over history, beyond its author's time.[97] Authors can collude in this in representing themselves as 'inspired' or even 'prophetic', the standard example being the narrator of epic who requests of the Muse that he 'sings', and so establishes his voice as vatic.[98]

The meaning of a text may not be reducible to what the time-bound author, in historical terms, thought he was doing, but for Augustine, the author's *intention*, his 'stretching towards', can result in him doing more than he could know. While not accorded omniscience, the author is seen as having the power of creation, which involves the imposition of order. Confronted by memory, Augustine finds it a 'huge cavern, with its mysterious, secret, and indescribable nooks and crannies' (*Confessions* 10.8.13). It is 'a vast and infinite profundity. Who has plumbed its bottom?' (10.8.15). Memory is 'a power of profound and infinite multiplicity [*profunda et infinita multiplicitas*]…See the broad plains and dens and caverns of my memory…I run through all these things, I fly here and there and penetrate their working as far as I can. But the end is nowhere [*finis numquam*]' (10.17.26). From its depths, 'things have to be brought together [*cogenda*] so that they can be known; that means that they have to be gathered [*colligenda*] from their dispersed state [*ex quadam dispersione*]' (10.11.18).[99] The author of the *Confessions* seeks to bring some degree of order into this infinite multiplicity, to 'gather' it together as best he might, but he is aware that this act is not going to bring him the satisfaction he desires: Augustine's human experience of time is as a *distention*.

How is this distention to be transcended? Augustine looks once more to the hand. 'See how my life is a distention [*distentio*] in several directions. "Your right hand upheld me" (Ps. 17:36; 62:9) in my Lord, the Son of man who is mediator between You the One and us the many, who live in a multiplicity of distractions by many things' (*Confessions* 11.29.39). Augustine goes on to express the hope 'that I may apprehend through him in whom I am also apprehended (Phil. 3:12–14) [*ut per eum apprehendam in quo et apprehensus sum*]', taking from the Bible the image of *grasping* to express the idea of holding still the movement of time. The 'hand' of God is to be the model for his efforts. His wish is that 'leaving behind the old days I might be gathered up [*a veteribus diebus colligar*] to follow the One, forgetting the past [*praeterita oblitus*] and moving not towards those future things that are transitory [*non in ea quae futura et transitura sunt*], but to "the things that are before me" [*sed in ea quae ante sunt*].' There is a contrast here between the things that are within time – the past, and the future that will be transitory – and those outside time, what Augustine calls 'the things that are before', *ea quae ante sunt*,[100] which with the use of the *present* tense [*sunt*] are pointedly contrasted with the past participle, *praeterita*, 'the things that have passed by'. Augustine looks towards transcending the process of organisation, with (for him) all its imperfections, 'not stretched out in distraction but extended in reach [*non distentus sed extentus*], not being pulled apart but by concentration [*non secundum distentionem, sed secundum **intentionem***]. It is in *intention*, the stretching out to point towards what is not time-bound but lies outside time, that he experiences an adumbration of an ideal order beyond the imperfect act of human ordering.

Augustine here develops a 'theology' of authorship alongside an authorial theory of God. The notion of authorial intention, we might say, 'points to' an assumed order *within* the text, but also to an assumed order *beyond* the text – God's 'intention'. We should not thereby assume that we can 'grasp' that latter order, however much we may aspire to, a totalising gesture which he sees as ultimately a divine rather than human prerogative. Moreover, we shall see that we should not assume it of the former either. The analogy of authorship to explore the human and the divine is just that – a metaphor which signals that the discussion is imperfect, uncompleted and lacking the finality for which one can only gesture towards God. The work of Roland Barthes looks to reverse the poles of the forcefield the *Confessions* generates, rather as Culler sought to do in his discussion of authorial omniscience. Augustine's discussion plays on its manipulation of grammatical tense, particularly in the pointed contrast between *ea quae ante sunt* and *praeterita*; *praeterita*, 'things that have passed away', conjures up the French tense known as the preterite, the narrative past tense. For Barthes, the preterite '*signifies* a creation: that is, it proclaims and imposes it'.[101] You need do no more than use a preterite, and you summon order into being. He explains,

> The part it plays is to reduce reality to a *point* in time, and to abstract from the depth of a multiplicity of experiences a pure verbal act, freed from the existential roots of knowledge, and directed towards a logical link with other acts, processes, a general movement of the world: it aims at maintaining a hierarchy in the realm of facts. Through the preterite, the verb implicitly belongs with a causal chain, it partakes of a set of related and orientated actions, *it functions as the algebraic sign of an intention.*[102]

Given that Augustine's discussion of *intention* sees it as a striving towards a transcendent meaning that is underpinned by the existence and presence of God, it would be easy to overlook the way in which these associations can be seen to inform ostensibly secular notions of authorship and of authorial desire 'directed towards' grasping a stable and transcendent order of meaning – a desire that 'aims at maintaining a hierarchy in the realm of facts'. The function of tense is not simply to place events in a temporal sequence. In the process of gathering from the infinite multiplicity, 'before' and 'after' extend beyond the purely chronological to the causal. Barthes continues,

39

Allowing as it does an ambiguity between temporality and causality, [the preterite] calls for a sequence of events, that is, for an intelligible Narrative. This is why it is the ideal instrument for every construction of the world; it is the unreal time of cosmogonies, myths, History and Novels. *It presupposes a world that is constructed, elaborated, self-sufficient, reduced to significant lines, and not one that has been sent sprawling before us, to take or leave. Behind the preterite, there always lurks a demiurge, a God or a reciter. The world is not unexplained, since it is told like a story*; each one of its accidents is but a circumstance, and the preterite is precisely this operative sign whereby the narrator reduces the exploded reality to a slim and pure logos, without density, without volume, without spread, and whose sole function is to unite as rapidly as possible a cause and an end.[103]

The Augustine who is the author of the *Confessions* of course remains forever committed to his theological beliefs, and a metaphysics of presence that continues to resonate in some theoretical accounts of literature.[104]

However, Barthes's essay 'The Death of the Author' is a reminder of how complicit with theological notions the concept of authorship is. The death of the Author (note the capital, otherwise the prerogative of God, and an allusion to the death Nietzsche had proclaimed) has its effects:

Time, first of all, is no longer the same. The Author, when we believe in him, is always conceived as the past of his own book: book and author are voluntarily placed on one and the same line, distributed as a *before* and an *after*: the Author is supposed to *feed* the book, i.e., he lives before it, thinks, suffers, lives for it; he has the same relation of antecedence with his work that a father sustains with his child. Quite the contrary, the modern *scriptor* is born *at the same time* as his text; he is not furnished with a being which precedes or exceeds his writing; he is not the subject of which his book would be the predicate; there is no time other than that of the speech-act, and every text is written eternally *here* and *now*.[105]

Barthes goes on to suggest that 'writing' viewed in this way 'can "no longer" designate an operation of recording, of observation, of representation', but a performative, a speech-act, and as an example he gives 'something like the *I sing* of the earliest poets'. The text, he continues, does not release 'a single "theological" meaning (the "message" of the Author-God), but of a multi-dimensional space in which are married and contested several writings, none of which is original: the text is a fabric of quotations, resulting from a thousand sources of culture.'[106] The traditional, 'theological', view of the text treats it like scripture, as harbouring a 'true' meaning put there by its author; readers, who believe in their Author as the ultimate source of the meaning of a particular text, subject it to the processes of commentary and allegoresis in an attempt to discern his 'intention'. Barthes regards the term 'author' as modelled on God and the God's-eye view to which Augustine aspired, and jettisons it in favour of 'scriptor', whom Barthes creates in the image of man rather than God. What he calls 'writing' is something that takes place within time, and, as 'a multi-dimensional space', it resembles nothing so much as Augustine's description of his memory. Moreover, you could be forgiven for seeing the Barthesian text generated within time by 'writing', 'a fabric of quotations', as looking remarkably like Augustine's *Confessions*, a network of citations from the Bible that is drawn from Augustine's memory.[107]

Barthes identifies his stance as, explicitly, countertheological:

> Thereby literature (it would be better, from now on, to say *writing*), by refusing to assign to the text (and to the world-as-text) a 'secret', i.e., an ultimate meaning, liberates an activity we may call countertheological, properly revolutionary, for to refuse to halt meaning is finally to refuse God and his hypostases, reason, science, the law.[108]

He sides with the perspective of the writer within time who positively embraces indeterminacy, and distances himself from those writers who adopt an authorial position (and those readers who collude with this view) that would arrogate God's knowledge, through concepts that lay claim to finality (he cites three, reason, science and the law) so as to suggest that the text, or the world (when viewed *as* a text), has an ultimate order and an ultimate meaning. Barthes is himself a very distinctive and even, dare one say it, knowing author (and Author), and there is much playfulness in what he writes here. His use of the rebarbative term 'hypostases' juggles with theological jargon. Stephen Prickett offers this commentary:

The original Greek meaning is, literally, 'that which stands under' something. In French, as in English, it is a theological term, meaning 'essence', or 'personal existence', as in the three 'hypostases of the Godhead' in the doctrine of the Trinity. Reason, science and law, three of the most commonly imposed external disciplines in reading a text are thus seen not just as aspects of God, but specifically 'personalities' of God in the sense of being like the persons of the Trinity.[109]

Augustine had sought analogues to himself (created in God's image) in the Trinity, seeing God the Father, the creator, in memory.[110] A 'countertheological' or 'revolutionary' view of authorship does not eschew theology — far from it — but within the 'economy' of ideas theological discourse sets in motion, Barthes happily shakes up priorities Augustine strives to establish and turns them around to point the other way. Meaning is, yes, the creation of an author and of authorial intention, but whereas Augustine would enshrine God as the *cause* and guarantor of meaning and of final distinctions between true and imperfect knowledge, Barthes would see God, and the idea that there is an ultimate meaning 'in' the world, as *effects* of this view of authorship and authorial activity. Barthes could be seen to set in play a wry typology, with his theology the antitype to that in the *Confessions*, as a challenge to the *authority* that texts which affect the viewpoint of the transcendent seek for themselves.

2

TIME FOR HISTORY

To encapsulate his thinking about time, Augustine used the illustration of reciting a psalm which he knew. The 'life' of this act, he suggested, was stretched two ways, into the memory and into expectation. The example of the psalm allows him to diminish the scale, from the psalm to its particular words and its individual syllables, or increase it, where the psalm is but part of a longer action. The scale can be further increased: 'It is also valid,' he continued, 'of the entire life of an individual person, where all actions are part of a whole, and of the total history of "the sons of men" (Ps. 30:20) where all human lives are but parts' (*Confessions* 11.28.38). Augustine significantly makes the psalm one which he *knows*: wherever he is in the psalm, he is aware of it as a whole. He knows what has been and what is still to come, what was the beginning and what will be the end. Augustine's example can point up both the possibilities and limitations of narrative. In the *Confessions*, the narrating self 'knows' more than the narrated self by virtue of his later position within time: the significance of any individual event changes in the 'light' of subsequent events, of what eventuates. Thus events within a life, whether narrated by oneself or by another, exist, in Frank Kermode's phrase, 'under the shadow of the end'.[1] That end moves on with time, and, as the scale expands to encompass 'the total history of "the sons of men"', the human viewpoint seems increasingly inadequate.

God alone, Augustine would have it, is in a position to know *this* 'text', and in a way not granted to his creatures within time. He alone can see it as a whole, for he 'spoke' and created it as having the form it does.

For Roland Barthes, behind even something so seemingly straight-forward as uttering a narrative past tense, 'there always lurks a demiurge, a God or a reciter', the time-bound writer's timeless alter ego (the Author) who imposes form and order on chaos and sprawl: 'the world is not unexplained, since it is told like a story.' For Barthes, 'reality' is that chaos and sprawl, and it is the role of narrative and its sovereign Author to 'reduce' that 'exploded' reality to 'a point in time' and to a 'slim and pure logos' whose 'sole function is to unite as rapidly as possible a cause and an end'. As we saw in Chapter 1, Augustine and Barthes occupy opposite poles of a field of theological thinking about time and texts. In this chapter, with Augustine and Barthes still very much in mind, I explore further the interplay of narrative and historical thinking and how historical narratives are constituted from the *interaction* of two perspectives, a 'human' one from 'within' time and the 'God's-eye view' from 'outside' time. The major point of reference throughout will be Virgil's *Aeneid*, which constructs a narrative that, for its own ends, artfully separates out these two perspectives. In the first section, I focus on the way in which various narrator-figures in the poem are given different temporal perspectives in such a way as to suggest that time and history as a whole have, in Aristotelian terms, a 'plot' with a beginning, a middle and an end. The *Aeneid* thus offers a dramatisation of the act of historical interpretation that (I go on to argue in the second section) is further worked out in the poem's reception. I suggest how complex narratives (like the *Aeneid*) can be 'condensed' into terms (like 'history' or 'empire') which, viewed as *metaphors*, express the movement of historical time seen from 'within', and, viewed as *concepts*, seek to offer a perspective that is not time-bound.

(DE-)CONSTRUCTING HISTORICAL PERSPECTIVES

The narrative of the *Aeneid* directs us to a particular 'point in time'. That phrase is, of course, Barthes's, though as my argument goes on a further set of inverted commas should begin to emerge: a particular 'point "in" time'. The first sighting we get of Aeneas in the poem's narrative comes amidst the storm the god of the winds Aeolus has raised at Juno's instigation as the Trojans are sailing from Sicily towards Italy, seven years into their wanderings after the sack of Troy. Aeneas and his men seem confronted by imminent demise: 'everything', the narrator remarks, 'threatens them with present death' (*praesentem ... viris intentant omnia mortem*, 1.91). The elements seem to be personified in the way they 'stretch towards' their future goal (*intentant*), while for the men (*viris*), death seems 'present', here and now (*praesentem ... mortem*). Under the shadow of what Aeneas assumes, at that moment, to be the end, the investment of passion in his repeated exclamations of his wish that he could have died fighting at Troy (1.94–101) emphasises his immediate sense of the meaninglessness of the intervening years of wandering. There is no overarching rationale to which he can gesture: those years seem to him pointless. Yet, as it turns out, this is not the end: Neptune intervenes to calm the storm, and Aeneas survives. However revealing it is of the depth of Aeneas's despair as he believes he is confronting imminent death, his own judgement of the meaning and significance of his life is not definitive, either at this or any subsequent moment of his life. With the passage of time, his life becomes a part of a larger story 'where all human lives are but parts'. My phraseology is derived from Augustine, but this is a crucial aspect of the narration of the *Aeneid*, the pagan text that was the favourite of the young Augustine, as the author of the *Confessions* attests (1.13.21–22).

Making land in Libya, Aeneas procures food for his companions, and reminds them that they are not unacquainted with setbacks, that they have suffered worse things, and that god will grant an *end* to these sufferings also (*o socii [neque enim ignari sumus ante malorum]/o passi graviora, dabit deus his quoque finem'*, 1.198–99). Aeneas is once more looking forward, albeit cautiously; the end which he had thought was immediate is now postponed, though it still provides the frame of reference for his feelings. Following a brief description of the meal they prepare, and of the sorrow they express for the companions they believe they have lost, the narrator of the *Aeneid* cryptically remarks 'and now it was the end, when Jupiter, looking down from the highest point of heaven...' (*et iam finis erat, cum Iuppiter aethere summo/despiciens...*,1.223).[2] The repeated word *finis*, emphasised by its position at the end of 1.199, and its obscure appearance in 1.223, assumes even greater importance in the scene in heaven that follows when Aeneas's mother Venus challenges her father Jupiter. 'From the beginning Jupiter is associated with the end', remarks Denis Feeney,[3] and that end lies well beyond the stopping point of the narrative, the death of Turnus at the hands of Aeneas in the closing lines of *Aeneid* 12. Beginnings and ends are clearly of importance to this narrative, but for greater understanding let us step into the theoretical and conceptual world created by narratological analysis.

Few narratives begin at the 'beginning', the earliest event referred to within the narration, or end at the 'end', the latest: the storm off Carthage and the death of Turnus do not constitute the absolute temporal limits of the *Aeneid*. The analysis of narrative characteristically operates with a distinction between *story* and *discourse*.[4] The distinction is offered as heuristic: the analyst, presented with a narrative – the 'discourse' – constructs a linear sequence of all the events alluded to in the discourse – the 'story' – so as to describe and interpret how this idealised, purely chronological, sequence of events is emplotted and evaluated by the narrator.[5] The narrative discourse of the *Aeneid* takes us from the storm which shipwrecks the Trojans on the shores of Carthage at the beginning of Book 1 through to the death of Turnus at the close of Book 12, a narrative 'present' that moves through the events that are represented as taking for the characters a year or so. However, the narrative of the *Aeneid* makes reference to a number of events that took place long before the fall of Troy. Juno's wrath, for example, is traced back to the judgement of Paris and the abduction of Ganymede by Jupiter (1.25–27). Evander recalls meeting the young Anchises (8.163), and there are intimations of an even more distant past as Evander draws the attention of Aeneas to the ruined cities on the site where Rome will one day stand (8.355–58). In a complex interweaving of times, we learn that Dardanus, the founder of Troy, hailed from Italy (3.167), so that when Apollo's riddling instruction to the Trojans to 'seek out your ancient mother' (3.96) is at length understood by the Trojans, they reappraise their arrival in Italy as a return. Arguably, the speech of Anchises in the Underworld (6.724–51) takes us back to the very creation of the cosmos. The latest event referred to in the story is the death of Marcellus, stepson of the Emperor

Augustus, lamented by Anchises in his prophetic catalogue of Rome's greatest figures (6.882–83). The poem's narrator makes a number of references that locate him, and the point of perspective of his narrative, in the time of Augustus.[6] Even this is not the ultimate temporal limit of the story. Extrapolate all those events variously referred to in the narrative and put them in an order of succession and you have the story which the narrative emplots.

Narrative discourse is characterised by what Gérard Genette called *anachronies*, in which the narrative refers backwards from its present to events that happened 'earlier' (Genette calls this 'analepsis') or forwards to those that happened 'later' ('prolepsis'). Genette cites as an inaugurating instance the opening eight lines of Homer's *Iliad*, where the narrator 'having evoked the quarrel between Achilles and Agamemnon that he proclaims as the starting point of his narrative (*ex hou de ta prōta*), goes back about ten days to reveal the cause of the quarrel in some 140 retrospective lines'.[7] The narrative plunge 'into the midst of events' (*in medias res*), followed by an expository analepsis, becomes one of the formal markers of epic, as Genette goes on to remark;[8] but it is also the 'point in time' to which Barthes has drawn our attention when he suggests that 'the world is not unexplained since it is told like a story', thus asking us not to draw any hard and fast distinction between narrative forms as diverse as 'cosmogonies, myths, History and Novels'.[9] Such expository flashbacks may be voiced by the narrator, but are frequently placed in the mouths of characters, as when Homer's Odysseus narrates his wanderings after the fall of Troy in Books 9–12 of the *Odyssey*, and Aeneas tells of his to Dido in *Aeneid* 2–3. In many narrative forms, prolepsis tends to be a more elusive figure.[10] Characters internal to the narrative at any one point within it may, of course, anticipate, desire or fear a particular outcome to events, as Aeneas does in the storm, without any guarantee that that *will* be the outcome. First-person narrators who are also characters within the narration, in Genette's term 'homodiegetic' narrators, may offer accounts of their past which are 'testimonies to the intensity of the present memory',[11] as is clearly the case with Aeneas's account to Dido of the fall of Troy. He opens his account with an address to the queen – 'you are ordering me to renew a grief that defies telling' (*infandum, regina, iubes renovare dolorem*, 2.3) – and the way in which he describes events (such as the discovery of the Horse outside Troy after the Greeks have seemingly retreated) are shot through with inflections of his knowledge of the outcome.[12] Narrators who are external to the narrative, whom Genette terms 'heterodiegetic',[13] can, of course, relate events that are subsequent to the moving 'present' of the narrative which the characters experience. However, epic's supernatural machinery provides it with a range of internal characters (gods, seers) and devices (prophecy, omens) that make prolepsis one of its most distinctive features.

All these narrators, internal or external, human or divine, seek to provide their narratives with meaning through the imposition of form, through emplotment. Aristotle's famous analysis of plot in the *Poetics* is no less amenable to the narratological distinction between story and discourse: 'by "plot"', Aristotle says, 'I mean the arrangement of the incidents' (*Poetics* 1450a4–5). Those incidents from which a plot is constructed may follow in linear sequence, but do not of themselves form a plot. Crucially, the plot must be a whole, which has a beginning, a middle and an end. A beginning, he says, is 'that which does not follow another thing of necessity [*ex anagkēs*]', that is, no necessary causal connection to what has gone before is asserted; an end, on the other hand, follows on by necessity or as a rule from something else, but has 'nothing after it', nothing, that is, that is seen as a necessary or plausible consequence of that end-point, and so would need to be included within the plot. So, 'well-constructed plots must neither begin nor end in a haphazard fashion' (*Poetics* 1450b27–33). Internal cohesion, consisting of necessary or probable causal connection between those incidents it contains, constitutes the well-formed plot. Such a plot will be a unity, and Aristotle's comments on this are worth citing at length (*Poetics* 1451a16–30):

> A plot [*muthos*] is not a unity, as some people think, if it is about one person. Many, infinitely many, things happen to one person, some of which do not combine to form a single entity; and so too an individual carries out many actions [*praxeis...pollai*] from which no unified action emerges [*ex hōn mia oudemia ginetai praxis*]. And so it seems that all those poets who have composed a *Heracleid*, a *Theseid*, and such-like poems have missed the mark, since they think that because Heracles was one man, a plot about him must also be a unity. Homer, exceptional as

he is in other respects, seems, by his artistry or natural genius, to discern this clearly also. In composing the *Odyssey*, he did not include everything that happened to Odysseus, such as being wounded on Parnassus, or his feigned madness when the army was being levied, since there was nothing necessary or probable connecting either of these incidents to the other. Rather he constructed the *Odyssey*, and likewise the *Iliad*, around the kind of unified action I mean.

Aristotle's theory links unity of plot (*muthos*) and unity of action (*praxis*) with *intelligibility*:[14] thus a life, be it Odysseus's or Aeneas's or Augustine's, is not to be understood in terms of all the 'infinitely many' incidents and actions that comprise it, but in terms of the form the emplotment imposes. That form, as so often for Aristotle, is conceived of as teleological: it looks towards the *telos*, the end or the goal. Always implicit in the events of narrative discourse is the Aristotelian relationship of necessary or plausible cause: 'because of this, then this...' Rather than being inert, events within a unified narrative discourse are dynamic and have a trajectory. This is a theory that has remained profoundly influential. In his analysis of Martin Amis's novel *Time's Arrow* (1991), which traces the life of a perpetrator of the Holocaust backwards from death to birth, Seymour Chatman suggests that narrative discourse is 'vectored', directing its readers from one moment to the next, usually in a forwards direction (Amis's novel is a rare exception), from an initial state of affairs to a final one.[15] Aristotle's thinking also lies behind Barthes's formulation that it is the role of the narrator to reduce an 'exploded reality to a slim and pure logos, without density, without volume, without spread', and 'to unite as rapidly as possible a cause and an end'.[16]

The narrated time that we are told elapses in the *Aeneid* as the narrative discourse moves from the start of Book 1 to the close of Book 12 may be no more than a year, but the narrator's summary in the opening sentence of the epic (1.1–7) suggests a span from the wanderings of Aeneas to the glories of his own time.[17] With its many analepses and prolepses, (the story that) the narrative (emplots) has an even greater temporal reach. But if the story gives the order of succession of events, it is the emplotment of those events into a unified whole within the narrative we read – their selection, which endows those incidents with not simply a temporal but a causal relationship – that endows them with their rationale and intelligibility. Within narrative, events do not sit inertly one after another, but are, as Chatman put it, *vectored* towards the end. A total narrative – the one gestured towards by Augustine – would show each and every event in its full intentional and consequential significance, and so offer total intelligibility, though, as Augustine remarks, this lies beyond human capacity; as Aristotle suggests, it would contain an *infinite* number of incidents. A narrative aims at intelligibility, and, so as to explain, has to have limits.

Following his initial summary of the story in the opening sentence, the narrator of the *Aeneid* asks the Muse to relate to him the *causes* (*Musa, mihi causas memora*, 1.8), and poses a number of questions about what motivated the events the poem emplots, in particular the role the goddess Juno played in them: 'in what had her will been offended, what caused her to grieve that she, the queen of the gods, drove a man renowned for his sense of duty to work his way through[18] so many misfortunes, to encounter so many hardships? Can heavenly minds feel such great anger?' (*quo numine laeso/quidve dolens regina deum tot volvere casus/insignem pietate virum, tot adire labores/ impulerit. tantaene animis caelestibus irae?* 1.8–11). On such a scale, any human perspective on events seems woefully inadequate. A human life is but part of that whole, situated somewhere (but where? What point in time?) within it. The human perspective is limited by its lack of knowledge, both of the past and of the future. Within the narrative of the *Aeneid*, Aeneas acts out that dilemma, and even the narrator of the epic presents himself as obliged to look beyond himself for an authority, the Muse, to answer the questions he poses. In resignation, Aeneas had said that 'god will grant an end [*finem*] to these things also' (1.199). The term *finis* in Latin can signify not simply an *end*, but a *trajectory* and a *goal* as well. Aeneas searches for a shape or form, in which the events which join beginning to end are meaningfully linked, so as to provide a rationale for the sufferings he and his people are undergoing and a belief that all will turn out to have been worthwhile in the end. He thus seeks to understand his own situation precisely in narrative terms. Virgil's exploration of the term *finis* continues in the scene in heaven that follows. What is the end of the events narrated? In which direction are they moving?

That scene, dramatised in terms of the present concerns of Venus and Jupiter, is a masterclass in the manipulation of narrative temporality, and of some of its most familiar tropes. Venus approaches her father (who is gazing down on Libya and is described as himself preoccupied, though the text is not entirely explicit about the cause of his concerns)[19] to express her anxiety about her son Aeneas. Without naming her, she cannot also suppress references to her continuing rivalry with, and suspicion of, Juno. She contrasts the current misfortunes of the Trojans with the promise[20] that there would come a time when their descendants the Romans would hold the whole world under their sway (1.234–37). In what feels like a veiled reference to Juno, she asks her father, 'Has some argument swayed you?' (*quae te, genitor, sententia vertit?*, 1.237). She says that she used to console herself thus for the destruction of Troy, balancing one fate with another (*fatis contraria fata rependens*, 1.239), but ill fortune continues to pursue the Trojans. Echoing what Aeneas said in 1.199, she asks Jupiter, 'what *end* of toils do you *give*?' (*quem das finem, rex magne, laborum?*, 1.241). In his response, Jupiter 'is carefully tailoring his prophecy to console Venus'[21] and, picking up on her words, immediately reassures her that 'the fate of your descendants remains unchanged, you'll see…nor has any argument swayed me' (*manent immota tuorum/fata tibi…neque me sententia vertit*, 1.257–60). He then launches into a rapid and selective proleptic narrative that vectors from Aeneas's arrival in Italy[22] through his death and the succession of Ascanius to the foundation of the city of Rome and way beyond. The significance of the toils endured by Aeneas and the Trojans is not to be assessed in terms of the present moment or the life of any of those involved, then or subsequently. 'On the Romans,' he says, 'I place bounds neither of fortune nor time' (*his ego nec metas rerum nec tempora pono*, 1.278), and, in response to Venus's question 'what end do you give…', he subtly alters the tense and syntax of her words to announce 'I have given dominion without end' (*imperium sine fine dedi*, 1.279). Her most pressing concerns will be resolved in the reconciliation of Juno to the dominion of the Romans (1.279–82), a start to which will be narrated in the closing book of the *Aeneid*; subsequently, that power will be significantly advanced by a lineage of her own which is 'to bound dominion by the Ocean,'[23] and who will bring in a new order of peace and justice (1.291–96). The sacrifices, it is implied, will have been worthwhile. This seems to offer the prospect of fulfilment in spatial terms, but Jupiter's speech is as much about *time*.[24]

Even if the latest datable events that can be specified in the *Aeneid* come from the Augustan period, the proleptic force of Jupiter's statement indicates that the *story* of the epic does not end there. Jupiter sketches a trajectory that intersects the narrator of the poem's 'present' in the Augustan Age en route to a future that stretches ahead *infinitely*. For narratologists, this can raise the intriguing conundrum of whether to classify the Virgilian narrator as a homodiegetic figure rather than a heterodiegetic one, internal to the narrative rather than outside it, as much one of the characters within it as Aeneas is – and no nearer the 'end' than he is. The narratee of the epic, anyone who identifies with the 'Romans' frequently referred to and even on occasion apostrophised, is no less in the midst of things than Aeneas or Virgil, no closer to the end, so readers too can be 'within' the narrative rather than looking at it from outside. A sense of an ending is offered, but it is a curious closure, which seems simultaneously an affirmation and a denial. 'Dominion without end' suggests there is no *end* to the toils, though they do have a trajectory, a goal, even if that is beyond the perspective of any individual at any particular point in time. The miracle of narrative endows those toils with an overarching purpose by offering the reader a fugitive glimpse of the 'God's-eye view' of 'the *total* history of "the sons of men"'.[25]

A fugitive glimpse is all it is, for Jupiter's speech is extraordinarily tantalising. Denis Feeney reminds us that 'Jupiter cannot be distilled out of the narrative, for he remains an agent, a character', and something more than harassed patriarch or everyday family guy. Feeney continues,

> Jupiter, to speak in social terms, is often seen in the poem presiding like a politic superior over an emerging consensus, preferring, if possible, not to force the issue. Vergil's tactfulness in this matter creates many unresolved areas of vagueness around Jupiter, Fate and Providence, and this comparative reticence has opened the path to readings of Jupiter as an omniscient, omnipotent, and imperturbable – even impartial – Providence.[26]

A century ago, the great Virgilian Richard Heinze introduced a shrewd note of caution:

> An all-powerful and all-knowing god, without whom and in opposition to whom nothing can happen, and who has himself relinquished his freedom to decide about anything and everything, is – perhaps – just about conceivable, but is completely unusable in an epic poem. Concessions must inevitably be made; the only question is, how can they be made as unobtrusively as possible?[27]

Jupiter's representation as a character within the narrative militates against any readings that would seek to find in him a vantage point from which the problems of evil and divine (in)justice would make sense.[28] The *Aeneid* is not a theological treatise, and the concessions (or prevarications) Virgil makes are not always unobtrusive, though they do show sensitivity to theological issues. 'Jupiter's perspective is, naturally, a commanding one,' Feeney concludes. 'It is the perspective of Fate, of Time, of history. It cannot be unsaid, undone.'[29] It is worth probing this perspective further.

'Fate' (*fatum*) is associated with the verb *fari*, to speak, and Fate in the *Aeneid* is sometimes identified with the utterance of Jupiter.[30] But the 'tactfulness' of which Feeney speaks does indeed bring a vagueness to Virgil's representation of Jupiter's relationship to Fate, not least its temporal aspect. He reassures Venus that the fate of her descendants remains unchanged (*manent immota tuorum/fata tibi*, 1.257–58), which suggests that, even if Jupiter is speaking to the moment so as to console Venus, matters are not being decided here and now. Moreover, the succession of future tenses that have dominated his prolepsis in 1.263–77 shift through the present tense in 278 to the perfect tense in 'I have given dominion without end' in 279, which might just be a reminder to Venus of the 'promise' she referred to in 1.235–37; somewhere, some time (neither specified nor itself narrated), it is implied, information along these lines has been communicated before. This is not an originary moment, no less, we may surmise, than the earlier occasion Venus has alluded to. In another brief analepsis in 1.19–20, the narrator tells us that Juno had heard that a race was rising from the Trojan stock that would one day overthrow Carthage: *sic volvere Parcas* (1.22). The accusative and infinitive construction makes this part of what Juno had heard, and so reveals what she understood to be the authority for this information – this is what the Fates were 'turning' – though, significantly, not the source from which she has learnt it: Jupiter? Venus? We are not told. Another case of a revelation of the future 'tailored' or 'packaged' for its recipient's consumption? Perhaps. 'Within' the poem's temporality, an originary moment is never attributed to Fate, and, as Jupiter remarks, the fates remain unchanged. Fate exists outside the poem's time; Jupiter re-presents it, as circumstances demand, within the poem's time. But he does also say, '*I have given dominion without end.*' He seems to be both inside and outside the poem's time.[31]

Jupiter's speech to Venus is introduced by the words *dehinc talia fatur*, 'then he speaks thus' (1.256). The verb *fari* is an archaic word which, in the words of Maurizio Bettini, 'represents a way of speaking that far surpasses other normal utterances in terms of its authority, efficacy, and credibility'.[32] As Bettini suggests, the verb has connotations of revelation and is associated with prophetic expression, a link that may be reflected in the way that *fari* is never found in the first person in the present indicative, but only in the future indicative. '*fabor*, rather than **for*, is the form that Roman authors employ: in other words, if a speaker wishes to perform an act of *fari*, he must project the moment of his utterance into the future,' Bettini remarks[33] – precisely as Jupiter declares to Venus in 1.262–63, when reassuring her that fate remains immoveable, 'for I shall explain at some length, since this anxiety is eating away at you' (*fabor enim, quando haec te cura remordet,/longius*). It may be, as Bettini suggests, that the utterances of Jupiter have a performative aspect, that is, they bring into being the events of which he speaks.[34] However, if this is the case, the temporality is thoroughly scrambled: *this* future-oriented 'revelation' (*fabor*) is presented as a corroboration of what has been said (*fata*) already. We will search for an originary moment of performative utterance, a moment of full *presence*, in vain. As a character and an agent, Jupiter does not stand outside the narrative's temporality. Augustine's God he is emphatically not. *Sicut Deus falsus erat, ita mendax vates*, Augustine remarks mordantly of Virgil: 'just as his god was false, so the poet is a liar.'[35]

'Liar' is a harsh judgement. If Virgil is elusive in his representation of Fate and its relationship with Jupiter, it is perhaps because he too was grappling with the sort of questions that exercised Augustine, a complex of theological issues comparable with those associated in the *Confessions* with the Word of God and how it operates within time and history. Indeed, when we examine the imagery in which Virgil seeks to gesture towards the notion of Fate, we may be reminded of the way in which reading a text was the metaphor, however inadequate, adopted by Augustine in his attempt to understand eternity.

When Jupiter announces his intention to speak of the future to Venus, he explains his action in 1.262 in a cryptic phrase that defies ready translation or interpretation: *volvens fatorum arcana movebo*. In his commentary on the line, R.G. Austin suggests that *arcanus* 'implies what is known to initiates only', kept away from public view, while *volvens* 'is probably a metaphor from the unrolling of a book', by which he means a papyrus scroll, though he qualifies the last statement by saying that *volvens* 'might be no more than "turning over" in the mind'.[36] A number of images may intersect in the word. The most intriguing gloss on these words comes in the story of the murder of Julius Caesar at the end of Book 15 of Ovid's *Metamorphoses*, which is clearly modelled on this scene, and, like so many Ovidian allusions to Virgil, works to deconstruct the ways in which Virgil's texts create their effects. When Venus attempts to hide her descendant Caesar in a cloud as, centuries earlier during the Trojan war, she had protected Paris from Menelaus, and Aeneas from Diomedes, Jupiter admonishes her (15.807–15):

Do you mean to disturb [*movere*] unconquerable Fate [*insuperabile fatum*] on your own, my daughter? You may go yourself into [*intres licet ipsa*] the abode of the three sisters [the Parcae]. There you will see the records of all that happens [*rerum tabularia*] on a vast structure made of bronze and solid iron, tablets which, being secure and eternal [*tuta atque aeterna*], fear neither the thunderings of the sky nor the wrath of the thunderbolt nor any ruinous collapse; there you will find engraved on everlasting adamant the destiny of your race. I myself have read them [*legi*] and noted them in my mind and shall recount them [*referam*], so that you may no longer be ignorant of what is to be.

Fate is given an unmistakably textual form, which is 'eminently Roman: heroically "bureaucratic", assuming the form of a state archive',[37] and paradoxically amusing in that this archive records the future as inexhaustibly as it does the past. It is explicitly 'eternal', not subject to the normal processes of destruction in time, not even by Jupiter's own thunderbolt. Ovid's Jupiter remarks to Venus that she has permission to enter the archives of the Parcae, implying that it is closed to others, which seems to pick up on the use of *arcana* by Virgil's Jupiter. Moreover, Ovid's Jupiter states that he has 'read' these records, and intends to 'recount' Fate (the future tense in *referam* picks up on *fabor* used by Virgil's Jupiter in *Aeneid* 1.261) by reference to this prior 'text'.

'Jupiter says he will open yet farther the secrets that lie in the book of fate', Virgil's commentator Conington explains.[38] The 'book' that Jupiter 'unrolls' in the *Aeneid* is metaphorically fleeting,[39] but Ovid's brazen literalisation can help us to sense its entailments. In the *Metamorphoses*, Jupiter represents himself explicitly as a reader, and the *rerum tabularia* – a phrase so aptly characterised by Bettini as 'bureaucratic' – that he reads look like nothing so much as the ordered, linear succession of events which narratologists term the idealised *story*. That story, as we discussed earlier, exists only as a theoretical construct to facilitate analysis of the narrative, but is regarded as logically prior to the actual narrative discourse which is said (and here the logical priority comes through clearly) to 'emplot' it. Virgil's Jupiter may be responsible for both the story (outside time) and the narratives he 'recounts': narrativisation is characteristically represented as a repetition of something that is, in some sense, already there, and Jupiter's speech to Venus contains intimations, at least, of repetition, though whether this is a repetition of an earlier telling or of Fate itself is again a matter of prevarication.

As a character within the poem, Virgil's Jupiter is the consummate rhetorician, an artful and politically astute narrator who 'tailors' or 'packages' his accounts to suit their immediate audiences, as when he configures a selective narrative of the future around Venus's lineage. In particular, he must equip his narratives with beginnings and ends so as to endow them with the unifying form that will grant them their intelligibility. With this in mind, look again at the verb Virgil uses of his Jupiter in 1.262, *movebo*, which is picked up by Ovid's Jupiter when he protests to Venus that she is preparing to alter Fate (*sola insuperabile fatum,/nata,* **movere** *paras?, Metamorphoses* 15.807–8). At the start of the second half of the *Aeneid*, the narrator calls upon the Muse Erato to guide him in telling of the battles Aeneas and his men have fought when they landed in Italy, a prayer that finds its climax in the words *maius opus moveo,* 'this is a greater theme I now set in motion' (7.45). The Muse is, as before (1.8), the guardian of the story that the poet, enmeshed in time and circumstance, can only narrate. In poetic contexts at least, *movere* has the status of a quasi-technical term for narrating 'to the moment';[40] Jupiter as a character and an agent within the *Aeneid* can only narrate thus. But he has just reassured Venus in 1.257–58 that the 'fates of your descendants remain unmoved' (*manent immota tuorum/fata*): unaltered, of course, but also in a form that lies beyond any particular time-bound telling of them. So, to paraphrase Ovid's Jupiter when he says to Venus in *Metamorphoses* 15.807–8, *sola insuperabile fatum,/ nata, movere paras?*: 'you want to go it alone and narrate Fate in your own way? That's not going to overcome it, my girl.'

The image of fate as a written text, and the very phrase *manent immota* recur in Helenus's description in *Aeneid* 3.443–52 of the cave of the Cumaean Sibyl, the prophetess who will accompany Aeneas on his journey to the Underworld. She foretells ('sings') the fates (*fata canit,* 3.444), and writes her prophecies on leaves, which she sets in order (*digerit in numerum,* 3.446), and keeps locked up in her cave. There they remain unmoved in their places and do not depart from their order (*illa manent immota locis neque ab ordine cedunt,* 3.447). Her filing system evokes the archive we saw in Ovid, and, in locking up the leaves in her cave, she tries to maintain a strict consecutive arrangement that reflects the order of Fate's unnarrated story. However, the slightest breath of wind when the door of her cave is opened by anyone coming in to consult her is sufficient to throw the leaves into disarray, and she makes no effort to replace them in their proper positions or to reunite the verses of her prophecies (*nec revocare situs aut iungere carmina curat,* 3.451). As a result, people go away disappointed. The stable, ideal order, the full knowledge of past and future, is disrupted by 'movement' of any kind. The imagery of movement recalls Aristotle's formulation in the *Physics* (4.11, 219a2–4) that time is not motion but has something to do with it

57

(*ti tēs kinēseōs estin*). Any attempt to set in motion the details of the story involves the imposition of beginnings and ends, and therefore offers only partial intelligibility. Moreover, the story is never told without a *motive*. The images of archive and book allow the *story*, rather than being simply a succession of inert and self-contained incidents in a purely chronological succession, to assume a shape or form that is not subject to change. The physical text acts as a symbol of something that persists over time, notionally unchanged. But Ovid's archive is like no archive we know. It preserves the records of past events, which is familiar enough, but the records of events yet to happen already exist in it as well. It is the same when Fate is figured as a book. Both images, it should be noted, suggest that what exists is not the events themselves but records of them, their representation in textual form.

This poses a metaphysical challenge to the standard narratological distinction between story and discourse. Whether the story is one of fiction or of fact, narratologists must make the assumption that the linear order of the story is the 'true' one, since it is only then that they can present the discourse as a modification of that order. Jonathan Culler puts it thus: 'narratological analysis of a text requires one to treat the discourse as a representation of events which are conceived of as independent of any particular narrative perspective or presentation and which are thought of as having the properties of real events.'[41] Two key terms are in play here, *representation* and *real*. They tend to crop up together, but their relationship can be construed in two opposing ways. The way that they are routinely deployed in narratology, as Culler formulates it, suggests that the events of the story are re-presented, and this term entails a logic that sees the story as anterior to or before the emplotment of its constituent events in any particular discourse. This is metaphysics as Plato would like it to be: the Form, eternal, unchanging, true and real, is prior to its representation, which is an imperfect replica of it. But, Culler suggests, that anteriority, assumed as a principle within narratological analysis, is in important respects misleading, as the story can be seen as an idealised extrapolation from the events in the discourse, which gives logical priority to the discourse. This can be readily grasped in the case of fictional narratives, but has purchase as well in respect of narratives like the *Aeneid* that could be regarded as factual or historical.

This is to reverse the poles of Platonic metaphysics. Reality, rather than being seen as prior to the act of representation, is seen as its effect. Much of the language we use presumes the Platonic take on metaphysics as the 'true' one. Even to speak of an 'incident' or 'event' colludes with this perspective, and it requires a reversal of the poles to envisage how a continuum of action can be constituted as an 'event' as a result of its representation, the imposition of boundaries that mark off its beginning and its end and so represent it as a unity. This is what Aristotle strives to do in the *Poetics* in thinking about what constitutes a *praxis*. In turn, in the *Physics* he isolates a period of time that can be measured in the mind by imposing at either end the boundary of a 'now' on the continuum of time. One 'now' is the point that marks the beginning, the other the end. This period can be of any length, from the instantaneous to the total history of the sons of men. And the former can be incorporated as part of the latter. These metaphysical tensions are encoded in the language we use. Is a factual narrative a record of things 'done' (*facta*, perfect passive participle of *facio*) by the characters, or things 'made' (*facta*) by the narrator?

Both the Platonic perspective and its counterpart see the act of representation as sovereign, though their metaphysical compasses take them off in opposite directions. From the former perspective, reality can take on a providential aspect, existing above and beyond any representation of it and not subject to change; from the latter, as the product of representation, reality is provisional in the sense of awaiting further re-presentations which will reconfigure it in ways as yet unforeseen. If Fate or the total history of the sons of men is thought of as a book, it is hard to get away from the idea that it has an Author. Augustine and Virgil both adopt a metaphysical perspective that is effectively Platonic. Humankind's role is to try, however imperfectly, to understand that Author and our role within his creation, although Augustine issues a warning not to get palmed off with shoddy gods like Jupiter, theologically undertheorised. Barthes cheerfully develops a metaphysical perspective that is the antithesis to the Platonic. For him, we encounter an exploded sprawl that writers seek to give shape to in their discourse, though if 'the narrator reduces exploded reality to a slim and pure logos', one effect of that success can ironically be to precipitate precisely the Platonic perspective and its sense that the discourse appears to be the imperfect representation of a pre-ordained reality. In Barthes's view, the writer deploys his discursive resources 'to reduce reality to a *point* in time, and to abstract from the depth of a multiplicity of experiences a pure verbal act, freed from the existential roots of knowledge, and directed towards a logical link with other acts, processes, a general movement of the world: it aims at maintaining a hierarchy in the realm of facts.'[42] In seeking to understand history, which in narrative terms is not simply the past, but the past-in-relation-to-the-present-in-relation-to-the-future, Virgil's narrator imposes his boundaries on the continuum of time and action to take us back to a point in time when Aeneas is shipwrecked on the shores of Carthage, a point when the future is already (to the narrator) and not yet (to Aeneas) known. From Aeneas's point of view, the narrator's knowledge would sound prophetic: what (for the narrator) happened was-to-happen. The effect is to make Aeneas's future feel determined. No human narrative is total, in its scope or in the intelligibility it offers. The passage of time obliges us to re-narrativise, but so does the limited intelligibility offered by existing narratives. Later circumstances and later texts oblige us to re-examine earlier ones, seeing them as fashioned of and for their moment, however right they may have seemed at the time. Virgil's masterstroke is to take this narrative logic and place the narrator of the poem and the readers within it, such that the future and what is-to-happen is, in some sense, already known. The following section will explore that qualification 'in some sense'.

LOOKING TOWARDS THE UNIVERSAL

Virgil's strategy of making Jupiter an internal narrator within the *Aeneid* allows the poem's *story*, Rome's rise to imperial dominion, to be equated with Fate or History. Howsoever this is emplotted or narrativised in particular circumstances to particular ends by particular historical actors 'within' the narrative, the story itself is assumed to remain unmoved and unchanged: for the Romans, there are 'no boundaries of space or time' (*nec metas rerum nec tempora*, 1.278) and 'dominion without end' (*imperium sine fine*, 1.279). Emplotment involves trajectory, and the teleological movement associated with the narrative of the *Aeneid* intersects in Jupiter's prophecy with the narrator's present in the Augustan age on its way into a future which is, strictly speaking, infinite in space and time. If the past and present of the poet's narrative are replete with specific historical detail, the future is not. You will search in vain for explicit references to, let us say, the successors of Augustus, the discovery of the New World, or the landing on the moon. The *Aeneid* sets itself up as the record of a prophecy that looks towards the end, but not in the sense of a specific content. 'Teleology,' Jacques Derrida has remarked, 'is, at bottom...a way of knowing beforehand the *form* that will have to be taken by what is still to come.'[43] In the ellipsis of the quotation, Derrida says that teleology is 'a negation of the future'. His take on teleology encourages us to think about what we mean by 'the future'. The Latinate *future*, from the future participle of the verb 'to be', suggests what 'is about to be', that is, it sees the future as a modality of the present, and, in a way, as already existing (*is* about-to-be). It thus reflects a metaphysics of presence. While we regularly anticipate ('capture in advance'), predict ('say in advance') or expect ('look out for') something, this, from Derrida's perspective, is not the future but (to use the metaphor of the scroll once more) the unfolding of what is anticipated, predicted or expected *from the point of view of the present*. Against this, Derrida frequently emphasises the etymological associations of the French *l'avenir*, what is to come (the *à-venir*). What is to come is in this sense *unknowable* in advance: who knows what may *arrive* in times to come?[44] For Derrida, teleology and the metaphysics of presence find their fullest expression in apocalyptic discourse – discourse itself and with it everything that speculates on vision, the imminence of the end, theophany, parousia, the last judgement' – without assuming that this gives *you* access to the truth.[45]

The narrator of the *Aeneid* does not know what will happen historically subsequent to its composition, but anticipates that *whatever* happens – good or bad, expected or unexpected – can be accommodated to the form it expresses; and in part, as we shall see in this section, that is reflected in the poem's reception. David Quint has suggested that there is a particularly strong collusion between narrative and power at work in epic discourse, not least in the *Aeneid*, where the narrative of history is associated with the acquisition of *imperium*:

> Epic takes particularly literally the axiom that history belongs to the winners. Imperial conquest of geopolitical space – the imposition of a single identifiable order upon different regions and peoples – becomes a process of history making. The *Aeneid* appears to identify history itself with a new idea of universal world history.[46]

The idea of a universal world history has been elegantly defined by one of its most recent practitioners, Francis Fukuyama: 'A Universal History of mankind is not the same thing as a history of the universe. That is, it is not an encyclopaedic catalogue of everything that is known about humanity, but rather an attempt to find a meaningful pattern in the overall development of human societies generally.'[47] Quint suggests that the narrative of this triumphal version of history takes on the shape of the well-made literary plot as defined by Aristotle in the *Poetics* in terms of a unity of action, with beginning, middle and end, and was so developed by the second-century BC Greek historian Polybius.[48] Polybius begins his history with the outbreak of the Second Punic War between Rome and Hannibal in 221 BC, and offers the following rationale for making this point in time the beginning of his narrative (1.3.3–4, my emphasis):

> Now up to this time the transactions [*praxeis*] of the world had been, so to speak, scattered, being as widely separated in their impulses and results as in their localities. But from this time, History becomes an organic whole [*hoionei sōmatoeidē*]: the affairs [*praxeis*] of Italy and Libya are interconnected with those of Asia and Greece, and *all lead up to one end* [*pros hen ginesthai telos*].

Previously history had been characterised by multiple, disconnected 'actions' (he shares the term *praxis* with Aristotle) or episodes, but now they are gathered up into a single coherent whole which leads up to one end (*telos*). That his notion of universal history is shaped by Aristotle's thinking is suggested also by his use of the adjective *sōmatoeidēs*, 'body-shaped', which recalls Aristotle's description of the unity of the well-made epic plot, a single and complete action (*mian praxin holēn kai teleian*) with beginning, middle and end, as 'like a single, whole living thing' (*hōsper zōon hen holon, Poetics* 1459a18–20).[49] Aristotle had claimed that poetry was more philosophical and more serious than history, because history speaks of particulars, events that have occurred (*ta genomena*, e.g. what Alcibiades did), whereas the job of the poet is to speak of universals (*ta katholou*), the sort of things that could occur (*hoia an genoito, Poetics* 1451a36–1451b11). Polybius's application of Aristotelian form to the past has the effect of suggesting that events themselves are invested with the kind of emplotment they would have in a work of literature, and have a teleological character, irrespective of any narrativisation of them.

The notion that History in this sense (capital H) has an end or goal is picked up in the title of Fukuyama's account of the triumph of Western liberal democracy at the end of the Cold War, *The End of History and the Last Man*. In an essay of 1989 from which his book was to emerge, Fukuyama makes clear his commitment to the notion of the *directionality* of history as manifested in (my emphasis) 'the *universalization* of Western liberal democracy as the *final* form of human government' in the context of the breach of the Berlin Wall:

> What we may be witnessing is not just the end of the Cold War, or the passing of a particular period of postwar history, but the end of history as such: that is, the end point of mankind's ideological evolution and the universalization of Western liberal democracy as the final form of human government. This is not to say that there will no longer be events to fill the pages of *Foreign Affairs*' yearly summaries of international relations, for the victory of liberalism has occurred primarily in the realm of ideas or consciousness and is as yet incomplete in the real or material world. But there are powerful reasons for believing that it is the ideal that will govern the material world *in the long run*.[50]

The 'End of History' does not crudely imply that events stop happening, nor that time stands still (though there are intimations of this to which we shall return), but that there seems to be a clear and indisputable *winner*, even if the process that leads to ultimate fulfilment is, for Fukuyama as it was for Polybius and for Virgil, as yet incomplete.

The End of History is, curiously, both already and not yet at hand, and the cessation of the ideological conflicts that marks 'the passing of a particular period of postwar history' ushers in, he maintains, the reign of peace. There will be setbacks along the way, he concedes, but the outcome is beyond doubt: to echo Derrida on teleology, we know already the form that will have to be taken by what is still to come. Events since 1989 may seem to have rendered Fukuyama's triumphalist tone somewhat hollow, but the logic of universal history allows those events to be seen, from a projected future retrospective point of fulfilment, as a temporary setback. The 'already but not yet' structure characteristic of teleological universalising narratives (whether of Empire or Western liberal democracy) asks us to accept that the phenomena that characterise 'the End of History' are present, albeit *imperfectly* (i.e. incompletely). Those phenomena are imperfectly present since, as Fukuyama puts it, 'victory… has occurred primarily in the realm of ideas or consciousness and is as yet incomplete in the real or material world.' Polybius significantly suggests that the idea that History has a shape and a direction can become internalised and itself play a part in the motivation of historical agents (1.3.6):

> For it was their victory over the Carthaginians in the war I have mentioned, and their belief that thereby the most important and greatest step towards universal dominion had been taken, which encouraged the Romans for the first time to stretch out their hands (*tas cheiras ekteinein*) towards the rest, and to cross with an army into Greece and Asia.

The image of stretching out their hands signifies the intentionality of the Romans, not simply to subjugate these lands but by their gesture to point to the overarching meaning of that particular act of subjugation.

What temporal experience is associated with this narrative of Universal History? The *Aeneid*, primarily through the figures of Aeneas and of the epic narrator himself, offers a dramatisation of what it means to enter that consciousness of being within History. Caught in the storm in the first book, Aeneas anticipates that he is very close to the 'end' of a particular story, one that is coterminous with his life, and evaluates his experience in that light. He believes he has nothing to look forward to, and he experiences his presumed end as demise. His despair leads him to wish that that demise had come earlier, an end from which, in his present circumstances, he believes he would have been able to perceive a (marginally) more satisfactory order or meaning to his life. This turns out not to be the end, of course, which recedes into the future, with Aeneas once more in the midst of things, and he can now anticipate a future for him and his men, one from which, as he tells them, they may be able to look back on the present hardships with some degree of pleasure: 'perhaps even these things at some stage it will be a pleasure to recall' (*forsan et haec olim meminisse iuvabit*, 1.203). 'These things' include encountering Scylla, Charybdis and the Cyclops (1.200–2), untoward episodes that would fall under the rubric of Derrida's *arrivant*:

> the future is necessarily monstrous: the figure of the future, that is, that which can only be surprising, that for which we are not prepared ... is heralded by species of monsters. A future that would not be monstrous would not be a future: it would already be a predictable, calculable, and programmable tomorrow. All experience open to the future is prepared or prepares itself to welcome the monstrous *arrivant*.[51]

For Derrida, being 'open to the future' involves welcoming the untoward when it happens, but Aeneas's strategy is rather different. He is keen to relegate the untoward to the past as part of a narrative that looks to a predictable, or, as Derrida puts it, a 'programmable tomorrow': 'through various disasters, through so many dangers, we are directing our course [*tendimus*, 'stretching'] to Latium, where the fates show [*ostendunt*] us a place to settle in peace' (1.204–6).[52] The monstrous is accommodated to a narrative that finds its end, grammatically as well as thematically, in the future perfect (*meminisse iuvabit*, 1.203). The arrival of Polybius's Romans may well be 'monstrous' and dubiously *welcome* to the inhabitants of Greece and Asia, but the Romans themselves are prepared for whatever hardship and sacrifice to achieve what they have 'stretched out their hands' towards.

In the shift of outlook in these two speeches of Aeneas we can feel the 'movement' of history, of time and circumstance, but it is also the movement of narrational perspective, for Aeneas is implicitly the narrator of his story at this point, and he imagines a future 'present' from which he will look back and view the events of the current present in a different, and more positive, way. This enacts the temporal distinction we explored in Chapter 1 between the narrated self and the narrating self, each with his own 'present', the division of temporal perspective which we saw to be constitutive of the understanding associated with narrative. Immediately following this scene, another narrator is introduced, Jupiter, a third- rather than first-person narrator, but one whose narration similarly imposes a division of temporal perspective, here a vast one: things may look bad now, his message is to Venus, but from a future 'present', they will look much more positive, as if to echo Aeneas's sentiment: *forsan et haec olim meminisse iuvabit*. Through signs and prophecies, through visiting another privileged narrator with precise and detailed knowledge of the 'future', his father Anchises in the Underworld, through gazing in puzzlement at the depiction of Roman history yet-to-happen on the shield his mother has had fashioned supernaturally for him, Aeneas (or, more precisely perhaps, the reader of this narrative) learns to adopt a perspective that transcends the limits of his own existence and to sense a significance in what has happened to him that seems lacking when viewed only within those narrow limits.

For the reader of the *Aeneid* to undergo that experience, the role of the poem's narrator is crucial. As we have seen, he represents himself and his readers as 'within' rather than 'outside' the (hi)story he narrates, and so without privileged knowledge of the details of the future beyond the historical moment of narration in the Augustan age or beyond the moment of reading, whenever that takes place. How does he negotiate this problem? In the description in Book 8 of the *Aeneid* of Aeneas's originary visit (as an uninvited but welcome guest)[53] to the settlement of Pallanteum, where the city of Rome will one day stand, Aeneas is guided across a site described to him by its present inhabitant, Evander, in terms of its past history. However, the epic narrator's voice superimposes on the site terms of description and names which cannot have been known to Evander or Aeneas, but which are familiar to the narrator and his audience: 'from here, Evander leads Aeneas to the Tarpeian seat and the Capitol, golden now, but in other times bristling with forest thickets' (*hinc ad Tarpeiam sedem et Capitolia ducit/aurea nunc, olim silvestribus horrida dumis*, 8.347–48). The juxtaposition of the deictic adverbs *nunc*, 'now', and *olim*, 'in other times', draws attention to the way in which two temporalities, that of Aeneas and that of the epic's narrator, are being brought together to provide a historical perspective that stretches across the centuries that divide them. Similarly a few lines later, 'conversing thus amongst themselves, they were approaching the dwelling of the humble Evander, and all around they could see the cattle lowing in the Forum of Rome and the chic Carinae' (*talibus inter se dictis ad tecta subibant/pauperis Evandri, passimque armenta videbant/Romanoque foro et lautis mugire Carinis*, 8.359–61). The narrative's 'present' is the time of Aeneas, centuries before the foundation of Rome and the building of its landmarks and districts, but these passages offer a view 'forwards' to a 'future', which also happens to be the narrator's 'present', when these features stand out in all their splendour.

One moment we can designate a 'present' is superimposed upon another such, but neither in itself offers a plenitude, and each is a complex temporality involving recollection of the past and anticipation of the future. Aeneas's experience of Pallanteum is moulded by Evander's historical description of it as experiencing a 'golden age' (*aurea.../saecula*, 8.324–25) of peace for its primeval indigenous inhabitants before a decline characterised by war and a migration of peoples that has brought Evander (and Aeneas) here (8.326–36). The immense passage of time and a trajectory of decline are further emphasised as Evander points out to Aeneas the ruins of two towns, Ianiculum and Saturnia, on the site (8.355–57). In turn, the narrator's 'present' looks back to a time when the site was 'bristling with forest thickets', but plots a trajectory of progress to the 'Capitol, golden now' (8.347–48): the trajectories of decline and rise have completed a cycle in returning the site to a golden age – an age characterised by the Augustan peace. That this may be an ongoing cycle is intimated in the ambiguous temporal adverb *olim*, which can refer to the past or the future: the Capitol, golden now, may one day be, as it had been in the past, bristling with forest thickets, no less a ruin than the settlements of Ianiculum and Saturnia.[54] However, that need not be a *definitive* end, for if such cycles or eddies are thought to exist within the movement of history, there will be a succession of rises and declines, advances and setbacks – some of which may well seem monstrous, in Derrida's sense, to those involved. David Wood remarks that History in this metaphysical sense 'is the unbroken transmission and development of meaning. Contingency, plurality, death, breaks, circles, regressions are all to be appropriated within a wider continuity.'[55]

A phenomenon gains historical shape, order and meaning only when the events it embraces can be viewed from the vantage point of the moment deemed (retrospectively, currently or prospectively) to be its end, and that end can be troped as fulfilment as well as demise. Both Aeneas, whether despairingly caught in the storm sent by Juno or wandering around Pallanteum suffused with hope, and the epic narrator of the *Aeneid* are, as we have seen, located within the movement of history. They are historicising as they go along, in the midst of time and circumstance, *anticipating* a moment, which they may believe to be proximate or very distant, that will mark a moment of ending or closure. For those historicising as they go along, the moment of closure on the significance of a chain of events lies at the point when a seemingly conclusive evaluation or judgement, seen in terms of fulfilment or demise, *will have* been made. Even the arch-rhetorician Jupiter in his prophecy to Venus asks her to look forward from that point to a moment at which she *will* be convinced that everything *has* come about as foretold: 'you will see the city and the promised walls of Lavinium, and...' (1.258ff.). For Aeneas in the storm, the moment that *will* establish that his travails *have not been* worthwhile seems imminent indeed. The tense I have been using, the future perfect (the 'completed' future), is emblematic of the closure anticipated by those historicising as they go along, but the closure is one contingent on events yet to happen: a historicisation made as one goes along anxiously awaits the moment of *its* historicisation. At some point in the future, will the Capitol, golden now, still be golden? The closure that any subsequent historicisation imposes is contingent on the moment, and the perception of circumstances, when it happens to arrive, and the closure so imposed determines the degree to which the earlier anticipated judgement is seen as 'right' or 'wrong'. So, Aeneas's evaluation of his life in the storm is seen, in the light of what subsequently happens, as wrong, his hopes as he walked around Pallanteum as perhaps well short of what was to transpire. The narrator of the *Aeneid* signals his awareness, in the cyclical pattern he attributes to history in its movement, of the historical situatedness of his own judgement and its contingency upon what will subsequently come to pass. This virtual invitation to look back on the Virgilian narrator was accepted by the humanist scholar Poggio Bracciolini, who in his *On the*

Vicissitudes of Fortune (*De varietate fortunae*) of 1448 depicted himself and a companion climbing the Capitoline hill in a self-conscious reprise of the tour of Evander and Aeneas. In Edward Gibbon's account of the passage in the very final chapter of his *Decline and Fall of the Roman Empire*, they 'reposed themselves among the ruins of columns and temples and viewed from that commanding spot the wide and various prospect of desolation'. In Gibbon's wonderful translation of Poggio, 'The forum of the Roman people, where they assembled to enact their laws and elect their magistrates, is now enclosed for the cultivation of pot-herbs, or thrown open for the reception of swine and buffaloes.'[56]

For those historicising as they go along, the 'present' moment and the judgement it encourages may be characterised by a sense of *provisional* fulfilment, as it does for the narrator of the *Aeneid* in the Augustan age, or, as for Poggio, demise; but at some point in the future, these 'same' things may very well look different. However, if the 'present' is regarded not as one of an ongoing or moving series of vantage points, but as the final one – which it will insofar as the 'present' is endowed with a sense of certainty and feels capable of passing a definitive judgement of 'right' or 'wrong' – that is to put an end to history and to adopt a God's-eye view, which is to see in the phenomena under review their direction and final meaning all along, as Jupiter does. However, such a *providential* view is not restricted to the gods. As the *Aeneid* demonstrates, narrative can be so orchestrated as to make that view available to any mere mortal, and that view can be internalised so as to become a modality of experience – as it is for Fukuyama (in 1989, at any rate).

To inhabit History as a concept or modality of experience is to have enormous self-belief. In the *Aeneid*, History is mapped on to *imperium*, and the plot of History is Rome's progress towards 'dominion without end' (*imperium sine fine*, 1.279). In his recent study of the meaning of the term *imperium*, John Richardson suggests that its primary association in the Augustan period was 'power', but it was coming to be associated with 'territorial extension as such', and 'in nine cases at least, this power is represented as of immense or even infinite extent.'[57] So, at the time of composition of the *Aeneid* (and, as the passages cited by Richardson suggest, the poem was crucial in this respect), *imperium* is coming to take on its now familiar connotations of 'empire'. Empire is characterised by transgression, the crossing of boundaries; it reacts to 'outside' by the desire to make it 'inside', until, in the Virgilian formulation, that boundary is rendered meaningless as empire becomes universal. From a temporal perspective, universal Empire (capital E) has an orientation towards a future that is *conceived of* as fully completed, a future that *will have been* achieved in its entirety: the future *perfect*, the completed future, is both its tense and its modality. This future, confidently anticipated (even if, conceptually, infinitely deferred), gets refracted back onto the present, as simultaneously already, but not yet, completed. On the shores of Carthage, Aeneas troped fulfilment as 'a place the fates show us to settle in peace' (1.204– 5). Thus the Augustan peace described in Jupiter's speech to Venus in 1.291–96 can already, but not yet, be the 'end of history'. The reign of peace does not preclude wars, but they are subsumed to its logic, as Anchises in the Underworld suggests. Beyond death, Anchises has access to the future as well as the past, as his description to Aeneas of the heroes of Rome yet to be born makes clear. In 6.851–53 Anchises speaks these words:

tu regere imperio populos, Romane, memento
(hae tibi erunt artes), pacique imponere morem,
parcere subiectis et debellare superbos.

Make it your business and don't you forget, Roman, to rule the nations with your dominion (this will be your science), and to impose civilized behaviour upon peace, to show mercy to those who submit and to crush the arrogant in war.

His apostrophe is notionally spoken to Aeneas, but it summons up an eternal present, the discursive present of reading we explored in Chapter 1. To everyone – no matter where, no matter when – who feels addressed by the vocative *Romane*, ethical confidence is married to the confidence of historical judgement, and the means, war, is justified by the end, peace. Such a Roman feels sure that he is, ultimately, *right* – historically, morally, politically, epistemologically.

The God's-eye view associated with this modality of experience, for all that it believes it has transcended history and circumstance, remains a view from within history, and subject to the pressures of re-narrativisation. The view of a god like Jupiter, as he appears in the *Aeneid* foretelling for the Romans dominion without end, has the capacity to be overtaken by events that seem to those involved to be *so* conclusive as to challenge the modality of experience it represents, and to compel re-historicisation. Such was the conclusion of Augustine, as he wrote *City of God* in the wake of the sack of Rome by Alaric and the Visigoths in August 410 AD. The idea that Rome was 'the Eternal City', which had become current in the Augustan period,[58] was not restricted to pagans, but was held by some Christians as well, 'who thought of the Roman Empire as the instrument of divine providence, and therefore, potentially, as an empire without end'.[59] The Christian writer Prudentius in his poem *Against Symmachus*, written after an earlier incursion by Alaric had been averted at Pollentia, south of Turin, in 402, clearly had no difficulty in appropriating the language of the Virgilian Jupiter when proclaiming of the emperor Theodosius that 'in short he sets limits neither of space nor of time, he points to empire without end' (*denique nec metas statuit nec tempora ponit/imperium sine fine docet*, 2.541–42).[60] The outcome at this juncture, defeat for Alaric, confirmed the logic, but the events of 410 showed Alaric's sack of the Eternal City as a monstrous *arrivant* that resisted attempts to accommodate it.

So, for many who inhabited the idea of Universal Empire as a modality of experience, the sack of the city was of traumatic psychological significance, an existential crisis. St Jerome wrote, 'I was so distressed that it was like the old proverb: I didn't even know my own name.'[61] For Augustine, the conclusion to be drawn was clear: 'all earthly kingdoms will have their end' (*finis erit terrenis omnibus regnis*, Sermon 105.8.11), and the sack of Rome definitively gives the lie to Jupiter's prediction of Rome as an 'empire without end'. He is inclined to forgive Virgil for his part in all this, but condemns Jupiter as a false god and a deceptive prophet (*Sermon* 105.7.10):

> Those who have promised eternity to earthly kingdoms...have lied in order to flatter. A certain poet of theirs brought on Jupiter to speak and he said of the Romans, 'For them I place boundaries of neither space nor time: I have granted empire without end.' Clearly this is not true...If

we wished to reproach and mock Virgil because he said this...he would say to us: 'Yes, I know. But what could I do, as a peddler of words to the Romans, but flatter them by promising something that was false? Still even in this I was careful: when I said, "I have granted empire without end," I brought on their own Jupiter to say it. I did not say this false thing in my own persona, but imposed the lying persona of Jupiter: as the god was false, so too was he a deceptive prophet.'[62]

From the vantage point of his present moment, Augustine feels certain enough to pass judgement upon Jupiter as wrong, but although he rejects Jupiter as a false god, and believes that no historical regime can fulfil the Virgilian prediction of 'empire without end', he nonetheless retains a commitment to it as an *idea* or *concept*: 'Terrestrial kingdoms undergo change; but he shall come of whom it is said, "And of his kingdom there shall be no end"' (*Sermon* 105.7.9). The power of Virgil's conceptualisation impressed itself upon Augustine also from the speech of Anchises. He quotes it in the preface to *City of God* to sum up the earthly city's desire to dominate others, in contrast to the divine law, which states that 'God resists the proud, but gives grace to the humble.'[63] In the terrestrial city of lived experience, we all crave peace (even, Augustine suggests, a monster like Virgil's Cacus [*City of God* 19.12]), and we fight wars to achieve it. The imperial prospect of universal peace becomes mapped into his scheme as the ultimate good, the *perfect* peace of eternal life, 'of such a kind and so great that nothing can be better or greater than it' (*City of God* 19.10). This peace is not only physical but intellectual. History as narrative, we have seen, is associated with the language of *movement* and *disturbance*. At the 'end of history' lies perfect peace, the peace that passes all understanding.[64]

Alongside the earthly city subject to the flux of history and associated with the flawed vision of a false god, Augustine proposes an equivalent under the providential guidance of the one true God,[65] revealed in a more secure form than Virgil's narrative, brilliant though that may be (*City of God* 11.1):

The City of God of which we are treating is vouched for by those Scriptures whose supremacy over every product of human genius does not depend on the chance impulses of the minds of men, but is manifestly due to the guiding power of God's supreme providence, and exercises sovereign authority over the literature of all mankind.

'The chance impulses of the minds of men' translates Augustine's phrase *fortuitis motibus animorum*, where the word *motus* ('movement') seems to connote the human being's entanglement in time, in language and in the necessity to narrate (*movere*). Augustine conceives of God as existing outside those constraints, and not needing to narrate. An acute awareness of the limitations of the human viewpoint within history was no disincentive to Augustine producing in the *City of God* a work of Universal History on the grandest scale.[66] As Donald J. Wilcox has put it, 'The *City of God* is not a historical narrative, but an essay on the meaning of history, and in it Augustine used historical events only as examples of his theory.'[67] Within human history, Augustine singled out two particularly famous examples of empires that were transient, Babylon and, following its sack, Rome (*City of God* 18.2), which he saw as the two most prominent episodes in the human will to power. He thus acknowledges the human capacity to see unity within time:

> his connection of Babylonian and Roman history indicated his commitment to a unified time whose significance could be seen by the human mind. He considered the two empires not as the greatest in fact but as the most important in fame. It was in the consciousness of those looking at the past that the empires of the world took on a unity, just as in the *Confessions* he showed that the unity of time itself depended on the creative activity of the human soul.[68]

This mammoth work falls into two parts. The first, a rebuttal of pagan accusations that the sack of Rome was the result of Christian neglect of the pagan gods, treats the City of God 'both as it exists in this world of time, a stranger among the ungodly, living by faith, and as it stands in the security of its everlasting seat' (*City of God* 1, Preface). In the second, he says, 'My task is to discuss, to the best of my power, the rise, the development and the destined ends of the two cities, the earthly and the heavenly, the cities which we find, as I have said, interwoven, as it were, in this present transitory world, and mingled with one another' (*City of God* 11.1).[69]

In a work with its own totalising pretensions, Augustine thus sets out to supplant the pagan Roman tradition and to make History and

Empire synonymous with Christian providence. It is clear to Augustine that Jupiter's prospective narrative of Roman history in the *Aeneid* as an empire without end has been shown to be conclusively wrong in the light of what he views as a closural event, the sack of Rome, and that this also strikes a fatal blow at pagan theological concepts. In his discussion of historical revisionism, Reinhart Koselleck suggests that, though history may be written by the victors in the short run, 'historical gains in knowledge stem in the long run from the vanquished... The experience of being vanquished contains an epistemological potential that transcends its cause, especially when the vanquished are required to rewrite general history in conjunction with their own.'[70] In particular, concepts assumed to be universal are shown to be specific to their historical moment and in need of rigorous re-theorisation if they are to be re-stabilised.

Nonetheless, it is also the case, in Augustine's exhortation to the people of Rome in *City of God* 2.29 to abandon their worship of pagan gods, that Virgil's conceptualisation of Empire as precipitated in the narrative of the *Aeneid* survives as a structure or shell for his own ideas:

> Take possession now of the heavenly country for which you will endure but the smallest hardship, and there you will reign in truth and forever. There you will find no hearth of Vesta, no Capitoline stone [i.e. statue of Jupiter], but the one true God who places no bounds of space or time but will grant an empire without end.[71]

Only such a God can know 'the total history of "the sons of men"'; in contrast, as he had argued in *Confessions* 11, the internal human experience of temporality renders all human historical judgements relative. In his work *On Christian Teaching* (2.28.44), he argues:

> Historical narrative also describes human institutions of the past, but it should not for that reason itself be counted among human institutions. For whatever has already gone into the past and cannot be undone must be considered part of the history of time, whose creator and controller is God.[72]

He seeks to open out a distinction between history in the sense of historical narratives, written by humans about human institutions within the human experience of temporality, and History, which he describes as an order of time, that is created by God, guided by his providence, and 'cannot be undone'. This he maps on to the doctrine of two empires, allowing him to relativise any human account of a human institution, such as the Roman empire. In accommodating their eschatological faith to pagan myth, many Christians like Prudentius had coupled the rule of Christ to the persistence of Rome. When the sack of Rome failed to coincide with the Last Judgement, the shock was theological as well as cultural. In separating out histories (plural) and History, empires (plural) and Empire, Augustine could argue that historical phenomena, on a scale from the smallest human action to the greatest empires, come and go, and, as Koselleck puts it, 'whatever might happen on this earth was thereby structurally iterable and in itself unimportant, while being, with respect to the Hereafter and the Last Judgement, unique and of the greatest importance.'[73]

Augustine's appropriation of the concept of Empire arises out of a sense that he is correct in seeing the sack of Rome as the 'end' of the Roman empire. But what if, in the passage of time, the sack of the city is viewed not as a definitive demise (imposing the boundary of a narrative end and so making Rome's empire into a historical episode) but as a temporary setback, a blip, that can be accommodated within Rome's destiny – as, Virgil's poem could suggest, were Aeneas's shipwreck, or, on a larger scale, the civil wars that had dominated the century before Virgil wrote? The fall of Troy, indeed, could be seen in terms not of rupture but of continuity, facilitated by a politically expedient change of name from 'Trojan' to 'Roman' (*Aeneid* 12.828). Such a re-narrativisation takes us back 'into' the story, and has appealed to those, from Charlemagne to Napoleon or Mussolini, from the Holy Roman empire to the European Union, who have laid claim to the historical heritage of the Roman empire, and it underlies the remarkably flexible doctrine of *translatio imperii*, the 'transfer' or 'carrying across' of Empire from one historical time and place to another.[74] Such an attitude accords with Augustine's notion of the structural iterability of historical phenomena, though it can accommodate or downplay as it wishes the theological imperative that drove his argument of the two cities. The sense that one is a part of that Empire is a recurrent trope in Western literature,[75] and is perhaps most memorably described by Henry James on the opening page of *The Golden Bowl*:

The Prince had always liked his London, when it had come to him: he was one of the Modern Romans who find by the Thames a more convincing image of the truth of the ancient state than any they have left by the Tiber. Brought up on the legend of the City to which the world paid tribute, he recognized in the present London much more than in contemporary Rome the real dimensions of such a case. If it was a question of an *Imperium*, he said to himself, and if one wished, as a Roman, to recover a little of the sense of that, the place to do it was on London Bridge, or even, on a fine afternoon in May, at Hyde Park Corner.

The passage well illustrates the ideology of *translatio imperii*: for the Prince, Empire has been moved across boundaries of space (Rome to London) and time (the ancient state to present London), but he has no difficulty in seeing himself, if he so wished, 'as a Roman', and as such, open to address in terms of Anchises's apostrophe in *Aeneid* 6.851. Across apparent historical rupture and change, Empire persists as a modality to be inhabited.

However, *imperium* may also be *translated* as 'power', allowing for a less immediately obvious but more sinister *translatio imperii*, and a less savoury image of what it is to inhabit that modality. In George Orwell's *Nineteen Eighty-Four*, O'Brien interrogates Winston Smith under torture in the Ministry of Love:

'There is a party slogan dealing with the control of the past,' he said. 'Repeat it, if you please.'

'"Who controls the past controls the future: who controls the present controls the past,"' repeated Winston obediently.

'"Who controls the present controls the past,"' said O'Brien, nodding his head with slow approval. 'Is it your opinion, Winston, that the past has real existence?'

Again the feeling of helplessness descended upon Winston. His eyes flitted towards the dial. He not only did not know whether 'yes' or 'no' was the answer that would save him from pain; he did not even know which answer he believed to be the true one.

O'Brien smiled faintly. 'You are no metaphysician, Winston,' he said. Until this moment you had never considered what is meant by existence. I will put it more precisely. Does the past exist, concretely, in space? Is there somewhere or other a place, a world of solid objects, where the past is still happening?'

'No.'

'Then where does the past exist, if at all?'

'In records. It is written down.'

'In records. And – –?'

'In the mind. In human memories.'

'In memory. Very well, then. We, the Party, control all records, and we control all memories. Then we control the past, do we not?'

'But how can you stop people remembering things?' cried Winston again momentarily forgetting the dial. 'It is involuntary. It is outside oneself. How can you control memory? You have not controlled mine!'

O'Brien's manner grew stern. He laid his hand on the dial.

'On the contrary,' he said, '*you* have not controlled it. That is what has brought you here...'[76]

Orwell tracks the disintegration of Winston's personality and individuality under the pressure of a torture that is mental as much as physical. 'Power is not a means, it is an end,' O'Brien tells him. 'The object of power is power.'[77] The role of the individual is, of himself, to subsume himself in the collective. O'Brien continues,

> God is power. But at present power is only a word as far as you are concerned. It is time for you to gather some idea of what power means. The first thing you must realize is that power is collective. The individual only has power in so far as he ceases to be an individual. You know the Party slogan: 'Freedom is Slavery'. Has it ever occurred to you that it is reversible? Slavery is freedom. Alone – free – the human being is always defeated. It must be so, because every human being is doomed to die, which is the greatest of all human failures. But if he can make complete, utter submission, if he can escape from his identity, if he can merge himself in the Party, so that he *is* the Party, then he is all-powerful and immortal.[78]

Mutatis mutandis (for this is at the heart of translation, a point to which we shall return), Winston must make like Aeneas: 'if he can escape from his identity, if he can merge himself in the Party, so that he *is* the Party', and not see himself in terms of his own life, but subsume his individual hopes, desires and memories to the cause so that he can truly recognise himself in the collective apostrophe (Anchises's *Romane*): Big Brother is watching you. And, in Winston's case, respond of himself to the Party's slogans 'Freedom is Slavery' – and 'War is Peace'. If it is 'a question of an *Imperium*', one says to oneself, Orwell, no less than Virgil, Augustine and Henry James, can be part of the response. Winston's earlier attempts to re-write the past at the Party's behest in his job at the Ministry of Truth, although effective and bringing him some job satisfaction, were crude (certainly in comparison with Virgil's).[79] This is not solely the province of (re-)narrativisation. Bringing another text into the argument, like Orwell's, can reconfigure the past *without changing a word* – formally, though the interpretative content of course changes over time. To conclude this chapter, I want to see what another theoretical appropriation of the concept of *imperium* can bring to this discussion.

Narrative is central to the development of nations and a sense of national identity,[80] and the *Aeneid* can certainly be seen as a national epic. Borders, which distinguish between inside and outside, are fundamental to the nation. As Ika Willis puts it, 'The nation – that is, the spatial extension of sovereignty, its inscription in terrestrial space – constitutes itself through the practices by which it determines its edges.'[81] However, the prospect held out to the Romans by Jupiter is of *imperium* without limits of space or time. In pondering the decline of the sovereignty of nation states in the face of the forces of globalisation, Michael Hardt and Antonio Negri appeal to *Empire* in this metaphysical sense:

> The concept of Empire is characterized fundamentally by a lack of boundaries: Empire's rule has no limits. First and foremost, then, the concept of Empire posits a regime that effectively encompasses the spatial totality, or really that rules over the entire 'civilized' world. No territorial boundaries limit its reign. Second, the concept of Empire presents itself not as a historical regime originating in conquest, but rather as an order that effectively suspends history and thereby fixes the existing state of affairs for eternity. From the perspective of Empire, this is the way things will always be and the way they were always meant to be. In other words, Empire presents its rule not as a transitory moment in the movement of history, but as a regime with no temporal boundaries and in this sense outside of history or at the end of history.

Although Hardt and Negri do not invoke Virgil here, this might almost be a commentary on Fate and History in Jupiter's speech. They continue,

> Third, the rule of Empire operates on all registers of the social order extending down to the depths of the social world. Empire not only manages a territory and a population but also creates the very world it inhabits. It not only regulates human interactions but also seeks directly to rule over human nature. The object of its rule is social life in its entirety, and thus Empire presents the paradigmatic form of biopower. Finally, although the practice of Empire is continually bathed in blood, the concept of Empire is always dedicated to peace – a perpetual and universal peace outside of history.[82]

In turn, this could be a paraphrase of the other key passage in which Empire is characterised, the climax of the speech of Anchises in the Underworld, where the Roman is enjoined to remember 'to rule peoples with your dominion…to impose civilized behaviour upon peace, to show mercy to those who submit and to crush the arrogant in war' (6.851–53). In offering what they term a 'genealogy of the concept' (and thus a historicisation of it), Hardt and Negri do trace it back to Rome and remark, 'Empire exhausts historical time, suspends history, and summons past and future within its own ethical order. In other words, Empire presents its order as permanent, eternal and necessary.'[83] Specifically, as they said earlier, Empire presents its rule not as a transitory moment in the *movement* of history. Empire, in seeking to erase 'borders' wherever it finds them, gestures towards a totality that also abolishes the temporal limits of beginnings and ends – the limits of nation and narration alike.

Hardt and Negri prefix the four-fold characterisation of Empire quoted above with this theoretical reflection: 'We should emphasize that we use "Empire" here not as a *metaphor*, which would require demonstration of the resemblance between today's world order and the Empires of Rome, China, the Americas, and so forth, but rather as a *concept*, which calls primarily for a theoretical approach.'[84] Recall the Prince in *The Golden Bowl*, who is a classic instantiation of the doctrine of *translatio imperii*. He experiences Empire both as *metaphor*, in Hardt and Negri's sense, as he contemplates the movement of history ('he was one of the Modern Romans who find by the Thames a more convincing image of the truth of the ancient state than any they have left by the Tiber') and as a *concept*, as he considers the 'truth' of the ancient state. Thinking metaphorically involves thinking hypothetically, *as if* London were Rome (and vice versa), or interrogatively, *what if* London were Rome (or vice versa)? So, the Prince thinks metaphorically to himself '*If* it were a *question* of an *Imperium*…and *if* one wished, as a Roman, to recover a little of the sense of *that*', and, in response to the hypothetical deictic 'that', points to where and when the transcendent concept may be experienced in the here-and-now: 'the *place* to do it was on London Bridge, or even, *on a fine afternoon*, in May, at Hyde Park Corner.' He adopts both the human and the God's-eye viewpoint, but only inhabits the concept fleetingly ('a little of the sense of that'), whereas in the world of *Nineteen Eighty-Four* or of aspirant globalisation, the hypothetical and the interrogative are to be abolished, difference is to be effaced, and the indicative is to reign unchallenged, linking terms that are interchangeable because identical: freedom is slavery, war is peace, the market is always right. The concept of Empire is to be inhabited not fleetingly, but permanently.

Empire deployed as a metaphor 'would require demonstration of the *resemblance* between today's world order and the Empires of Rome, China, the Americas, and so forth'. Empire is a metaphor, in Hardt and Negri's parlance, when it involves thinking about Empire *within* the continuing processes (the 'movement') of history as a series of discrete historical phenomena: empires rise and fall – that is, have beginnings, middles and, if one believes that one's historical judgement is *right*, ends that make of them narrative episodes. The *concept*, however, has a different temporal character: like the Prince, one can continue to see oneself, 'if one wished', as *still* a Roman, or to think, as Ika Willis has put it, 'the Empire never ended';[85] one can inhabit this concept in all its totalising reach, in which all boundaries of time and space are transcended. As the example of the Prince indicates, both are in play in the experience of *translatio imperii*. Treating Empire as metaphor can offer a genealogy, a history, of the concept that leads from *imperium* in Virgil's *Aeneid* to the City of God in Augustine, through O'Brien's chilling disquisition to Winston Smith in Orwell's *Nineteen Eighty-Four* to Hardt and Negri's own critique of capitalism and globalisation. But if this is to happen, any distinction between '*imperium*', 'God', 'power' and 'globalisation' must be fleetingly (one hopes) abolished. What are perceived as boundaries, whether of geography, historical period, culture or language, must be both acknowledged *and* – in the end – elided. The concept of *concept* and the concept of *Empire*, in the totalising sense that the narrative of the *Aeneid* presents us, are isomorphic.

This can lead to confusion. As Willis remarks, 'The question of the survival of Empire is complicated by the fact that '"Empire" is – implicitly or explicitly – one of our primary *conceptual* tools for thinking survival in the first place'.[86] In the temporality of discourse, concepts (and not simply the concept of Empire) can be configured as principles or terms of analysis in such a way as to suggest that they transcend the occasion of their invocation, that they have a *universal* application not constrained by boundaries of space or time. If investment in a concept is total, if it is taken, in the end, to be *true* (albeit imperfectly understood or realised in the here-and-now), it takes on the aspect of Universal Empire, its dominion reaching over all time, past, present and future, the utopian temporality that satisfies the craving for certainty. Discourse on ideas is not an exercise of pure thought. If Virgil invokes *imperium* and O'Brien 'power' with this totalising investment, they also mobilise these concepts 'within' History to the end of conferring, precisely, *ideological* legitimacy in the here-and-now. Reconfiguring such concepts as metaphors opens them up to being seen as historically specific and conceptually imperfect, as Hardt and Negri seek to do in their critique of globalisation. Concepts can thus be seen to have their histories. They come into being, metamorphose and pass away as matters of concern, preferred terms of analysis and modalities of lived experience.[87]

One further question that *translatio imperii* poses is that of translation in its linguistic aspect. Imperial thinking aspires to the stability not only of concepts, but to the stability of their expression as well. It aspires, therefore, to transcend the limitations of human language that Augustine felt so keenly. Virgil's *Aeneid* holds out the prospect of the universality of Latin culture[88] and of Latin as a universal language,[89] and the status of Latin over the succeeding centuries is an important aspect of the poem's reception, as Latin becomes the established language of the Church, the law and the academy.[90] It is a telling detail in *The Golden Bowl* that when the Prince thinks conceptually of Empire, it is 'the question of an *Imperium*' that goes through his mind: for him, the Latin term continues best to capture the concept he fleetingly inhabits. The totalitarian world of *Nineteen Eighty-Four* looks forward, if that is the phrase, to the 'final adoption' by the year 2050 of Newspeak, a language in which, 'so far as it could be achieved', a word was 'simply a staccato sound expressing *one* clearly understood concept', stripped of any associations and so 'impossible to use … for literary purposes or for political or philosophical discussion. It was intended only to express simple, purposive thoughts, usually involving concrete objects or physical actions.'[91] Newspeak aspires to the status of the language of Adam before the Fall, or what the philosopher Richard Rorty terms a 'final vocabulary'[92] – when words are not seen as performing any mediating function at all, when they simply 'say what they mean' without any ambiguity, or any alteration of meaning in their reception across time and place. Such words would be pure concepts, incapable of being metaphorically 'carried across' (the image encoded in the Greek term *metaphora*) the limits of their 'proper' reference, so as to generate new meanings through the assertion of resemblance and difference.

So, when Hardt and Negri seek to think *metaphorically* about Empire, what this involves is the 'demonstration of the resemblance between today's world order and the Empires of Rome, China, the Americas, and so forth', and they want to take Empire within history, and mobilise it towards a new argumentative end. This also involves the assertion of resemblances and equivalences on the linguistic level: how is *imperium* to be *translated*, to be 'carried across' (as the imagery of the Latin term suggests)[93] perceived boundaries of language and culture, time and place? As 'power'? As 'empire'? As 'globalisation'? As 'God'? The process, moreover, operates not simply at the level of the single word, but discursively and dynamically at the level of form and intention. In *Nineteen Eighty-Four*, the goal of the Party is the final adoption of Newspeak, and to this end old documents are translated into Newspeak. Of the Declaration of Independence ('We hold these truths to be self-evident, that all men are created equal … That whenever any form of Government becomes destructive of those ends, it is the right of the People to alter or abolish it …') it is said,

It would have been quite impossible to render this into Newspeak while keeping to the sense of the original. The nearest one could come to doing so would be to swallow the whole passage up in the single word *crimethink*. A full translation could only be an ideological translation, whereby Jefferson's words would be changed into a panegyric on absolute government.[94]

Translation involves processes of compression, expansion and reconfiguration towards new ideological ends, as the history of a text like the *Aeneid* can suggest. The 'true' or 'proper' meaning of a word like *imperium* or of a text like the *Aeneid* is, within time, a process of endless contestation, and to grasp it we would need to be immortal. But to hold a truth to be self-evident, here, now – there's a mighty notion. What concepts would one inhabit, if one *wished*, more than fleetingly?

3

DETERMINATION

In the previous chapter, I explored the way in which literary characters can inhabit a concept as a modality of experience, and how a concept such as *imperium* (whether we translate it as 'empire' or 'power') can exert a totalising grip on those who internalise it in the form in which it is 'condensed' out of a narrative like the *Aeneid*. But in life no less than in literature, some people display a strong sense of trajectory in their beliefs and behaviour, a determination to strive towards some end or other. In this and the next chapter (for an arc of argument will span the two), I extend the analysis to consider how individuals may come to insert themselves into narrative structures and to see themselves as characters emplotted (by themselves, by some higher power or by some idea) in such a way that they view their actions as in some way (pre-)determined. The issues of determinism and free will are associated with the question of whether time is, in a metaphysical sense, 'open' or 'closed', and an 'economy' of free will and determinism operates even in those (con)texts where one or the other seems to dominate. As in earlier chapters, the argument is structured around a major text, here Sophocles's *Oedipus the King*, which in its reception has been drawn into passionate, though arguably one-sided, debate about the issues of free will and determinism. In the first section, I engage with Gary Saul Morson's strong metaphysical assertion

84

that '[r]eal time is an ongoing process without anything resembling literary closure' to probe initially how classical literature goes about representing issues of free will and determinism in narrative, before exploring how the providential aspect associated with the prophecy that plays so important a role in these representations is occluded, though not necessarily thereby eliminated, in later attempts to 'uncover' or *determine* 'latent' or 'hidden' patterns of historical causation. Issues surrounding determinism and free will can thus be seen to be no less important for interpretation as they are for narrative. The second section then uses a range of orthodox and unorthodox approaches to Sophocles's *Oedipus* to probe the challenges posed by attempts to determine the meanings of texts, and to consider the question what is literary interpretation for? What is its *end*?

PLOTTING DETERMINISM AND FREE WILL

For most characters within narratives, the experience of time is asymmetrical. The past is, to some extent at least, known, but the future for the most part can only be a matter of doubts, hopes, fears and wishes; events will appear contingent, their shape or goal uncertain. The future is a matter of prognostication, of more or less informed conjectures; it has not been experienced in the way that the past has been experienced. From the character's point of view, the future doesn't (yet) exist to be known: the future 'presents' itself – makes itself felt in the present – as a range of choices, decisions to be made. For some (though by no means all) people 'in the world', this is their assumption about their experience, and it goes along with a metaphysical assumption that time is 'open'. However, as readers they may be aware that, although they might not have got to that part of the book yet, the character's future has already been written, and, no matter how often the book is read, the events will follow the same path. If they reflect on this, they may come to the conclusion that the freedom the characters think they have is illusory. This may translate into a metaphysical assumption that time is closed and that our actions are, really, determined. Both assumptions draw a firm distinction between 'life' and 'literature'. Gary Saul Morson knows where he stands, and avers, 'Real time is an ongoing process without anything resembling literary closure.'[1] First of all, let us put these distinctions between 'life' and 'literature', 'determinism' and 'free will' under some initial pressure.

A third-person heterodiegetic narrator 'outside' the world of the text, in the knowledge of what is to transpire for the characters 'within' it, may decide to share that knowledge with the reader. As Morson observes, the Russian critic Mikhail Bakhtin referred to this as the narrator's 'essential surplus' of knowledge.[2] As we saw in Chapter 1 with Augustine's *Confessions*, this can be a feature of first-person, homodiegetic narratives also, where a temporal distinction is opened up between the narrating self and his earlier narrated self. A feature of many Greek and Roman texts is that some of that essential surplus is distributed to characters within the narrative, often in complex ways. Thus Odysseus in Books 9–12 of the *Odyssey* takes on the role of an internal, first-person narrator to recount to the Phaeacians his adventures in the ten years since the fall of Troy. Odysseus tells how his earlier self travelled to the Underworld and there received a prophecy from the prophet Teiresias (11.97–137):

> So he spoke, and I, holding away the sword with the silver
> nails, pushed it back in the sheath, and the flawless prophet,
> after he had drunk the blood, began speaking to me.
> 'Glorious Odysseus, what you are after is sweet homecoming,   100
>
> but the god will make it hard for you. I think you will not
> escape the Shaker of the Earth, who holds a grudge against you
> in his heart, and because you blinded his dear son, hates you.
> But even so and still you might come back, after much suffering,
> if you can contain your own desire, and contain your companions',   105
>
> at that time when you first put in your well-made vessel
> at the island Thrinakia, escaping the sea's blue water,
> and there discover pasturing the cattle and fat sheep
> of Helios, who sees all things and listens to all things.
> Then, if you keep your mind on homecoming, and leave
> these unharmed,   110

you might all make your way to Ithaka, after much suffering;
but if you do harm them, then I testify to the destruction
of your ship and your companions, but if you yourself get clear,
you will come home in bad case, with the loss of all your companions,
in someone else's ship, and find troubles in your household,   115

insolent men, who are eating away your livelihood
and courting your godlike wife and offering gifts to win her.
You may punish the violences of these men, when you come home.
But after you have killed these suitors in your own palace,
either by treachery, or openly with the sharp bronze,   120

then you must take up your well-shaped oar and go on a journey
until you come where there are men living who know nothing
of the sea, and who eat food that is not mixed with salt, who never
have known ships whose cheeks are painted purple, who never
have known well-shaped oars, which act for ships as wings do.   125

And I will tell you a very clear proof, and you cannot miss it.
When, as you walk, some other wayfarer happens to meet you,
and says you carry a winnow-fan on your bright shoulder,
then you must plant your well-shaped oar in the ground, and render
ceremonious sacrifice to the lord Poseidon,   130

one ram and one bull, and a mounter of sows, a boar pig,
and make your way home again and render holy hecatombs
to the immortal gods who hold the wide heaven, all
to them in order. Death will come to you from the sea, in
some altogether unwarlike way, and it will end you   135

in the ebbing time of a sleek old age. Your people
about you will be prosperous. All this is true that I tell you.'[3]

In terms of narrative temporality, this passage is extremely complex. The prophecy of Teiresias, an extended prolepsis within the four-book analepsis of Odysseus's account, is deftly emplotted so as to distribute the essential surplus. Its rapid forward trajectory intersects with three 'presents', that of Odysseus's narrated self in the Underworld; that of his narrating self in the court of the Phaeacians; and that of the present of narration of the *Odyssey* as a whole, which ends shortly after the slaying of the suitors. In the chronology of the story, the prophecy is delivered to Odysseus after he has blinded the Cyclops and incurred the wrath of his father Poseidon (11.103), but before his men kill the cattle of the god of the sun Helios on the island of Thrinacia (11.107–9), and before he is shipwrecked on the island of Scheria, the home of the Phaeacians, who will return him to Ithaca (11.115), where he will kill the suitors in his palace (11.119). Teiresias's speech intersects with the temporality of Odysseus the narrated self hearing the prophecy in the Underworld at 11.103 and with that of Odysseus the narrating self on Scheria at 11.113, but continues on beyond the events surrounding Odysseus's return to Ithaca with which the Homeric narrator concludes his narration in Book 24 to encompass not only Odysseus's subsequent travels inland far from the sea (11.121–25), where he will appease Poseidon (11.126–34), but also, following his return home, his death in old age from the sea (11.134–36). 'All this is true that I tell you,' Teiresias adds (11.137). Odysseus's future seems at this stage already largely determined, if not in every detail. Teiresias does give the narrated Odysseus some wiggle-room in relation to the cattle of Helios ('if you keep your mind on homecoming, and leave these unharmed,/you might all make your way back to Ithaka', 11.110–11; cf. 11.104–5), and the slaying of the suitors ('either by treachery, or openly with the sharp bronze,' 11.120), but Odysseus at the moment he narrates the prophecy to the Phaeacians already knows that the possibility Teiresias held out to him of coming home with all of his crew if they do not kill the cattle is not what eventuates. For all that the Homeric narrator seems to nod towards the human experience of possibility and choice, his emplotment, through a prolepsis internal to the narrative – prophecy of the future as already known – creates a strong sense of the future as more or less inevitable.

Nowhere is this sense felt so powerfully as in Sophocles's *Oedipus the King* (*Oedipus Tyrannus*) and it is similarly the effect of an emplotment that offers its characters through prophecy this essential surplus of knowledge. The story the play emplots, to put it far too simply,[4] is the fulfilment of the prophecy that Oedipus will kill his father and marry his mother, in spite of his best attempts to evade the future that has been foretold. The essential surplus of knowledge offered to Oedipus is pitted against the human experience of choice, and the latter is decisively revealed to be illusory. The tragic climax comes in the stark realisation on the part first of Jocasta, and then of Oedipus, that what they had believed to be their freedom of action is no such thing. *Oedipus* is a play that Aristotle turns to repeatedly in the *Poetics*. For Aristotle, plot is the most important part of tragedy, and key features of what he calls 'complex' plots are reversal (*peripeteia*) and recognition (*anagnōrisis*), which he defines as a change from ignorance (*ex agnoias*) to knowledge (*eis gnōsin*, 1452a29–30). One such plot is *Oedipus*, and the transformation the plot engineers for its protagonists is not simply to Oedipus's realisation of his real identity and relationship to Jocasta, but also from a false belief about the world they inhabit as one in which they assume they have some freedom of action and can thwart what the prophecy says will happen to them, to the knowledge that that world is really deterministic, and that this was going to happen all along, for all their efforts.

In his book *Narrative and Freedom*, Morson is a man with a mission, and *Oedipus* is a prime exhibit of what he seeks to contest. He suggests that there 'seems to be something intrinsic to narrative art itself that predisposes it, more or less, to a deterministic perspective.'[5] He argues that '[i]t appears that literary structure is not neutral with respect to philosophies of time…and we may say that narratives, insofar as they rely on structure, are predisposed to convey a sense of fatalism, determinism, or otherwise closed time.'[6] Narratives have the Aristotelian structure of beginning, middle and, crucially, end. In contrast, '[i]n our own lives, most of us know by experience that there is never a point when all loose threads are tied together, at least not until the end of history or the Last Judgement. Real time is an ongoing process without anything resembling literary closure.'[7]

The 'end of history' or the 'Last Judgement', as we have seen in earlier chapters, would imply the shaping of our lived experience *as* a text by an author, who need not necessarily be God, but is in one way or another modelled on God. Morson argues forcefully against this view, and explains,

Life as it is experienced does not have closure or an Aristotelian ending, a point at which continuation is unthinkable and at which all loose ends are tied up. Lives end but they are not completed. Closure and structure mark the difference between life as it is lived and as it is read about; and real people live without the benefit of an outside perspective on which closure and structure depend...In Bakhtin's terms, that is because 'finalization' (the sense of a completed whole) demands radical 'outsideness': an end requires an external standpoint.[8]

A more dynamic view of Aristotelian literary structure could be advanced. In the *Poetics*, he suggests that 'beginning' means that which does not 'of necessity' follow on from a preceding event, but can give rise 'naturally' to some later fact or occurrence; while by contrast an 'end' is an event which 'naturally' occurs after a preceding one, whether 'of necessity' or 'as a general rule', but after which there need be nothing else (1450b27–30). The classic fairy tale observes this in its assertion that nothing before 'once upon a time' or beyond 'they lived happily ever after' is deemed to bear upon the interpretation of its plot. However, Aristotle is making a strong theoretical point about how a plot can suggest causal connections between its events, whether of necessity or as a general rule – so granting to narratives explanatory potential. The act of emplotting eschews a pure temporal succession (...this, then this, then this... *ad infinitum* in either direction) in favour of suggesting meaningful relationships (because of this, then this) by the imposition of the boundaries he suggests. These boundaries may enclose just two events. E.M. Forster famously suggested that 'The king died and then the queen died' is a story, but 'The king died and then the queen died of grief', with its hint of a causal connection between the two events, is a plot.[9] A plot could encompass many more – though not an *infinite* number, for then there would be no boundaries. For Morson, 'real time' and 'life as it is lived' looks like one damned thing after another.

Closure is not the only literary effect that is absent from the experience of 'real' time, Morson suggests; omens and prophecy are absent too. He quotes the philosopher Arthur C. Danto on the disconcerting quality of prophetic discourse:

A prophecy is not a mere statement about the future, for a prediction is a statement about the future. It is a certain *kind* of statement about the future … an *historical* statement about the future. The prophet is one who speaks about the future in a manner which is appropriate only to the past, or who speaks of the present in the light of a future treated as a *fait accompli*.[10]

We will be returning to probe the implications of this statement in a while, but for the moment, let us just note how Danto is firmly of the belief that we cannot (or at least should not) make about the future the kind of statements we make about the past. Nor, according to Morson, do we experience anything like literary foreshadowing:

For those who believe in omens, the future leaves its mark on the present, much as a thunderstorm in a novel may occur *in order to* indicate a catastrophe to come. If the event caused by the future is detectable only by the reader, we speak of foreshadowing. If it is recognized as a sign by the character, he will have discovered an omen. Conversely those people in real life who believe in omens are implicitly treating real time the way we would treat time in a narrative. For good reason, the already written book or scroll is a standard metaphor for fatalism.[11]

By contrast, foreshadowing in *Oedipus* is 'no mere artistic device', but rather 'conveys the temporality that is supposed to govern the real world. Not fate but temporal openness proves to be a mirage, as time is shown to be essentially oracular.'[12]

Morson points to the way that the play brings together two temporalities and two ways of knowing, the one associated with Oedipus, who can draw inferences and plot causal relationships from past and present events better than anyone else, but who dismisses the signs of the future, the other with Teiresias, who, as Oedipus contemptuously observes, could not solve the riddle of the Sphinx (391–98), but who knows the future all along, and can detect a kind of backwards causation as the present is pulled forwards, for all the efforts of Oedipus and Jocasta, to its prescribed destination. These two opposing temporalities and ways of knowing collide in the encounter between Oedipus and Teiresias, and '[t]he one in which the future shapes the present proves more powerful.'[13] The audience, or readers, of the play are aligned with the perspective of Teiresias, Morson suggests, because we know the outcome:

> Of course, Tieresias [sic] has this knowledge *within* the represented world, because he is a prophet; he has it because the gods of his world have revealed it to him. By contrast, we know the whole story because we exist *outside* the represented world and have heard the story before. The two positions are not identical but are nevertheless crucially similar in one respect: we resemble Tieresias and differ from Oedipus because we are able to assess events as they happen in terms of their inevitable outcome.[14]

But the audience simultaneously identifies with the temporal experience of Oedipus, because a life lived without a quasi-historical knowledge of the future corresponds with their own. 'Our experience of time in *Oedipus*,' Morson concludes, 'is therefore double: we can imagine what each act of the hero feels like, and we also see what it "really" is.'[15] Contingency and determinism thus play off against each other in *Oedipus*, but also in narrative more generally. Morson explains this at the level of the reader's experience:

> Readers of literary narrative have a double experience: they both identify with characters and contemplate structure. Alternating between internal and external views, they not only project themselves into the character's horizon but also view the character's entire world as a completed aesthetic artifact. One perspective gives them process, the other product; one an open future, the other a future that has long since been determined. It is therefore possible, indeed easy to read literary narratives as emblems of utterly closed time in which characters falsely believe they are free, just as we mistakenly sense our own freedom, which is a mirage if determinism or fatalism is true.[16]

For the readers of any narrative or the audience of any play, two temporalities interact, and Morson sees the metaphysical implications of this acted out in *Oedipus* itself, where they collide. On his reading, the play suggests that, whatever our experience, 'real' time is closed; but he wants to assert that the time *he* takes as 'real' is open.

We might object that *Oedipus* is just a play, that we can willingly suspend disbelief (in prophecy, in a rigid metaphysical determinism) for the sake of appreciating the literary power of the tragedy, and that we can walk away from any metaphysical messages we see it as conveying as we walk away from the theatre or close the text. Morson suggests that larger and more subtle forces are at work. He points to Bakhtin's suggestion that narrative develops insights into temporality which are then 'transcribed' into philosophical discourse,[17] although the narrative dimension is then often buried and forgotten. Thus we could see concepts such as *determinism* or *free will* as precipitated out of narratives such as the *Odyssey* or *Oedipus*, or at least out of certain traditions of reading them.[18] Morson then suggests that, in making global assumptions about temporal closedness or openness, people

> tacitly accept that time must essentially be one sort of thing, so that (let us say) a metaphysical assertion of determinism is applied across disciplines – to psychology, sociology, and history as well as to biology and physics. It may come to affect how people conduct their daily lives. The history of the past few centuries has offered many examples of such broad applications of a doctrine, supposedly proven by a given science, to the rest of culture.[19]

Even though this makes him duly hesitant about elevating temporal openness to a metaphysical assumption himself, Morson declares his ethical and ideological commitment to a view of human time as open, so that we can exercise the freedom to choose; the Russian novels of ideas that he examines in his book 'exhibit, and often explicitly advocate, a temporality close to the one which I wish to explore and *recommend*'.[20] Although he questions whether it is misleading to assume a single temporality for all disciplines and all aspects of experience, his application of the term 'real' to time and the world comes close to making the sort of metaphysical assertion he cautions against. The word 'real', and the associated verb 'realise', mobilise that process of viewing some *thing* (Latin *res*) as a metaphysical whole – time, a text, a person, an idea – which (to turn Bakhtin's observation on transcription through 180 degrees) narrative has conceptualised in terms of a structure involving beginning, middle and end (so that we can imagine ourselves standing outside it). The adjective *real*, without inverted commas, points to metaphysical investment that is otherwise gestured to in indicative uses of the verb *to be* ('Real time is an ongoing process...').

Morson mentions a range of disciplines, but let us focus on history for the moment. The world of the *Odyssey* or of *Oedipus* is avowedly a remote one, which the modern world has no difficulty in calling 'fictional', and the readers of the epic or the spectators of the tragedy can easily imagine themselves standing outside the plot, so as to subscribe to, or not, the temporal worldview they take the plot to represent. The issue of the essential surplus of knowledge becomes more complicated if we return to the *Aeneid*. The narrator, and reader, know more of what will happen to Aeneas than he does himself, though in the particular epic world he inhabits, he gains intimations of the future through supernatural means, in particular omens and prophecies. So, some of that essential surplus is distributed to the characters within the narrative by means familiar from the *Odyssey* and *Oedipus*. However, given that the Virgilian narrator presents himself, and asks his readers to see themselves, as no less 'within' the story than Aeneas – his world is linked in time to our world, it is suggested – some of the essential surplus is vouchsafed to the narrator and readers of the work as well as to Aeneas, and it is done so once more through the device of prophecy. However, what Jupiter foretells to Venus is a sequence of events in Roman history that intersects the present of Virgil's narration in the time of Augustus and heads off towards a future without end. At the dramatic moment of Jupiter's speaking in the narrative when Aeneas is shipwrecked on the shores of Carthage, the specific events he mentions have not 'yet' happened, though by the age of Augustus they have. Jupiter views prophetically the events that the Virgilian narrator looks back on. To recall Danto's formulation, prophecy is 'an historical statement about the future. The prophet is one who speaks about the future in a manner which is appropriate only to the past, or who speaks of the present in the light of a future treated as a *fait accompli*.' In this formulation, a similar logic of repetition applies to both prophecy and history, save that in prophetic discourse, the historical events are seen to 'repeat' the narrative, while in historical discourse, the narrative is seen to 'repeat' the events. Knowing the end of the sequence of events he prophesies, Jupiter can see its structure as a whole. From this emerges the trope of destiny, when the end is achieved which has been foreseen from the beginning, when the sequence of events can be seen, in the imagery of the journey or the path so frequently invoked in discussions of determinism, to have reached its anticipated *destination*.

Jupiter interrupts his narrative of the future – his *historical* statement about the future – with the words *sic placitum* (1.283): the verb suggests that this structure of events 'has found favour' with the god and is his will, a neat convergence of narration not simply with knowledge, but with desire as well.[21] Moreover, the association of the verb with decisions of the Roman Senate (senators would give their assent to a motion with the word *placet*) gives it also connotations of legal authority binding on the future, 'thus it has been decreed'. This, it has been decided, is what *will* happen in history. The words *sic placitum* imply that what will happen is the result of an act of *decision*, one which could have gone otherwise. This establishes an interplay of free will and determinism within the poem, an 'economy' of competing terms. And, like all economies, it has its winners and its losers: Jupiter, or Fate, is represented as enjoying the luxury of a choice that is ultimately denied to the human characters within the narrative, implicitly including its readers – whatever beliefs they hold on their own freedom of choice or action.

The *Aeneid* may be seen to mobilise another economy and to distribute functions that are united in the figure of the narrator. It is the explicit representation in the person of Jupiter within the narrative of the view forwards of the future from the narrative's present as *known*, its end and its significance already *determined*, that has made the *Aeneid* the paradigm of teleological narrative. The association of the view forwards with the god makes the view not merely prospective but *providential*. In this dramatic allegory of the act of narration and of historical understanding, Jupiter can view the structure as a whole and so becomes the figure of the narrator. But the immediate (though not ultimate) end towards which Jupiter looks is the Virgilian narrator's present, by which time this sequence of events constitutes the past, not the future. It is Virgil (and here I want to open out a bit of space between Virgil the poet and the Virgilian narrator represented within the poem) who has chosen the elements of the story, its beginning- and end-points, and its mode of presentation. Virgil takes the events of

Roman history, and, by giving them a beginning, middle and prospective end with respect to his present, makes of them a literary artefact, one structured by the trope of destiny and the associated sense of historical determinism the narrative of the poem dramatises: *sic placitum*. There is an irony here: in distributing the functions of the narrator as Virgil does, the Virgilian narrator is represented as less than divine, yes, but also as less than human, for the narration of a human author incorporates this providential aspect, however much it may strive to occlude it.

The poem elicits the reader's desire for order, and offers that desire immediate (though not yet ultimate) fulfilment in the Augustan present. As a human, Virgil cannot *know* what the future holds, as Jupiter is represented as doing, but is aware nonetheless that the present he inhabits is a transient moment, and that time and circumstance *ad infinitum* will fuel in future readers a desire for revision. He allows Jupiter to project a further (indeed, ultimate) *telos*, power without limits of time and space, within which Virgil's narrative can be continually revised and 'translated' as they will by future readers. And, crucially, he allows Jupiter to do one thing a human narrator within time, you would think, 'ought' not to be able to do, and which is (as we shall explore further in Chapter 5) seen as an attribute of the divine – impose an end or limit on an infinite sequence. In grappling with the challenges of historical representation, Tolstoy suggested in the final chapter of *War and Peace* that 'there can never be absolute inevitability' in historical writing because 'to imagine a human action subject only to the law of necessity, without any freedom, we must assume a knowledge of an *infinite* number of spatial conditions, an *infinitely* long period of time and an *infinite* chain of causation.' On the other hand, 'to imagine a man perfectly free and not subject to the law of necessity we must imagine him alone, *outside space, outside time* and *outside dependence on cause.*'[22] Virgil was able to short-circuit this problem by means of a device that was no longer available for Tolstoy because no longer theologically plausible to him, the representation within the narrative of an embodied providential perspective.

Although it is the explicit representation within the narrative of the perspective forwards from the narrative's present in the figure of Jupiter that has made the *Aeneid* the paradigm of teleological narrative, the implication of this argument is that all narratives, whether they be histories or fictions, can have a teleological character and a providential aspect *by virtue of having a narrator*. This is usually only apparent if the perspective forwards from the narrative's present is rendered explicit in some way, for example by a narrator's comments on the narrative's present in the light of what is yet to happen ('little did they know that…'). Livy, in his enormous year-by-year annalistic history of Rome 'from the foundation of the city' (*Ab urbe condita*), similarly emplots the foundation of Rome under the shadow of its present greatness. When Romulus and Remus set out from Alba Longa to found a new settlement, Livy attributes this providential aspect to them: the population willing to join the enterprise 'easily justified the hope that Alba would be small, Lavinium would be small in comparison with [*prae* also suggests 'before'] the city [*ea urbe*] that would be founded' (1.6.3). Even before its foundation, Rome is already proleptically the *urbs* it would turn out to be. Livy explicitly points to his own narratorial perspective as he invokes the trope of destiny: 'but, as I believe [*ut opinor*], the origin of so great a city and the beginning of the greatest empire after that of the gods was due to the fates [*debebatur…fatis*, 1.4.1].' He doesn't put himself forward as knowing this absolutely; he is a human narrator, and it is an act of faith or belief that drives the composition of his work. Contrariwise, if this forward perspective is suppressed (or, in the metaphor of economy, differently distributed) by various rhetorical means, the teleological and providential aspect of narration can be occluded, as when the Virgilian narrator presents himself as passively transcribing history ('Muse, recall to me the causes…', *Aeneid* 1.8) rather than actively emplotting it, as Jupiter does.

Danto recoils against the notion that prophecy treats the future as a *fait accompli*, but we might be equally wary of treating the past simply as a *fait accompli*, a set of 'facts' simply waiting to be transcribed. Augustine suggested in the *Confessions* that, though the truth may be 'there' for God, human narrators have to *make* it (*veritatem…facere*, 10.1.1) as best they can. The narrator's role in relation to the historical past, in selecting the plot elements and giving them their particular narrative structure, can be seen as a more active process than the Virgilian narrator, or Danto, suggest. Above all, we might come to question Danto's decisive demarcation of historical time into past, present and future. Ranke's famous characterisation of the historian's task as to tell it *wie es eigentlich gewesen* ('how it actually happened' or perhaps 'how it was in its own right') continues to cast a long shadow. Virgil's meditation on fate via Jupiter's 'utterances' raises the possibility that any attempt to order the past in relation to the present, to say 'this is how it was', by virtue of its narrative structure incorporates, albeit at a level that usually escapes attention, the claim 'this is how it was-to-be'. Morson's anxiety that there 'seems to be something intrinsic to narrative art itself that predisposes it, more or less, to a deterministic perspective' seems to be not unjustified.

A thoroughgoing historical realism, which sees no place for authorial or readerly desire for the end (Jupiter's self-satisfied *sic placitum*), can unwittingly succumb to its own mode of determinism. It sees as necessary causal connections what from a later perspective, with its essential surplus of knowledge as it writes the history of that earlier explanation, might look far more like historically contingent plausible ones. Morson does, however, say 'more or less', and, rather than see determinism itself as inevitable (something itself knowable only if we had infinite time, as Tolstoy reminds us), we might invoke what I earlier described as economies of free will and determinism. Narratives of universal history, as we saw in the last chapter, explicitly 'detect' a plot within 'events themselves'. History written in the Judaeo-Christian tradition (Augustine's *City of God* is a prime example) sees historical events as directed by God towards his purpose: the essential surplus of knowledge associated with a human narrator is thus attributed in an absolute sense to God as Providence.[23] However, although Augustine's deity is omniscient, he has given men free will, albeit that this is compromised by original sin, making them prone to evil rather than good.[24] This opens out the space in *City of God* for a subtle combination of divine providence and the autonomy of human agency in history.[25]

Although Enlightenment rationalism is usually associated with a secularisation of thought, historical events are often seen as controlled by natural, economic or other imperatives regarded as universal, but which look like surrogates for God (in Barthes's formulation 'God and his hypostases – reason, science, law'), and can be associated with an arguably less nuanced determinism than Augustine had formulated. Thus in *The Wealth of Nations*, Adam Smith uses the image, deeply sedimented theologically, of the 'Invisible Hand' to characterise the economic necessity that guides humans to be the unwitting agents of the common interest even as they believe they are purposefully promoting their own selfish ends. For Kant in the *Idea for a Universal History from a Cosmopolitan Point of View* (1784),

> the manifestations of the will in human actions are determined, like all other external events, by universal natural laws. When the play of the freedom of the human is examined on the great scale of universal history, a regular march will be discovered in its movements; ... Individual men, and even whole nations, little think, while they are pursuing their own purposes ... that they are advancing unconsciously under the guidance of a purpose of nature which is unknown to them.[26]

For Hegel in the second draft of his 'Philosophical History of the World' (1830), this guidance is provided by Reason: 'world history is governed by an ultimate design ... whose rationality is ... a divine and absolute reason ... The overall content of world history is rational and indeed has to be rational; a divine will rules supreme and is strong enough to determine the overall content.' The human perspective on this is imperfect, and it is the task of philosophy to divine the structure of Reason's 'ultimate design': 'The actions of human beings in the history of the world produce an effect altogether different from what they themselves intend', while 'philosophy should help us to understand' – not the world as it is, but – 'that the actual world *is as it ought to be*' (note the optative ascribed to the providence of Reason).[27] The shadows cast by this are indeed long. As Genevieve Lloyd remarks, 'Providence may now be largely "lost" from our secular consciousness; but it continues to exert an influence on our thoughts and on our lives.' The scare-quotes around 'lost' are certainly justified if, as I have suggested, providence, however occluded, can be associated with any act of narration.[28] Most people may no longer believe in prophecy, but if you believe that history, or the world, is in some way *intelligible*, are you committing yourself to some version of providence, albeit a weaker one? Hegel avers that 'The sole aim of philosophical enquiry is to eliminate the contingent' – an aim it can only achieve if it can step outside time. As you exit the theatre, can you be entirely sure that you have stepped outside the metaphysical discourses which intersect *Oedipus*?

OEDIPUS WRECKS HIMSELF?

In the light of the foregoing discussion, let us return to *Oedipus*. Teiresias has knowledge of the future within the represented world because he is a prophet; we outside the represented world know the whole story because we have heard it before. Morson is not alone in taking it for granted that knowledge of the myth on the part of the audience is presumed, and thus '[e]ven a first viewing (or reading) of the play therefore exhibits some characteristics of rereading.'[29] Such presumed knowledge seems blindingly obvious. In *Odyssey* 11.271–74, Odysseus recounts how in the Underworld 'I saw the beautiful Epikaste, Oidipodes' mother,/who in the ignorance of her mind had done a monstrous/thing when she married her own son. He killed his father/and married her, but the gods soon made it all known to mortals.' In his commentary on the play Roger Dawe draws attention to the early to mid-fourth-century BC comic poet Antiphanes, who says that 'you have only to say the word "Oedipus" and everyone knows all the rest – his father Laius, his mother Jocasta, his daughters, his (male) children, what will happen to him and what he did.'[30] And even in more recent times, those unfamiliar with Sophocles's play may, thanks to Freud, know that Oedipus killed his father and married his mother. In this pared-down form, it has become one of the most familiar of all Greek myths. That prior knowledge would certainly allow the audience to view the action from 'outside' the represented world, and it facilitates what Morson describes as the play's 'distinctive effect… foreshadowing and the dramatic irony it enables'. The words the characters use are doubly determined, by the meanings the characters intend, and by the meanings those same words take on in relation to the structure as a whole; the characters say more than they know. But this may do less than justice to Sophocles's play, in two ways. The trope of destiny operates also in genres such as epic, where, as we have seen in the case of Virgil's *Aeneid*, the boundary between 'within' and 'outside' the represented world can be manipulated in different ways by the narrator, and foreshadowing and dramatic irony are prominent features. It is all too easy to paraphrase the play so as to make it sound like a third-person narration rather than a dramatic mimesis. Furthermore, the prior knowledge of the myth is, as Morson suggests, significant, though perhaps in ways he does not address, for how might a 're-reading' in a 'first viewing' – an interesting inversion of chronological order – come about, and what effect might that have?

First, what makes tragedy distinctive as a form? Narratological theory has it that the time taken to narrate and the time narrated are most closely aligned in characters' direct speech. This is when the characters' experience of time and the viewer or reader's seem most closely to coincide. This effect is felt most keenly – one is tempted to say most 'dramatically' – in drama, where the story is 'told', in the *absence* of a narrator's voice, entirely through the speeches of the characters, and the action unfolds, scene by scene, in what for both characters and audience is the 'same' time. Though spectators and characters may be spatially separated within the theatre, and so 'outside' and 'within' the represented world respectively, time seems to pass at the same rate for both. As Morson suggested, the spectators of a play such as *Oedipus* may or may not be familiar with the precise way the plot will develop or be resolved (and so share the suspense of some of the characters) while also being at some level aware, or in expectation of, an artistic structure to their viewing experience.

Yet, against the dramatic illusion that the 'life' of Oedipus is being 'lived' before the audience's eyes, 'Oedipus knows what Sophocles wants him to know, and at the time Sophocles wants him to know it.'[31] The author of that artistic structure, like the gods 'within' the world represented, remains unseen or unheard; the action seems to be *presented* (the act of mimesis that was such a cause of concern to Plato's Socrates in Book 10 of the *Republic*) rather than mediated or re-presented by a narratorial voice, except in those details the audience recognises as foreshadowing or dramatic irony. The play contains what seem like false trails (or, at least, complications) without which the plot of *Oedipus* as Sophocles has contrived it would not 'work'.[32] Thus Creon recounts that when Laius was killed, all his servants were also killed except one, and that this sole survivor reported that Laius was struck down not by a single brigand, but by many; Creon remarks that, of the things which he saw, that was the one thing the survivor was able to say for certain (118–23). The survivor's account generates a delay in solving the initial problem confronted by Oedipus at the outset of the play's action – who killed Laius? – without which the full revelation of Oedipus's identity and what he has done would not have time to emerge. The issue of 'one or many?' sows confusion not simply for Oedipus but for the audience as well in what follows: the audience too know what Sophocles wants them to know, and at the time when Sophocles wants them to know it.[33]

The exact content of the oracles delivered to Laius and Jocasta at the time of Oedipus's birth and to Oedipus when he goes to Delphi shortly before the carnage in which he is involved at the place where three roads meet is similarly a matter for report in the play, resulting in a remarkable haziness in a play where the issue of the reliability of oracles seems pivotal to the development of the plot. However, the lack of first-hand knowledge arguably reflects the way that the will of the gods, or fate, as existing outside the human experience of time cannot be fully known within it, requires mediation through the oracle and 'translation' into the inevitably incomplete terms of human discourse. The last account (*logos*) of these oracles given by the herdsman in 1176 – 'the word was that he would kill his parents' (*ktenein nin tous tekontas ēn logos*) – does not simply reprise the confusion of singular and plural in respect of the killer(s) of Laius. Spoken as it is after Jocasta has rushed from the stage after guessing Oedipus's identity in 1072 and before the announcement in 1235 that she has taken her own life, it raises the possibility that the oracles were not in fact fulfilled long before the action of the play begins, but are being finally fulfilled 'now', in the death of Jocasta as well as of Laius, as the action unfolds in the 'real' time of the audience as well as the characters.

Morson is just one amongst a number of critics who are defiant in the face of what they see as the affirmation of determinism in the play. John Peradotto argues that the place of *Oedipus* as a central part of the literary canon should be secured – but 'as a powerful paradigm of theocratic and prophetic rhetoric in need of exposure'.[34] – He starts from the conundrum that Aristotle

- who subjected the concepts of chance and accident to such meticulous analysis in the second book of his *Physics*, and dismisses the view of those who grant chance the status of a genuine cause on the grounds that it is something divine and mysterious (*theion ti... kai daimoniōteron*, 196b7–8)
- who in the *Poetics* seeks to correlate his views of poetry with his views on metaphysics, and regards the best kind of plot as that in which things happen in accordance with probability or necessity (*kata to eikos ē anagkaion*, 1452a24)

makes his paradigm of tragic composition *Oedipus*, 'a play so riddled with chance, so crippled by coincidence, as to be ruled out of serious consideration by the scientist's touchstones of probability and necessity.'[35] In the *Poetics* Aristotle draws a sharp qualitative distinction between 'episodic' plots in which things simply happen one *after* another (*met'allēla*, 1451b35) and those in which things happen *because* of one another (*di'allēla*, 1452a4). In practice, this distinction can be harder to make than it looks. For E.M. Forster, 'the king died and then the queen died' is not a plot, whereas 'the king died and then the queen died of grief' is. But now re-read the first. It is a narrative, in that it links two events in temporal succession, though in terms of narrativity it is less rich and lacks the explicit causality that the addition 'of grief' gives to the second; but *qua* narrative it prompts the question 'is anything *there* in the juxtaposition of these two events?' Is there? For the moment let us give Aristotle the benefit of the doubt. Is it possible he admired *Oedipus* not in spite of, but because of, the pressure the play's 'coincidences' placed on his criteria of plausibility and necessity? We shall be returning to this.

Peradotto's strategy is to re-read a number of 'crucial' moments in the play as, precisely, coincidental (i.e. he gives the answer 'no, there's nothing *there*') and so not causally linked. Thus, of the arrival of the Corinthian messenger (924) who tells Oedipus of the death of his presumed father Polybus, he says,

Change the play to bring him in twenty minutes earlier or later and the tragedy dissolves. His arrival is timed to coincide with the arrival of Laius' herdsman summoned by Oedipus for questioning, and occurs immediately *after* Jocasta's prayer to Apollo for a clear resolution. Things like that do not appear to happen by accident. It is perceived as happening not simply *after* (*meta*), but *because of* (*dia*) Jocasta's prayer…Such events are…products of verisimilitude, cultural products, or contrivances of a poet – what, from the perspective we are assuming, we would call contingent. The arrival of the messenger can be said to happen *di'allēla* only if we posit – as the poet or cultural convention or belief may force us to do – a divine agent *causing* what we would otherwise call a *contingent, coincidental* occurrence.[36]

'Things like that do not appear to happen by accident': Peradotto repeatedly intones this ironic mantra as he surveys key incidents in the plot in turn. 'Remove any one of these coincidences, an easy thing to do given their infinitesimal plausibility, and the *Tyrannus* collapses like a house of cards,' he says, and adds of the specific mimetic rather than diegetic form of narrative that tragedy adopts, 'the superficial deletion of the author's voice actually gives him greater dominion over the discourse…and disables his audience's power to produce meaning.'[37] This could almost be Plato's condemnation of mimesis, and weighs heavily if, as Peradotto suggests, even so great a metaphysician as Aristotle, with his robust attitude to chance and causality, could still be seduced by Sophocles's craft. And, with what I have said about Forster's examples in mind, rather than disabling the audience's power to produce meaning, does the mimetic form of tragedy trigger it? Quite apart from the audience, what about Oedipus himself?

Perradotto's observations on the plot are powerful, but perhaps Aristotle's views on chance, and on *Oedipus*, can be made more congruent than he would have them. Michael Wood is a cautious but admiring reader of Sophocles's craft, and in his book on oracles and prophecy, *The Road to Delphi*, homes in on Oedipus's account (*Oedipus* 800–13) of how he and a stranger (whom Oedipus at this stage comes to the conclusion must be Laius, 813–14) both arrive at the same moment 'at the place where three roads meet':[38]

For a predestined meeting, this seems horribly random and contingent: harsh words, jostling, a scramble, rising anger, a small massacre. Daniel Mendelsohn, in an essay in *The New York Review of Books*, wittily writes of Oedipus' 'problems with road rage.' But of course this is just how prophecies work: through the contingent, not against it or in spite of it. And the true contingency here is not whether the two men, meeting, have to fight, but whether they have to meet. This is where the seemingly trivial question of the two actual itineraries looms very large. Couldn't father and son have missed each other, simply by arriving at the crossroads earlier or later? They could if they were not living out a tale of brutal destiny. But then the destiny begins to look like a matter of time as well as space.[39]

As the title of Wood's book suggests, his central concern in this discussion is how the itineraries of the two men lead them to meet. These events are not presented in the drama, though they are narrativised by the characters within it. In his own account of events, Oedipus tells how he went to Delphi, after hearing from a drunken reveller in Corinth that he is not the son of Polybus (779–80), to enquire about his true parentage, but instead received the alarming news that he is fated to kill his father and marry his mother (789–93). He flees from Delphi, his destination anywhere but Corinth (794–96). Laius, according to Creon's earlier account (114–15), was on his way from Thebes to consult the oracle,[40] 'so people said' (hōs ephaskon), and 'he did not take the further and expected step of returning in a way that would have matched his departure.'[41] There is little in the way of hard-and-fast information here. Creon relies on hearsay, and even the reason why Laius was going to consult the oracle is not reported. A road from Delphi to Thebes without any intersections could have had Oedipus and Laius on the same path, with quite an extended 'window of opportunity' for the fatal encounter. But this is a route where 'three roads meet': the road from Delphi forks, to Thebes in one direction, to Daulis in the other. The fork in the road, had Oedipus decided to make for Daulis, diminishes that window of opportunity. The plot of the play seems to revolve agonisingly around issues of timing: *if* Oedipus had arrived at the crossroads just a few minutes earlier, and *if* he had taken the decision to head for Daulis rather than Thebes... As Wood implies, the possibility that things *could have* gone otherwise, and by such small margins, makes what *did* happen all the more shocking, and so prophecy, rather than being undermined by our sense of the contingent, works on it – thus enabling Sophocles to generate those emotions of pity and fear which Aristotle saw as the mark of the best tragedies, and in particular *Oedipus* (*Poetics* 1452a1–33).

The way in which prophecy plays with our sense of the contingent is not peculiar to tragedy: recall how Teiresias in *Odyssey* 11 leaves the future in some respects 'open' for Odysseus. *If* he and his men leave the cattle of Helios unharmed, they might *all* make their way back to Ithaca. They didn't, of course – as Odysseus knows at the point when he is recounting the prophecy to the Phaeacians. However, few would apply the term *tragic* to this in the way they would to *Oedipus*. Prophecy, if we accept Danto's formulation of it as a *historical* statement about the future, is narrative in form, and it is one of the tasks of narrative to represent a sequence of events in time, in historical discourse of the past, in prophecy of the future. Although characters within narrative such as Oedipus may experience time as open, the future pressing upon him with possibilities and decisions to be made, the author has his essential surplus of knowledge. In *Oedipus*, the author of the tragedy can efface himself, while leaving the presumption of emplotted structure for the audience. Peradotto observes that 'From a semiotic and narratological perspective…the actions of Apollo are identical to the constitutive actions of the author, while those of Oedipus, Jocasta, and the rest are but *products* of those constitutive actions.'[42] We can observe in turn that, just as the characters in *Oedipus* have to assess the oracles of Apollo and act accordingly, the audience of the tragedy has to 'divine' the intention of its absent author – and try to interpret accordingly.

What is involved for either characters or audience? To explore this further, let's return to the issue posed not by the number of Laius's assailants but by the confusion it entails. Is this simply a dramaturgical device to facilitate the development of the plot and so allow Oedipus to learn his 'real' identity? There's a further complication. Oedipus, by his own admission, has murdered a traveller and, he emphasises, *all* his attendants (*kteinō de tous xumpantas*, 813) on his way from Delphi to Thebes, whereas Jocasta had said that *one* of the attendants of Laius escaped the carnage (753), and we eventually meet him, for, in another of the play's 'coincidences', he is also the Theban herdsman to whom Laius gave the infant Oedipus for exposure on Mount Cithaeron. Oedipus sees hope for himself in this discrepancy: if this man stands by his account, Oedipus is not the killer of Laius ('one cannot be equal to many', he says in 845). Jocasta reassures him that the man cannot go back on what he has said, since the city heard him, and not just she alone (850). She sends for the man, who eventually comes on the scene at 1110. In the meantime, the messenger from Corinth who enters at this point to announce the death of Polybus has shifted attention to the question of Oedipus's origins, and it is to this that the herdsman directs his remarks when he arrives; the issue he was summoned to resolve, the circumstances of Laius's murder, simply never arises. But when the herdsman reveals Oedipus's origins, Oedipus responds as though the herdsman had implicated him in the murder of Laius: 'all is clear, all come to pass…I have been revealed as born from whom I ought not, joining with whom I ought not, killing those I should not have' (1182–85). Whether the traveller that Oedipus killed *was* Laius is never explicitly spelled out in the play, though Oedipus himself jumps to that conclusion, as do most readers and viewers: we *know* that Oedipus killed his father and married his mother, don't we? *Everybody* knows. But *how* do we know? And *why* is the play so hazy about details when, if it is the grand affirmation of prophecy, fate and a deterministic worldview it is so generally taken to be, it could surely have made everything as completely 'clear' as Oedipus has come to believe it is?

Sandor Goodhart suggests that the issue of numbers can point to a rather different way of interpreting the play. Why does Oedipus jump to the conclusion he does, abandoning 'even the evidence of his senses in recollecting that he killed *all* those he encountered at the crossroads', as Peradotto puts it?[43] Because he inserts himself in the narrative of the prophecy, accepting that it is 'true': he jumps to *its* 'conclusion', the closural point of its narrative. And why do we? On the basis of the received myth, whose conclusion we all know. In narrative terms, the myth and the prophecy are structurally similar, though they employ different tenses, past and future respectively. Both are 'historical statements' (as Danto would have it) about Oedipus. Just as Oedipus comes to accept the authority of the prophecy, the critical tradition, Goodhart suggests, overwhelmingly accepts the authority of the myth.[44] This *is* what happens to Oedipus, isn't it? Recall Morson's comment that even a first viewing of the play is like a re-reading: the myth is granted a priority in the interpretation of the tragedy. The structure of repetition associated with narrative is operative here. Just as Oedipus conforms to the prophecy in his interpretation of events, so the audience conforms to the myth in theirs. And just as Oedipus neglects the loose ends, the *inconclusive* elements, that could lead him at least to question some aspects of his new-found belief in the prophetic narrative of himself, so critics marginalise or repress the details in the text that would conflict with their assumption that what Sophocles has given us is a dramatisation of the familiar story, an exploration of the flaws of Oedipus that led him to his destined end and the revelation of his 'true' identity.

Goodhart suggests that these loose ends might serve a rather different purpose: 'Rather than a critique of Oedipus via the myth, Sophocles' play is a critique via Oedipus of us,' he says,[45] particularly an *uncritical* adherence to 'the primacy of mythic expectations', to a prior narrative which thus *predisposes* us to interpret the play in the received way, just as a prior narrative, the prophecy, predisposes Oedipus to 'realise' his identity, which is the identity the prophecy had prepared for him. Oedipus is, by his own admission, a murderer, but if we are prepared to entertain the possibility that Oedipus has jumped to the wrong conclusion and may not have killed *Laius*:

> Suddenly, a new reading of Sophocles' play opens up to us. Sophocles has shifted our traditional focus entirely. Rather than an illustration of the myth, the play is a critique of mythogenesis, an examination of the process by which one arbitrary fiction comes to assume the value of truth…Oedipus discovers he is guilty of parricide and incest…less by uncovering certain unhitherto obscure empirical facts than by voluntarily appropriating an oracular logic which assumes he has always already been guilty. Oedipus becomes 'Oedipus' by assuming the myth *a priori*, by assuming he has been so all along.[46]

The 'arbitrary fiction' which comes to assume 'the value of truth' is the prophetic narrative into which Oedipus inserts himself so as to become the 'Oedipus' of the myth we all know, the genesis of which the play explores in Oedipus's surrender to the assumption that this is what *must* have happened, even though the evidence does not point to that unequivocally. This is *not* to say that Oedipus did not kill Laius: the play never resolves that question, and critics who try to 'prove' that he didn't[47] are on a hiding to nothing (though no more so than those who assert, against the unresolved discrepancies, that he did).

By taking the possibility seriously – *what if* Oedipus did not kill Laius? – it also becomes possible to suggest that the play is addressing the issue of contingency not only for the characters 'inside' its world and showing what happens when they abandon it in favour of determinism, but is also putting under scrutiny the determinism that the structured narrative of the received story imposes on viewers and the critical tradition 'outside' as well, when they abandon the notion that the play could be about something other than they *pre*sume it to be: 'We restore the myth, it would seem, *only from the outside* and only at the expense of the play Sophocles has given us.'[48] If we treat our lives as if they possessed the shape of particular narratives, then we can run into trouble, and this is a time-honoured theme of literature, ancient as well as modern. Don Quixote sees himself as a hero of romance, and, disastrously, both Flaubert's Emma Bovary and Tolstoy's Anna Karenina see themselves as heroines out of romantic novels. Anna accommodates everything that happens to her to a plot that revolves around a grand passion. Fatalistically, she sees herself as having no choice, and attributes nothing to chance; the death of the trainman at the opening of the novel when she meets Vronsky she herself deems 'an evil omen', and of course she commits suicide at the end by throwing herself under a train.[49] Erotic narratives, which often take on a strong teleological shape in anticipated consummation (or failure), lend themselves readily to this theme, but more generally while narrative aims at explanation and knowledge, it is also structured by desire – for the end: *sic placitum*.[50] Literature also enjoys representing figures well known from classic earlier treatments in the process of 'becoming themselves', or indeed resisting 'becoming themselves'. Ovid's epistolary narratives, the *Heroides*, have in recent years been seen as such complex discourses of 'self-realisation'. They represent figures such as Penelope or Dido writing letters to the men they love at a specific point 'within' the stories that are familiar from Homer, Virgil and other canonical texts.[51] On Goodhart's reading, *Oedipus* is a warning about (self-)realisation: what if Oedipus has prematurely fallen prey to a narrative about himself, so as to become what the narrative had said he was all along?

In suggesting that adherence to the 'truth' of the myth performs the same function for those 'outside' the play as adherence to the 'truth' of prophecy does for the characters 'inside' it, the stakes are very high. To question that myth, as Goodhart argues *Oedipus* itself just might do, is 'to play havoc with a legend that for twenty-eight hundred years has remained curiously intact. It is to raise serious questions about those for whom the myth has remained constant whether in Sophocles' world or our own.'[52] Goodhart's article is iconoclastic, in some eyes even heretical, and it has had limited impact on the criticism of Sophocles or beyond. Its subtitle, 'Oedipus and Laius' Many Murderers' sounds deceptively simple for a piece that raises such major issues.[53] It is not only literary critics who are in his sights:

> In the famous passage of *The Interpretation of Dreams* in which Freud links psychoanalysis with the Oedipus myth, Freud is astonishingly clear about the relation that he finds between the two. 'The action of the play consists in nothing other than the process of revealing with ever mounting delays and ever mounting excitement – a process that can be likened to the work of psychoanalysis – that Oedipus is himself the murderer of Laius, but further that he is the son of the murdered man and of Jocasta.'[54]

For Freud, the play *reveals* the truth not only about what Oedipus has done but what he 'is', and in likening the action of the play to the work of psychoanalysis, the latter becomes a process of revelation or discovery of the truth about the analysand and the desires that were there all along. Goodhart draws out the implications:

> The outcome of the therapy, for Freud, which we might assume to be open-ended, is thoroughly determined in advance ... The patient for Freud must discover himself Oedipus and must confess his crimes at the level of desire to the doctor who knew that truth in advance and who, with his wise silence and prophetic eyes, has assumed throughout the position of Teiresias ... The production of an 'Oedipus complex', the 'Oedipalization' of the patient, is an enabling condition for the psychoanalytical cure.[55]

For Freud, Goodhart suggests, the Oedipus myth, thus confirmed in Freud's reading of the plot of Sophocles's play, has taken on the status of a scientific truth, universal, and so applicable to humankind in all times and all places;[56] the possessor of that truth takes on the role of the prophet in that, come what may, *he knows what must eventuate.*[57] The determinism assumed in the plot of the play is transferred into the determinism of the system, and within its teleological structure, the form that the future will take is already known, and is associated with necessity, even if the content is contingent and variable. Equally, the past is configured by the system believed to be true and universal: Oedipus in the play instantiates the 'Oedipus complex'.

For Goodhart, the gravity of the issues at stake is itself thematised within the play.[58] After Jocasta has left the stage to summon the Theban herdsman in an attempt to establish what happened to Laius at the crossroads, the chorus of Theban elders anxiously express a conventional viewpoint on the action (899–910). No more will they go in reverence to the shrines at Delphi, at Abae or at Olympia, if these oracles do not fit (*harmosei*), so that mortal men can point at them with the hand (*cheirodeikta*) – the gesture that signifies transcendent truth in the here-and-now; the worship of the gods, they say, is perishing (*ta theia errei*). Those viewers and critics who assert 'but Oedipus *does/did* kill his father and marry his mother' to ground their assumption that Sophocles's plot *must* affirm the traditional myth similarly gesture, by their use of the indicative, to a perceived truth that is no less structured around a narrative than the prophecy is for the Theban elders – save that the elders are waiting anxiously upon events to find out whether or not the oracle *does* fit, rather than confidently assuming it *has to* or *will*. The notion that Sophocles's plot *might* complicate the myth and maybe leave it more open than it is usually assumed to be is prompted not by the corresponding indicative statement 'Oedipus didn't kill his father' but by the hypothetical question '*what if* he didn't?' Goodhart's deconstructive reading works to break down boundaries erected by critics between 'inside' and 'outside', in the case of his essay specifically the boundary between literature and criticism. On his reading, the play has already initiated a searching critique of our susceptibility to particular narrative structures even when we pride ourselves, like Oedipus, on our critical acuity, while criticism, buoyed by its assumption of independence and its belief that it knows, ends up by reproducing the myth.[59]

That literary texts might 'pre-empt' critical and theoretical approaches (and even be a bit better at them) – a common ploy of deconstructive criticism – offers an unsettling inversion of the 'normal' temporality assumed in criticism, that criticism comes *after* the text, and *reveals* what it is saying. Aristotle's theory of tragedy in the *Poetics* could be a case in point. Just before the messenger from Corinth appears to announce the death of Polybus, Jocasta has prayed to Apollo to give some clear resolution (*lusin tin'... euagē*, 921); later on, Oedipus says it was Apollo who brought his terrible woes to completion (*telōn*, 1330), thus seemingly fulfilling Teiresias's prophecy at 376–77: 'Your fate is not to fall at *my* hands – Apollo, whose concern it is to work these things out (*tad' ekpraxai*), is sufficient to that.' Apollo is to the oracle as the author is to the plot, and it has been pointed out that the term Jocasta uses of 'resolution' (*lusis*) is the word Aristotle will use for the *dénouement* of a plot;[60] Oedipus's language in turn 'anticipates' Aristotle's concern with teleology, just as Aristotle's term for an event that can be construed as a whole (*praxis*) 'echoes' Teiresias's words. Aristotle's enthusiasm for *Oedipus* could be explained on the grounds that there is a congruence between it and his theory of tragedy – to the extent that he is content to exclude or marginalise any element that doesn't 'fit': thus Oedipus's ignorance of how Laius died (*Oedipus* 112–13) lies 'outside the plot-structure' (*exō tou mutheumatos, Poetics* 1460a29). In particular, Terence Cave sees the prominence given in the *Poetics* to *anagnōrisis*, and to texts in which recognition is a key motif (particularly the *Odyssey* and *Oedipus*), in terms of the whole work's interest in 'fictions of knowledge', and wonders whether Aristotle, 'being interested in epistemology, could not help "discovering" epistemological themes and structures in literary works'. He continues,

> Aristotle's poetics is a powerful instrument, not because it provides an accurate account of how tragedies do or should work, but because it absorbs the narrative structure of a group of literary texts into a discourse deeply concerned with modes of cognition, and in the process transforms them: in the context it provides, the plays perform a heuristic role. It is by no means clear that they perform this role anywhere but in the *Poetics* – or, *mutatis mutandis*, in later versions of poetics. There is an important sense in which the things we see in literature are not there until we see them.[61]

Following from Cave, we could say that the perceived narrative structure of *Oedipus* is absorbed not only in the *Poetics*, but also in Freud and, *mutatis mutandis*, in Goodhart's ostensibly anti-determinist deconstructive reading as well.

Many critics have similarly configured *Oedipus* as a fiction of knowledge.[62] It is, needless to say, far more than that. The *Poetics* is a text in which Aristotle the epistemologist can be interested in tragedy as an exploration of causality, but also one where Aristotle the theorist of rhetoric can be interested in its capacity for emotional impact, which he suggests is one of its most vital features. The tragic effects of pity and fear, he argues, are more likely to be aroused through clear causal connections between events than if they seem arbitrary or fortuitous; but even chance events can have a great impact when they appear to have a purpose. He goes on to relate the story of how the statue of Mitys fell on his murderer when he was looking at it; such things, Aristotle says, do not *seem* to happen without reason (*Poetics* 1452a4–10). His commentator D.W. Lucas extrapolates that such events 'are more striking when they have the kind of chance connexion which is so appropriate that they seem to be directed by a higher purpose' and speaks of 'providential coincidence'.[63] Terence Cave likewise glosses that 'this is an accident for which the spectator will infer a providential motivation'.[64] The spectator will *provide* a chain of causation which maybe isn't 'there' at all, and in this verb it is possible to sense the trope of providence which 'foresees' (*pro-videre*) the end – although it retrojects this view forwards towards the end from the vantage point of the end, as being there all along. J. David Velleman uses Aristotle's story of Mitys's murderer to probe the kind of understanding that narrative offers, and suggests that 'the sequence of events *completes* an emotional cadence in the audience' (my emphasis). A murder may well prompt strong emotion, a feeling of indignation or a desire for vengeance, and when the murderer meets with a fitting comeuppance, that emotion is gratified: 'Although these events follow no causal sequence, they *provide* an emotional resolution, and so they have a meaning for the audience, despite lacking any causal or probabilistic connection.'[65]

The *Poetics* may thus be seen no less as a fiction of emotion than as a fiction of knowledge, and the two fictions need not be conclusively demarcated from each other. Velleman sees a continuum between the story of Mitys and the story of Oedipus, which means that the latter, for all that its events may strike us as coincidences and implausible to boot, for all that we consciously reject the notion of fate, nonetheless resonates with an emotional pattern we are familiar with, that of being undone by our own best efforts: 'Not knowing why it happened, we ought to question whether it really did happen that way; but knowing how it feels, we have a sense of understanding, and we mistakenly allow our skepticism to be allayed.'[66] Velleman's general point about the understanding offered by narrative, and particularly the narrative of historical events, is that the closure experienced may be emotional as much as intellectual:

> Insofar as historical discourse conveys understanding by organizing the past into stories, what it conveys is not an objective understanding of how historical events came about but a subjective understanding of how to feel about them...The storytelling historian thus brings his audience to some emotional closure about a course of events viewed in retrospect...Having made subjective sense of historical events, by arriving at a stable attitude toward them, the audience is liable to feel that it has made objective sense of them, by understanding how they came about. Having sorted out its feelings toward events, the audience mistakenly feels that it has sorted out the events themselves: it mistakes emotional closure for intellectual closure.[67]

His remarks are worth remembering when it comes to connecting events in accordance with plausibility (especially in texts that, like *Oedipus*, may challenge the limits of what we can accept as plausible) or necessity (the statue of Mitys falling on his murderer certainly causes his death in a very strong sense, but that's hardly what the story 'explains' to us). Moreover they will resonate strongly with those who seek to understand narrative in terms of desire and its satisfaction, most notably in Peter Brook's *Reading for the Plot*, which bases its theory of narrative on Freud. We may thus see Freudian psychoanalysis as both a 'fiction of knowledge' *and* a 'fiction of emotion', and perhaps appreciate the dangers that can accompany any attempt to *reduce* a text, be it Sophocles's, Aristotle's or Freud's, to the terms of one category of analysis to the exclusion of others. But this also raises the possibility that the issue of causality, and, if you will, the relationship between plausibility and necessity, is not simply a metaphysical or epistemological phenomenon, but a historical one as well that narratives help to probe, and that the boundary between necessity and plausibility will be re-negotiated by narratives in the future in ways that we cannot foresee.[68]

When Cave remarks that there is an important sense in which the things we see in literature are not there until we see them, he is striving to resist the temptation that goes with determinism to universalise a present insight. Goodhart succumbs to this with his suggestion that the perceived meaning has been there all along, had we but seen it: 'The play raises all the questions we would ask; it has *already* undertaken the "deconstruction" we would now "innocently" begin ... Translating these questions into a context in which answers are defined, we have *preempted* Sophocles' interrogation for our own.'[69] In speaking of *translating* the questions that *Oedipus* raises, he suggests that criticism involves a re-writing of the text into a discourse in which – unlike tragedy – 'answers are defined'. There is a sense in which, for Goodhart, this act of translation is a betrayal: *tradutorre traditore*, as the old saying has it. Returning to these issues some years later in a book which has the subtitle *Reading the End of Literature*, Goodhart asks what is the end or goal of literature? What are we doing when we write commentary *on* literature? In the revised essay on *Oedipus* which forms the book's first chapter he characterises this commentary as philosophy: 'Whether we read literature as philosophic moralism or philosophic history, we read literature through philosophy, and not the reverse.'[70] Goodhart offers a synchronic generalisation, but this perspective has a very influential diachronic, historicising counterpart, which sees tragedy as *supplanted* by philosophy.[71] Arguing against the notion that tragedy is in some sense universal, Jean-Pierre Vernant says that

> if the impact of tragedy depends on stimulating an emotional complex that we all carry within us, then why was tragedy born in the Greek world at the turn of the fifth and sixth centuries? Why did other civilisations know nothing of tragedy? And why was the tragic seam so rapidly exhausted in Greece itself and its place taken by a philosophical type of thought that did away with the contradictions upon which tragedy constructed its dramatic universe, by accounting for them rationally?[72]

In Vernant's use of the word 'rationally', we can see one of Barthes's three hypostases of the Author, reason. The counterpart arguments developed by Goodhart and Vernant converge on the notion that philosophy as a genre, a kind of writing, projects a structure that raises the expectation of answers.

For Goodhart, criticism is formally more like philosophy than it is like literature, but when he suggests that 'we may legitimately say that great literature is already "about" the criticism that will come along and attempt to displace it',[73] he is not saying that philosophy takes precedence over literature and thereby 'explains' it (or vice versa), rather that when we talk *about* 'literature', we are not 'saying' what literature 'says', we are saying something *different*, and that translation is, crucially, one of form as well as content. And yet, criticism often feels at its most satisfying when it seems to us to be saying the *same* as what we believe literature is saying, when any process of translation or paraphrase, any effect of the passage of time and circumstance, seems to be effaced. Pierre Menard, 'Author of the *Quixote*' in Borges's short story on the assumptions that drive literary commentary, confronts these challenges as he sets out laboriously to re-create Cervantes's novel word for word, an exercise that would, on the face of it, produce an absolutely identical text.[74] However, for all his efforts, Menard produces an incomplete text (only the ninth and thirty-eighth chapters of the first part, and a fragment of chapter twenty-two). The project is left unfinished – hardly even started – at his death, as he confronts what he finds to be the insurmountable problems, theological and metaphysical as well as linguistic and literary, entailed by the critical desire for identity over time. But the 'new' work is magnificent in its own way, as the narrator emphasises: 'Cervantes's text and Menard's are verbally identical, but the second is almost infinitely richer. (More ambiguous, his detractors will say, but ambiguity is richness).'[75] Even such a translation that painstakingly maintains the 'literal' form of its original transforms it, arguably even for the better.

As he seeks to address the issue, Goodhart casts it in theological terms. He argues that we are bound to betray whatever knowledge it is that literature offers us not by challenging its 'truth' but by appropriation, by claiming as that 'truth' our necessarily partial readings.[76] If criticism believes it ends up saying what literature was saying all along, and the critic apprehends that as a revelation so powerful that, in a flash – of recognition – he or she 'discovers' what was 'there all along', a feeling so inescapable that it can recuperate all earlier attempts to evade it, we are, Goodhart argues, dealing with a 'truth' that is 'prophetic'. The prophetic, he suggests, is one name

> for the logic of the diachronic, for a repetition founded not upon difference but upon sameness or identicality, upon 'more of the same', a logic, that is to say that recognizes…the *drama* in which human beings are engaged and names in advance of the end of those dramas *in order that we may gain the option of giving them up if we so choose.*[77]

The spectre of the deterministic world to which Oedipus surrenders by seeking to re-present perfectly in his own actions the narrative of the oracle haunts this account, but the world does not *have* to be so, Goodhart argues, echoing his own configuration of Sophocles's text as leaving contingency open as a possibility; and what from a different perspective is the philosophical problem of free will and determinism is 'translated' into the terms of 'drama', and figures human beings as within that drama, and so in the midst of time.

However, his fiction of knowledge as open-*ended* hints at the very determinism from which Goodhart would choose to escape. The dream of a final resolution of the issue that vexes him is formally entailed by the critical discourse in which he is writing in a way that does not arise for Sophocles's tragic text. Borges's narrator draws attention to a feature of Menard's work which has struck him, 'his resigned or ironical habit of propagating ideas which were the strict reverse of those he preferred'.[78] It's a common experience (at least it is for the present writer) that, over time, one can look at what one has written and come to the exact opposite of one's previous conclusion. Free will and determinism, for all that we desire them to be resolved, are not so easily separated out for us that what we believe to be our choice may not later look like an illusion. In our imagination, perhaps, in the fictions of knowledge we invent and in our capacity to 'place' ourselves where we will, in the midst (of time) and at the end (of time), our quest *feels* far from pointless. In his fiction of knowledge, Borges's narrator recalls a communication from Pierre Menard: "My undertaking is not difficult, essentially," I read in another part of his letter. "I should only have to be immortal to carry it out." Shall I confess that I often imagine he did finish it and that I read the *Quixote* – all of it – as if Menard had conceived it?'[79] Fantasy and wish fulfilment play their part in the act of interpretation. In the reversal *Oedipus* emplots, Oedipus moves from the assumption that he has freedom of action to the belief that prophecy is 'real' and that the world he inhabits is deterministic. We do not have ultimate answers to the question of what the play 'really' says (or of whether the world 'really' is deterministic or not) – we should have to be immortal, as Pierre Menard says, to carry that out – though, as Borges's narrator confesses, we often indulge ourselves by imagining precisely that the task has been completed: *sic placitum. Oedipus* can be re-written as a fiction of knowledge, or a fiction of desire, but it has the potentiality to be infinitely re-written, and in forms we cannot prophesy. We should have to be immortal to encompass all that the text could mean.

4

SELF-DETERMINATION

The sense that events or judgements can be viewed from a 'God's-eye view' authorial position 'outside' time may underlie our sense of their intelligibility, but if not subject to interrogation can give rise to a determinism that can be experienced in life no less than in literature. We saw in Chapter 3 that one form such interrogation could take was the hypothetical question 'what if...?' This chapter extends that argument by looking first at the current vogue for counterfactual history, taking as its text Livy's discussion of what might have happened had Alexander the Great lived and turned his attention westwards, which I examine primarily for what perspectives can be developed from it about historical methodology. Far from being the marginal exercise it has often been taken to be, counterfactual thinking starts to look central to historical interpretation – if, that is, the behaviour of historical actors itself is seen already to have a narrative aspect. This section brings into dialogue with Livy Jorge Luis Borges's famous story 'The Garden of the Forking Paths', which forms a bridge to the second section in which this assumption is explored in relation to one philosopher, Galen Strawson, who is convinced that 'life' does not have this narrative aspect, and another, Martin Heidegger, who in his theory of temporality, I suggest, seeks to confine the authorial viewpoint 'inside' time and make it the basis of how human beings order their lives and behaviour.

Let us begin by recapitulating a few points that will be developed further here. The use of the indicative, in the essential surplus of knowledge that plays around its use in narrativising what we think we know, brings with it intimations of a deterministic perspective: 'Oedipus killed Laius at the point where three roads meet'. Hypothetical questions such as 'what if Oedipus had reached the point where three roads meet a few minutes earlier?' or 'what if it wasn't Laius that Oedipus killed?' are ways of interrogating the determinism we read out of or into Sophocles's play. 'What if...' questions are at the centre of the recent debate over what has come to be known as 'counterfactual history' and its methodological implications for the writing of history more generally. What if the Emperor Trajan had exploited the steam technology that was available to him?[1] In a detailed historical survey which introduces a collection of counterfactual historical essays,[2] Niall Ferguson suggests that it is by no means a recent phenomenon, though often explicitly presented as marginal to mainstream historiography. For all its vogue in recent times, it remains a sub-genre of historiography, safely corralled in collections that give graphic warning of their provenance.[3] So-called 'mainstream' history in an avowedly counterfactual mode is less common,[4] though counterfactual speculation is a feature, albeit often an implicit one, in what Ferguson characterises as revisionist works of history, 'not altogether surprisingly, in that most revisionists tend to be challenging some form of deterministic interpretation.'[5] Revisionism will be one of the major themes of this section.

Amongst historians, counterfactual history is variously regarded indulgently as a *jeu d'esprit* in which reductive explanations (Cleopatra's nose, in Pascal's famous example) humorously play with the limits of plausible explanation; or dismissively as a 'parlour game', or as '*Geschichtswissenschlopff*, unhistorical shit', by E.H. Carr and E.P. Thompson respectively, both socialist historians with deep ideological commitments to the *form* of their explanation. Ferguson suggests a link between their methodological commitment to determinism in historical explanation and their antipathy to counterfactual speculation.[6] He relates the current popularity to the rise in interest in the role of narrative in historiography – itself a manifestation of the 'linguistic turn', the renewed interest in modes of representation that marks the critique of realism and determinism in both the humanities and the sciences. He sees its counterpart in physics in chaos theory,[7] which suggests that even within deterministic systems, specific initial conditions can soon give rise to unpredictable outcomes even when successive events are seen as causally linked.[8] So-called 'chaotic' systems are, in an image we shall shortly be examining, *non-linear*.

The 'what if...?' question mobilises the revisionist critique of determinism in historical narrative, but also in critical interpretation and methodology – where it can meet with an equally supercilious reaction, as we saw in Chapter 3. As Ferguson's survey shows, once you start looking for instances of counterfactual speculation, they start presenting themselves readily even in historical writing that methodologically embraces a deterministic stance. One of the most famous instances in a classical text comes in Book 9 of Livy's history of Rome from its foundation, and it will form the basis for a discussion here that goes beyond the limits Ferguson allows himself. As noted in Chapter 3, Livy offers an explicitly providential viewpoint on the events he narrates, though the phrase *ut opinor* suggests that the providential viewpoint is a matter of authorial faith (1.4.1). In the strictly annalistic, or year-by-year, form Livy's narrative adopts, it has reached the late fourth century BC in Book 9, and the Romans' wars against their neighbours, the Samnites. Livy tells of the infamous disaster of the Caudine Forks, when the Roman army was trapped in a valley with narrow defiles at either end which the Samnites blocked once the Romans had entered it. The soldiers were spared their lives only by submitting to humiliating terms and the ignominy of going under the yoke as the Samnites jeered, before returning to a hostile reception in Rome (9.2–7). After a heated debate amongst the Roman leadership about what to do next, the Romans march back into Samnite territory, the enemy are reduced in a siege, and forced in turn to go under the yoke (9.8–15). 'Scarcely any other victory of the Roman people is more glorious for its sudden reversal of fortune,' Livy remarks (9.15.8), and much of the credit for this is given to the consul Lucius Papirius Cursor. Livy devotes an extended eulogy to him (9.16.11–19), which concludes, 'People even mark him out in their minds as a match in generalship for Alexander the Great, if Alexander had turned his weapons against Europe after he had conquered Asia' (*quin eum parem destinant animis magno Alexandro ducem, si arma Asia perdomita in Europam vertisset*).

Comparisons between great Greeks and Romans is a favourite theme in classical literature,[9] but this one has drawn attention for the surprise of its introduction (prompted by Livy's own remarks, it is usually referred to as a 'digression') and for the counterfactual premise of the comparison: what if Alexander had turned his weapons to the West?[10] Livy's answer is triumphantly chauvinistic: Alexander is only accounted continually successful because he died before his luck could change; he had effectively shot his bolt after the conquest of the East, and was becoming progressively more unstable; but above all, each of the Roman generals he would have encountered, and there were many of them, was his equal, and he would have been trounced (9.17–18). Whatever one thinks of the historical insights the exercise affords, there is undeniably a strong sense of the 'retrospective wishful thinking' to which Ferguson suggests counterfactual thinking can be prone.[11] This is emphatically a discourse of desire: Livy (fore)sees Alexander's defeat as inevitable, to the even greater glory of Roman history. The counterfactual question, far from putting under interrogation Livy's deterministic story of Rome's inexorable rise to world domination, serves to endorse it.

There is a supplementary counterfactual here: what if Alexander *had lived* and turned his weapons to the West?[12] Chronologically, the war against the Samnites and the disaster of the Caudine Forks roughly coincides with the death of Alexander after the conquest of the East (323 BC), so, within an annalistic framework, it does not seem wholly arbitrary to introduce the question at this point.[13] But why introduce it at all? Why invest what could be seen as just a 'coincidence' with such weight? Livy's methodological uneasiness is explicit and worth close attention (9.17.1–2):

> *nihil minus quaesitum a principio huius operis videri potest quam ut plus iusto ab rerum ordine declinarem varietatibusque distinguendo opere et legentibus velut deverticula amoena et requiem animo meo quaererem; tamen tanti regis ac ducis mentio, quibus saepe tacitus cogitationibus volutavi animum, eas evocat in medium, ut quaerere libeat quinam eventus Romanis rebus, si cum Alexandro foret bellatum, futurus fuerit.*

Nothing could seem less to have been the object of my research [*quaesitum*] from the outset [*principio*] of this work [*operis*] than that I should turn aside [*declinarem*] more than is right [*plus iusto*] from the order [*ordine*] of events and, by interspersing the work [*opere*] with embellishments, that I should seek out [*quaererem*] pleasant detours [*deverticula amoena*], as it were, for my readers and mental relaxation for myself; but the mere mention of so great a king and commander calls out into the open those thoughts which I have often silently cast my mind over, so that it's a pleasure [*libeat*] for me to inquire [*quaerere*] what would have been the outcome for Roman history if war had been waged with Alexander.

The pursuit of pleasure and the pursuit of knowledge are here set against each other. The imagery suggests that writer and readers are on a journey together, and that this episode will lead them to stray from the route. A *deverticulum* is where one would break one's onward progress for a rest; the addition of the adjective *amoenus* suggests that such a place would be, as travel guides solicit us, 'worth the detour'.[14] This 'digressive' counterfactual episode is a *jeu d'esprit*, a distraction from the serious business of what, after all, Livy twice refers to in this passage as his 'work' or 'task' (*opus*). There are two journeys involved here, and both follow the same 'route'. One has been made by the 'order' of the 'things' themselves, the events of Roman history (*ab **rerum** ordine* is picked up by *Romanis **rebus*** later in the sentence). Their route is a direct one (*ordo* refers to the succession of events, but can mean a straight line).[15] This dictates the itinerary to be followed by the second journey, which is that of Livy's work itself as it moves from the past (the foundation of the city) to his own times (the present of the work's composition in the time of Augustus), mapping those events in its rigidly chronological, annalistic framework.

The route and destination dictate also his rate of progress, and explain his reluctance to turn aside (the verb *declinare* suggests deviation from a route). Livy's massive history, which covers more than seven hundred years, actually needs to move rather more quickly than 'the events themselves' if he is to catch up with them, which he never quite does, for the writing of his history itself takes time, and he only has a single life's span. His narratorial 'present', towards which he is journeying, has slipped in Book 9 some years since he began Book 1 in about 30 BC, and will slip the best part of his lifetime (he died in 17 AD) by the time he gets to the final book, Book 142, which deals with the events of 9 BC. Detours are thus rarely to be indulged, for he is always playing catch-up.[16] Apart from the delay it involves, this counterfactual episode, which introduces the prospect of protracted wars against Alexander that spread far into the future of this counterfactual byway, sits uneasily within the annalistic form of the work. The inhospitality to the episode of the annalistic framework, and the intrusiveness of wishful thinking, is seen, for example, in Livy's eagerness to add to the list of contemporary great Roman generals who could have defeated Alexander those of the generation after Alexander's actual death in 323 BC. This leads Livy to invent a war between Carthage and Alexander before he can turn his attention to Rome, in order to use up time, so that, in this imagined scenario, those generals too would be able to confront him.[17] Narratives of the past may need, as Augustine puts it, to *make* the truth (*veritatem… facere*), but the last thing a historian wants is to be seen to make it *up*, and Livy is in danger of laying open to unwelcome scrutiny the aspect of desire and fulfilment that is part of his fictive craft. Knowledge of Roman history, the professed object of his search or quest (the verb *quaerere* is used three times in various forms), will best be served if he follows the same route as precisely as he can (repetition without difference is the ideal to which his work aspires, just as, he believes, the events themselves repeat Fate), and so he must crave indulgence for this break in the journey, and present it, precisely, as a met*hodo*logical *aberration*, a wandering from the theoretical path (Greek *hodos*) which he has set himself to follow.

Livy's work has a point from which it sets out, a starting point (*principium*), 'from the foundation of the city', but, in terms of a journey whose destination is *already* known, *principium* shades from 'beginning' to 'guiding principle' in 9.17.1. His methodology is, to use the journey imagery, the route-map which will take him by the direct route to the destination, which he already knows, because he is, in part, already there, as his narrating self looks back on his narrated self trying to catch up. If Roman history has a pre-ordained destiny, a route along which History's events can march (to use Kant's image), so does the author of the *Ab urbe condita*. In the opening sentence of the preface to Book 1, he sets himself the task of writing the history of Rome, and is already looking forward, very cautiously, to looking back on himself from the imagined moment of completion: 'Whether I am about to undertake a task worth the effort if I shall have completed the writing of the history of the Roman people from the beginnings of the city I don't quite know, nor, if I were to know, would I dare to say it' (*facturusne operae pretium sim si a primordio urbis res populi Romani perscripserim nec satis scio nec, si sciam, dicere ausim*). The image of the journey in Book 9 gives us a momentary glimpse of the process by which Titus Livius fulfils his self-appointed destiny of becoming 'Livy, the historian of Rome's rise to power'.

To indulge in a brief detour at this point is attractive not simply because it coincides with the time of Alexander's actual death. Thematically, it is an interesting moment as well. The narrative of the Caudine Forks, which immediately precedes the counterfactual episode, tells of how the Romans were going to the aid of their allies in Luceria, deep in Samnite country. Two routes, we are told, were available to them, one through the Caudine Forks, the other skirting the Adriatic through open country, though 'long almost in proportion to its safety' (9.2.6). The Romans take the direct route, which results in disaster – though if one takes a slightly longer view, the vengeance they subsequently take on the Samnites for their humiliation leaves them stronger, *eventually*, as the narrator from his vantage point is aware. But scroll back a little, and you will reach a point, a turning point, if you will, where the *decision* was made to take the shorter, more dangerous, route rather than the longer, and safer, one. From the perspective of the Romans as they approach it, this is where three roads meet, the road they are on and the fork which will take them in one direction or the other. The decision the Romans make is far from trivial in its consequences.[18] Livy doesn't – or chooses not to? – narrate the reasons for the Romans' decision, other than to note that 'their deliberations were only on the route to be taken' (9.2.5), moving quickly to the outcome, their entrapment in the Caudine Forks.

Why the reticence? This reference *could have* prompted a counterfactual question (what if the Romans had decided to take the less direct route?), but in this case didn't. Elsewhere within the narrative of the Caudine Forks and its aftermath, Livy does focus at some length on the process whereby the historical actors arrive at their decisions, notably the debate amongst the Samnites (to which we will return) about what to do with the Romans when they have become trapped in the Caudine Forks (9.3.3–13). Livy has his methodological approach, one he has on principle decided from the outset to follow, that privileges the narrator's viewpoint from the vantage point from which he can view events from the perspective he regards as their eventual outcome. From this perspective, the boundaries he has imposed on the episode define it not as 'the humiliation of the Romans' but 'the humiliation of the Romans leads them to turn defeat into victory'. However, if we focus on the brief reference to the two roads, we can 'recognise' in it the perspective of those within the narrative who are faced with choice without certain knowledge of the outcome, a perspective he has sidelined. Livy knows, as the Romans involved didn't, that at a later juncture they *did* take the alternative route – and it leads to victory.

The narrator too has been faced with choices about how to narrate this episode, though the process in this case is not brought to our attention. When Livy subsequently asks his explicitly counterfactual question about Alexander, he represents himself as approaching a point where three roads meet: faced with a decision whether or not to ask the question, whether or not to stray away from his predetermined course and head off down the side-road, he makes the choice to do so. In so doing, he makes clear that, as a narrator, he is not simply a passive figure who can do no other than follow events. Such counterfactual speculation, he suggests, is an aberration, even though he admits that it has frequently been part of his thought processes (*quibus* **saepe**... *cogitationibus volutavi animum*), albeit a part that he has kept to himself (*tacitus*) and not brought out into the open (*in medium*), presumably because he is too obviously 'making up' the story he tells of Rome and Alexander. Many readers of Livy follow him in suggesting the rarity value of the episode,[19] though at the price of paying less attention to what he says about his silent cogitations, which concern thinking about what might have happened had some particular circumstance been different. 'What if Alexander had lived' is the counterfactual speculation he brings forward for our explicit consideration. But 'what if the Romans had taken the other road to Luceria' could provide another opportunity, though in this case it is a 'road' Livy himself does not take.

The fork in the road, the point at which it is possible to take more than one direction, is a common trope (a term that itself suggests a 'turning') for decision-making, as in Robert Frost's poem 'The Road Not Taken'. It is also, as we have seen in the case of *Oedipus*, a key plot element around which the debate over determinism and free will rages. What follows will take a little time, but is *not* a digression. Borges's short story 'The Garden of the Forking Paths' is a metaphysical fable that explores this image.[20] It consists of two nested and interlocking stories, the outer a spy thriller in which the motive for a mysterious murder is revealed, the inner in which the solution to a scholarly problem is suggested. In the outer story, Yu Tsun, a Chinese spy working in England for the Germans during the First World War, hears that a British agent called Richard Madden has intercepted another German spy, and is hot on Yu Tsun's trail. Before he is arrested or killed, Yu Tsun must find a way of surreptitiously communicating to the Germans the name of a town in France, the site of British artillery, that they should bomb, but in such a way that the Germans will pay attention to the message amidst the uproar of war, and the British not find out. Yu Tsun's ruse, as emerges at the end of the story, is to look up a name in the telephone book. However, unlike Augustine consulting the *sortes biblicae*, Yu Tsun does not open the book at random. He takes a train to the village of Ashgrove, narrowly evading Madden at the station, and finds his way to the house of a Stephen Albert. After conversing with Albert (during which Albert recounts the solution to the scholarly problem which is the subject of the inner story), Yu Tsun shoots him. Just then, Madden arrives and apprehends Yu Tsun. His Chief in Berlin deduces that the name of the town that was to be the target of the German bombs was Albert, and that the news reports of so unaccountable a crime were the means to communicate the secret to the Germans. Yu Tsun has devised a plot, which he resolutely carries through to its end in the full knowledge of the likely consequences for himself, while his Chief, in the classic style of the espionage thriller,[21] 'deciphered this mystery', thus retrospectively re-creating what his agent was up to. Both Yu Tsun's 'plot', prospectively towards its end, and the Chief's re-creation, retrospectively from the end, are linear, and both involve a strong sense of closure. All this is recorded in a statement dictated and signed by Yu Tsun after his arrest, which also contains his reflections about his experience of time as he has carried out his plot.

The story revolves around three... shall we call them 'coincidences'? They are, of course, from the internal narrator Yu Tsun's perspective, though not from the demiurge of this world, the Author Borges's. As chance would have it, Albert is a Sinologist, who, as it happens, has been studying the work of Ts'ui Pên, who, it turns out, is the great-grandfather of Yu Tsun. Albert relates how Ts'ui Pên was involved, so it was said, in two projects, a novel and an infinite labyrinth, but after his death there was no sign of the labyrinth, and only what appeared to be some rough drafts from the novel. However, Albert turned up a new piece of evidence, a letter in which Ts'ui Pên wrote: '*I leave to the various futures (not to all) my garden of forking paths.*' Albert concluded that the novel and the labyrinth are one and the same: Ts'ui Pên's manuscript is not unfinished, but a completed fragment from an infinite book, which represents Ts'ui Pên's understanding of time – as infinite, a garden of paths forking 'in time, not in space',[22] as Albert goes on to explain:

> A broad rereading of the work confirmed the theory. In all fictional works, each time a man is confronted with several alternatives, he chooses one and eliminates the others; in the fiction of Ts'ui Pên, he chooses – simultaneously – all of them. *He creates*, in this way, diverse futures, diverse times which themselves also proliferate and fork... In the work of Ts'ui Pên, all possible outcomes occur; each one is the point of departure for other forkings. Sometimes the paths of this labyrinth converge: for example you [Yu Tsun] arrive at this house, but in one of the possible pasts you are my enemy, in another, my friend.[23]

Albert's scholarly theory invokes closure no less than Yu Tsun's activities and his Chief's detective work do, but his comments on Ts'ui Pên's manuscript point to an important difference with Ts'ui Pên which they share: he *creates* whereas they *re-create*.[24] And herein lies the problem for counterfactual historians as they indulge their creative imaginations. Choose a fork in the road, and follow the path you know was not taken. Is that a direct route to some known destination, or does it fork in turn? And so on: the possible futures proliferate *ad infinitum*. Allow Alexander to live, and only a little way on you have him waging a war against Carthage. The implication is that after conquering Carthage, he meets inevitable defeat at the hands of the Romans. Livy had the sense to stop there, thus denying posterity the spectacle of Hannibal, the censor from Africa, intoning before a rapt assembly of the Senate and People of Rome, with the vatic pomp accorded only to the native speaker of Latin raised by the dictates of a stern mother, that Corinth must be destroyed.[25] *Geschichtswissenschlopff!*

But…what if the thought processes that go into such speculation are not unconnected with thinking historically more generally? Stephen Albert does the classic thing in the situation he finds himself in. Confronting a stranger in his house (what Derrida would call an *arrivant*), he keeps talking, keeps the stranger's attention while trying to work out what to do. So, he explains further to the clearly curious Yu Tsun the meaning of his great-grandfather's work. At the same time he is thinking out loud as he tries to understand the situation he finds himself in *now*. Albert suggests two examples to Yu Tsun, the first relating to the possible futures of this situation:

> Fang, let us say, has a secret; a stranger calls at his door; Fang resolves to kill him. Naturally, there are several possible outcomes: Fang can kill the intruder, the intruder can kill Fang, they both can escape, they both can die, and so forth. In the work of Ts'ui Pên, all possible outcomes occur; each one is the point of departure for other forkings.

In Ts'ui Pên's model of time, whenever there are two or more possibilities, each occurs in a different universe: all choices are always made somewhere, every possibility is an actuality, and so universes proliferate *ad infinitum*.[26] The second example is no less significant: 'Sometimes, the paths of this labyrinth converge: for example, you arrive at my house, but in one of the possible pasts you are my enemy, in another my friend.' Albert tries to understand his present situation not only by thinking about the outcomes of possible courses of action in the future, but by speculating on possible *pasts* as well: has Yu Tsun come as a friend or as an enemy? Looking forwards there is a 'fork' of possible courses of action; but look backwards, and there is a fork which converges at the point you are at *now*. Which of two possible paths, Yu Tsun the friend or Yu Tsun the enemy, has led to this point Albert finds himself in? Only time will tell, as what eventuates establishes one of the paths as the 'correct' one; and so the direct route to the determined historical past is created – as all but one road at *each* fork in the past is dismissed as 'counterfactual'. A narrator who insistently structures his history in terms of a known outcome will give a strong sense of events as determined; contrariwise, if the temporal perspective of the narrated is foregrounded, the element of choice and the quest for understanding and knowledge of their present on the part of those narrated is also foregrounded for our attention.

A frequent feature of Livy's narrative is precisely that he represents the point of view of his historical actors, through the medium of the speeches he puts in their mouths at what we have got into the habit of calling *crucial* moments.[27] We have seen how Livy doesn't narrate how the Romans came to the decision to take the shortcut through the Caudine Forks, but he does focus in first on the deliberations of the Romans trapped there (9.3.1–2) and then at greater length on the Samnites wondering what to do with them. He tells us that 'not even the Samnites' (*ne Samnitibus quidem*) had a 'plan' for making use of these 'so happy events' (*tam laetis…rebus*, 9.3.4). They are thus uncertain both about what to do in the future, but also how they have come to be in this unexpectedly welcome situation. Here, at any rate, is one reason why Livy may have chosen not to represent the Romans' debate about the shortcut. We share the Samnites' puzzlement at the Romans' unfathomable decision to expose themselves to an unnecessary risk. But consider also that, with his essential surplus of knowledge of what eventually happened, Livy is aware that the counterfactual alternative (why didn't they take the longer, safer route?) is *actualised* in the subsequent expedition, when they do take that route (as the brief reference to Papirius marching along the coast in 9.13.6 suggests),[28] and achieve victory and revenge.

However, the Samnites themselves do not know what to do in what they might well see as a 'turn' of events they had not anticipated. So they agree to send a message to Herennius Pontius, the aged and infirm father of their general Gavius Pontius, asking his advice. Livy has earlier introduced the father as being 'by far the most outstanding in foresight' (*patre longe prudentissimo*, 9.1.2).[29] He suggests that the Romans should all be released unharmed without delay. The Samnites reject this advice, and the messenger is sent once more to seek an alternative opinion. The old man then suggests that the Romans should all be put to death. When he has received these replies, 'contradictory, as if the responses of an ambiguous oracle' (*discordia inter se velut ex ancipiti oraculo responsa*, 9.3.8), his son is convinced that the old man's wits have gone, but he bows to the consensus that Herennius be summoned and consulted in person. When he arrives, he doesn't change his advice, and speaks only 'to give the reasons' for it. His first opinion (which he prefers) would lead to lasting peace with a powerful people by doing them an immense favour (*cum potentissimo populo per ingens beneficium perpetuam firmare pacem amicitiamque*, 9.3.10); his second would postpone war for many generations while the Romans sought to recover from their losses. Like Stephen Albert in Borges's story confronted in his home by Yu Tsun, Herennius tries to understand the present crisis in terms of the question 'have you arrived friend or enemy?' While the urgency of the situation obliges him to focus his attention on possible futures (spare the Romans or slaughter them?), his preference for the first course of action suggests a possible *historicisation* of the situation which would configure the Romans as 'friends'.[30] Prospectively, of course, but also retrospectively? Could it be that this possible future also *brings into being* a past in which the Romans' war upon the Samnites looks like an aberration? A path which in the past that forked in the direction of 'enemy' will have rejoined at this juncture the main road which was called, as roads are in virtue of their destination, 'friend'? The other alternative conjures up a main road that was always heading directly for 'enmity'. Gavius Pontius canvasses the old man's opinion: 'what if a middle *way* were adopted' (*quid si media via consilii caperetur*, 9.3.11), let the Romans go unhurt, but impose the legal humiliations associated with defeat. 'That idea of yours,' the old man replies, 'is one which neither makes friends nor removes enemies' (*ista quidem sententia... ea est quae neque amicos parat nec inimicos tollit*, 9.3.11):[31] the humiliation will rankle, and the Romans will not be satisfied until they have exacted revenge. This 'middle way' is precisely the course the Samnites eventually do follow, and they recognise in the aftermath that they should have heeded the advice Herennius has given: 'Too late and in vain they praised the advice of the older Pontius, alternatives between which they had fallen' (9.12.1).

Stephen Oakley suggests that 'Herennius Pontius is a classic warning figure, resembling many in tragedy',[32] the value of whose advice is only recognised after the reversal of fortune – a *peripeteia* – has taken place when the Samnites face retribution in the subsequent encounter. This is a reminder of how historiography and other genres cross-fertilise in pursuit of both understanding and effect.[33] Relevant too is Werner Suerbaum's observation that the 'warning figure' is an embodiment within the text of the counterfactual historian,[34] though, in the light of my discussion, we could see Herennius as one who is historicising 'as he goes along', as a figure not simply of the counterfactual historian, but of the historian *tout court*. Counterfactuals are explored by historians of every stripe as they go along when they are trying not simply to decide where to go next, but to understand where they have got to *now*. Cast the mind back to the remark with which Livy introduced the Alexander episode: 'people even mark him out in their minds as a match in generalship for Alexander the Great, if he had turned his weapons against Europe after he had conquered Asia' (*quin eum parem destinant animis magno Alexandro ducem, si arma Asia perdomita in Europam vertisset*). Who are these 'people' who are the unnamed subjects of the third-person plural verb *destinant*? Livy's contemporaries in their counterfactual 'parlour games'? Perhaps, as this could be a glance towards the Roman literary genre of the *suasoria*, an educational exercise in which the student is asked to take on the persona of a figure from history debating the pros and cons of taking a particular course of action at a specified crucial moment in a famous situation. A collection of such exercises and the titles of others survive in the works of the famous rhetorical teacher the Elder Seneca, and the practice extended beyond the rhetorical schools to the literary culture more generally.[35] The exercise involves the familiar economy of free will and determinism (the first-person character is confronted by choice, but the impersonator and audience know the outcome of that choice), and does not simply offer rich possibilities of pathos and irony as the character puts forward a vision of the future different from what we 'know' happened, but is also a way of subjecting accepted models of historical understanding and of motivation and plausible cause to interrogation through contemplation of antecedent possibilities that were not, in the end, actualised. Faced with the crisis they find themselves in *now*, the protagonists of the *suasoriae* are represented also as trying to understand which of the possible pasts still available to them at that moment led to the situation they find themselves in – one of which will *determine* the choice they make, and how they are viewed historically.

The *suasoria* had become a formalised exercise in particular social settings, but Livy's choice of the word *destinant* could refer to a much broader phenomenon. The syntax of his conditional sentence as a whole is intriguing. The pluperfect subjunctive of the protasis 'if he had turned...' gives way to the present indicative of the apodosis 'people mark him out...', and this could signify not simply Livy's immediate present, but a habitual present, with a broader historical frame of reference. A generation after Alexander's death, Italy *was* invaded by a Greek king, Pyrrhus of Epirus. Plutarch, in his *Life of Pyrrhus*, written a century after Livy's time but drawing on sources that were likely to have been available to him, quotes a speech made in 280 BC by Appius Claudius Caecus against a treaty with Pyrrhus:

> Where is your usual boldness of speech in the face of all men to the effect that if the great Alexander himself had come to Italy and attacked us in our youth and our fathers in their prime he would not now be celebrated as undefeated, but either fleeing or dying somewhere here he would have left Rome more glorious?[36]

The implication of these words, if correctly reported, is that already in 280 BC the question 'what if Alexander had invaded Italy?' was commonplace. Niall Ferguson suggests that counterfactual speculation is only plausible if it reflects future alternatives that can be taken to be 'real' in the thoughts of contemporaries, as Livy has taken pains to do in the case of the philosophical arguments of Herennius in the debate amongst the Samnites about what to do with the Romans trapped in the Caudine Forks. In the sense that what actually transpired was often not the outcome that contemporaries expected, 'the counterfactual scenario was more "real" to decision-makers at the critical moment than the actual subsequent events.'[37] What Ferguson regards as 'the methodological constraint' of counterfactual speculation (one that he imposes on himself and the contributors to the collection he compiled) is that 'counterfactuals should be those which contemporaries contemplated'.[38]

the historian must make no anachronistic assumptions on behalf of his historical characters. Retrospective counterfactual speculation ('what if Alexander *had* invaded Italy') forms part of the argument deployed by Appius Claudius in a debate about what the Romans *are to do* in the face of the threat posed by Pyrrhus. The habitual present tense of *destinant* in Livy 9.16.19 may thus be accorded a theoretical aspect: to locate counterfactual speculation about Alexander in the context of the late fourth century BC is not anachronistic. On the methodological level recommended by Ferguson, Livy is exonerated. It also serves to suggest that for people, like Livy himself and students in the rhetorical schools, who are still practising this speculation three centuries later, it is not anachronistic either. Just as Appius Claudius is historicising 'as he goes along', deploying a retrospective counterfactual speculation to serve his ideological aims in the present, so too may be the author of the *Ab urbe condita*. Ruth Morello interprets the significance of the episode in the context of the Augustan principate as an implicit critique of one-man rule.[39] An exercise that can seem formal and conventional may not be without repercussions when it is viewed 'within' time.[40]

Livy's own account of how he came to include the Alexander episode allows us to glimpse the temporality of his narrating self, indulging in a time-honoured exercise of counterfactual speculation, but also the temporality of his narrated self, faced with the choice of whether or not to include the Alexander episode. We know the answer to that dilemma, of course, but the glimpse afforded offers us an understanding of the decision and a meta-understanding of theoretical issues involved, as Livy confronts the methodological question associated with counterfactual speculation: does it come upon us as 'friend' or 'enemy?' In a similar spirit, we could see Ferguson's musings about counterfactual thinking as marking a point where the practice of history is not sure where it has got to or where it is going, a need to examine possible futures for the discipline which also involves tracing back possible paths which converge on the present aporia – and suddenly we notice coming up behind us and joining us here a path long dismissed as a 'trivial' side-road but on closer inspection revealing signs of heavy traffic, the 'counterfactual'. Could the 'counterfactual' turn out to have been the main road 'after all'? And, *pace* those who like to see Livy's episode as the first instance, does the road go back yet further? As Cave remarked of Aristotle's *Poetics*, there is an important sense in which the things we see in literature, historiography included, are not there until we see them,[41] until, through the mechanism we refer to as *recognition*, we 'realise' that they have been there all along, had we but known. Even historians long thought to be given methodologically to determinism begin to show signs of a friendly interest in the issues of choice and decision-making. Any methodology for which a universalising validity is claimed creates this effect of drawing attention to traces of the past that have been overlooked previously, or re-configuring those traces, so that historical actors, and writers, in the past are seen to do what we now believe or want them to have been doing. We *make* them our own, in that appropriation of the truth Sandor Goodhart cautioned us to be vigilant for.

One further brief discussion will act as a coda to this section. It has, of course, been *recognised* since antiquity that Herodotus is the 'father of history' (Cicero is but the first to refer to him thus).[42] Does anything he does 'provide' evidence for the argument above? As one who is engaged in an emerging style of thinking, the historical, the shape or rationale for which is not yet (even now) defined, his methods presumably do not appear to him fully armed, like Athena from the head of Zeus, but are being developed as he goes along. Like many of his successor historians, he 'stages' the decision-making process as a speech or speeches. Let us focus in on the tense debate between the king of Persia, Xerxes, his general Mardonius and Xerxes's uncle Artabanus (7.8–11) that precedes the invasion of Greece in 480 BC, and rehearses the arguments for and against it. Christopher Pelling offers a concise summary of the more remarkable features of this quite extraordinary episode:

> No scene shows an uneasy court dynamic more clearly than this, the most elaborate set of speeches of all – and appropriately placed, marking the most momentous decision of the history, for Xerxes has determined to invade Greece. 'Xerxes has determined...': the phrasing may seem odd for a debate when he is calling for advice, but the decision has already been taken. 'I have called you here so that I might pass over to you what I have in mind to do' (7.8a.2). 'This is what must be done; but, so that I may not seem to be self-willed, I place the matter before you, bidding anyone of you who wishes to express his opinion' (7.8d.2). Several phrases in

that sentence capture mantras of Greek, especially democratic debate: 'to express his opinion'; 'place the matter before you', literally 'into the middle', where all around may regard it as equally theirs; 'anyone who wishes', so familiar from Attic decrees. But it is only 'so that I may not *seem* to be self-willed'. This is already a travesty of debate, at least as Greeks would understand debate.[43]

Such a travesty of debate that it would not be unreasonable to assume that Herodotus has made it up, and that nothing of the kind actually took place in the court of a tyrant whose mind was already made up and whose will was binding. The so-called debate may indeed be counterfactual in that brute sense: Pelling goes on to call it a 'phantom-sequence', but emphasises that the arguments adduced are not crass, and 'the complexities only become clear once the later narrative has offered its perspectives.'[44] But it is not only at the level of the narrative's, or the historian's, later perspective. Opinions are expressed by the characters in terms of possible futures, and, in particular, futures that could *prospectively turn out* to be counterfactual. Thus Mardonius says the Greeks are averse to risk, but should he be wrong, and the Greeks be so foolish as to engage with the Persians, then they will learn that the Persians are the best soldiers in the world.

Herodotus is grappling with the problem of how the Persians came to do what, with the benefit of hindsight, turned out so disastrously in their decisive defeats at the battles of Plataea and Salamis. Put another way, Herodotus is not interested purely in telling what actually happened (his audience knows the Greeks won), but also in tackling the problem that what *was to* happen, in the determination of Xerxes (and the expectation of others), was not what *did* happen. The debate is 'staged' by Herodotus not in advance of the decision (for the course of action has already been determined – by Xerxes), though well in advance of its consequences. Why does he choose this scenario at all, if the decision has already been made? Artabanus respectfully suggests to Xerxes that, without a debate in which both sides of a question are expressed, it is impossible to choose which the better course is, and that otherwise, one can only accept whatever has been proposed; but if there's a debate a fair choice can be made. Pelling remarks how the mantras of *democratic* debate colour the scene. If what *will* happen, or the truth, is already determined, there is no place for democracy and its debates about what is the better course, or what possible futures lie open; contrariwise, democratic debate asks questions of knowledge, truth – and power. The modern Xerxes who would rule us *know* that competition is part of human nature and you can't buck the market, so why have a debate? Herodotus does not permit either his narrated characters or (unlike Livy or Appius Claudius in Plutarch on Alexander) himself as narrator, to indulge in speculation on the basis of a circumstance at that stage already known not to be the case. Nonetheless, his skilful retrojection from the present to the past of the conventions of Athenian democratic debate onto exchange of speeches in the court of Xerxes facilitates the historical elucidation of choice and motivation by evaluating choice in terms of plausible alternatives that were not adopted.[45]

The art of historical narrative, Barthes suggests, is to reduce reality to a point of time. According to Reinhart Koselleck, any such point – any given 'present' – is simultaneously a 'former future', and this has consequences for the writing of history. As David Carr puts it in his review of the 1985 English translation of Koselleck's book *Vergangene Zukunft* (*Futures Past*),[46]

> Because its subject-matter is persons and their lives and actions, it must treat what is ultimately constitutive of them as persons, their possibilities and their future. Thus the subject-matter of history is in an important sense not fact but possibility; or, more precisely past possibilities and prospects, past conceptions of the future: futures past.[47]

As Carr elsewhere suggests, if such temporal configuration inheres in experience itself, then this counts against the view 'that such structure is overlaid or imposed upon experience by a retrospective and "literary" effort extrinsic to experience itself'.[48] This is diametrically opposed to Morson's view that 'real time is an ongoing process without anything resembling literary closure.'[49] Carr draws attention to how Koselleck's views on history are deeply influenced by the German philosophical tradition.[50] Koselleck does discuss Hegel and Kant, but he never so much as mentions the elephant in this particular room, Martin Heidegger. In any discussion of time and temporality, Heidegger is a very big beast, indeed for some a rogue. He will make his presence visible shortly.

BEING 'IN' TIME

One supposition of this style of scholarly argument, then, is that not only narrators but the historical agents they represent within their work shape action according to the structures of narrative – and so do we in our everyday experience. Some, and my example here will be the philosopher Galen Strawson, strenuously resist this notion. In a trenchant essay entitled 'Against Narrativity', Strawson widens the argument to embrace a dizzying array of disciplines:

> Talk of narrative is intensely fashionable in a wide variety of disciplines including philosophy, psychology, theology, anthropology, sociology, political theory, literary studies, religious studies, psychotherapy and even medicine. There is widespread agreement that human beings typically see or live or experience their lives as a narrative or story of some sort, or at least as a collection of stories.[51]

He cites, for example, the psychologist Oliver Sacks, who says that 'each of us constructs and lives a "narrative"... this narrative *is* us, our identities'; the philosopher Charles Taylor, for whom 'a basic condition of making sense of ourselves is that we grasp our lives in a *narrative*' and have an understanding of our lives 'as an unfolding story'; and Paul Ricoeur, who argues 'How, indeed, could a subject of action give an ethical character to his or her own like taken as a whole if this life were not gathered together in some way, and how could this occur if not, precisely, in the form of a narrative?'[52] Strawson first of all sets up a distinction 'between one's experience of oneself when one is considering oneself principally as a human being taken as a whole, and one's experience of oneself when one is considering oneself principally as an inner mental entity or "self" of some sort – I'll call this one's self-experience.'[53] And this leads to a further distinction, between what he calls 'Diachronic' and 'Episodic' self-experience, the former that in which 'one naturally figures oneself, considered as self, as something that was there in the (further) past and will be there in the (further) future', the latter, by contrast, that in which 'one does not figure oneself, considered as a self, as something that was there in the (further) past and will be there in the (further) future.'[54] These he describes as 'styles of temporal being' and as 'radically opposed.'[55]

The world can be divided up, he suggests, into Episodics and Diachronics, and he has no doubts about how he sees himself: 'I have absolutely no sense of my life as a narrative with form, or indeed as a narrative without form. Absolutely none. Nor do I have any great or special interest in my past. Nor do I have a great deal of concern for my future.'[56] He is equally confident about others:

> Among those whose writings show themselves to be markedly Episodic I propose Michel de Montaigne, the Earl of Shaftesbury, Laurence Sterne, Coleridge, Stendhal, Hazlitt, Ford Madox Ford, Virginia Woolf, Jorge-Luis Borges, Fernando Pessoa, Iris Murdoch … Freddie Ayer, Bob Dylan … Diachronicity stands out less clearly, because I take it to be the norm (the 'unmarked position'), but one may begin with Plato, St Augustine, Heidegger, Wordsworth, Dostoyevsky, Graham Greene, Evelyn Waugh, and all the champions of Narrativity in the current ethico-psychological debate. I find it easy to classify my friends, many of whom are intensely Diachronic, unlike my parents, who are on the Episodic side.[57]

An impressive herd of sheep, to be sure; and the goats don't look all that bad either. To get some purchase on Strawson's argument, let's return to one of his Episodics, Borges, and our old friend (or will he, in the context of this argument, turn out to have been an enemy?), Yu Tsun.

At the opening of the account he has dictated after his arrest, on discovering that a fellow agent has been apprehended and that the 'implacable' Madden is after him, Yu Tsun is convinced that he will die that day and is initially at a loss what to do. He goes back to his room and throws himself on his bed, looking through the window at the 'six o'clock sun'. He recalls his feelings: 'It seemed incredible to me that that day without premonitions or symbols should be the one of my inexorable death.' As it turns out, this is *not* the day of his death, for he lives long enough, at least, to dictate the statement we are reading. But his experience of time is what Morson would call 'real' time, in that Yu Tsun experiences no omens or foreshadowing. It also suggests, from what he says subsequently, that his experience of time is what Strawson would call Episodic: 'Then I reflected that everything happens to a man precisely, precisely *now*. Centuries of centuries and only in the present do things happen; countless men in the air, on the face of the earth and the sea, and all that is really happening is happening to me …' There is an Aristotelian feel to his *self-centred* experience as he recollects it: time as a succession of *nows*, the past or (except for the certainty of a death he believes imminent) the future not 'really' existing. While at this moment, there are 'countless men' involved in the war, they have hardly any existence for him; there is little but a residual sense of his own life as part of the 'total history of the sons of men', as Augustine put it, of a self that is distended across time in memory and anticipation. For Strawson, we may recall, Episodic self-experience is that 'one does not figure oneself, considered as a self, as something that was there in the (further) past and will be there in the (further) future.' But it is a flash of memory, significantly painful, 'the almost intolerable recollection of Madden's horselike face' that banishes what Yu Tsun with the benefit of hindsight dismisses as 'these wanderings', and spurs him to action: 'I said out loud: *I must flee.*' The future opens out for him as a time *for* action, and 'in ten minutes my plan was perfected.' He has devised a 'plot' with the desired *end* that he *will have* alerted (future *perfect*) his Chief in Berlin. Yu Tsun then relates how his earlier self became the protagonist of the plot he had devised.[58]

In pursuance of his plot, he takes the train to Ashgrove, rushing to catch the eight-fifty. The next leaves at nine-thirty, and he just makes the earlier, unlike the pursuing Madden, whom he glimpses vainly running down the platform as the train departs. The few seconds' difference make for a close escape, but he now has a precious 40 minutes' start on Madden. He proceeds through the coaches, and as a man with a mission (emphatically self-imposed), his experience of the present is different from what it had been as he lay on his bed in his room. His attention is heightened, and directed outwards from himself towards his fellow passengers. These he sees not in the abstract as things but as people who show detailed traces, recognisable to him, of life outside their immediate presence in the carriage, traces which suggest a rich diachronic (or, in Strawson's sense, Diachronic) experience: 'a few farmers' (whose occupation obliges them constantly to pay heed to time and the seasons); 'a woman dressed in mourning', whose clothing expresses the way she figures herself, considered as a self, in Strawson's definition 'as something [*sic*] that was there in the (further) past' – a wife – 'and will be there in the (further) future' – a widow; 'a wounded and happy soldier', looking forward to a future that is so different from the past which has left him maimed. There was also 'a young boy who was reading with fervour the *Annals* of Tacitus', immersing himself, that is, in a literary structure imposed by its author, and eagerly looking forward to what comes next.[59] As Yu Tsun takes his seat in the train, and thus *within* a symbolically significant mode of transport heading for *its* destination without any prospect of deviation, there is nothing for him to do for the duration of the journey but to reflect as, and on, his new-found diachronic self as he moves towards his self-imposed end: 'I told myself that the duel had already begun and that I had won the first encounter by frustrating, even if for forty minutes, even if by a stroke of fate, the attack of my adversary.' Living out the plot Yu Tsun has fashioned for himself, Madden's failure by but a few seconds to catch the same train seems 'a stroke of fate'. Whereas his earlier episodic self had seen no omens, now 'I argued that this slightest of victories foreshadowed a total victory', and, buoyed by that interpretation of events past and future, he also argues that his consequent feeling of 'cowardly felicity proved that I was a man capable of carrying out the adventure successfully', thus casting himself forward in his imagination to the moment when he will be able to look back on his enterprise from the vantage point of its successful end and see himself as its brave and resourceful hero all along.[60]

Confusingly for the clear distinction Strawson wishes to set up, Yu Tsun is, at different times and in different circumstances, both an episodic sheep with no story to tell of himself, and a diachronic goat, the hero (or, it may be, from a later perspective the villain) of his own quest, embodying at one moment an Aristotelian take on time, at another an Augustinian one. And, although Strawson pens Borges himself in with the Episodics, Borges's divergent representations of Yu Tsun's self and, in 'The Garden of the Forking Paths' more generally, of time as both finite and closed *and* infinite and open could suggest that Strawson has prematurely foreclosed the debate Borges has taken such pains to open up, thus stepping outside that debate and, with the essential surplus he assumes this gives him over Borges, deeming Borges to be *really* an Episodic.[61] We're not finished yet. Let us return to Yu Tsun deep in thought on the train to Ashford, philosophising on what it is to *be* the diachronic self he now finds himself to be, and presenting (as one does) the outcome of those deliberations as directive for humankind hereafter, descriptive *is* shading into prescriptive *ought*:[62]

> I foresee that man will resign himself each day to more atrocious undertakings; soon there will be no one but warriors and brigands; I give them this counsel: *The author of an atrocious undertaking ought to imagine that he has already accomplished it, ought to impose upon himself a future as irrevocable as the past.*

Morson has a perceptive comment on this: 'To act resolutely in the present, one must, strangely enough, adopt a species of fatalism. The exercise of will is enabled by the belief (or imagination) that the desired future is in any case already irrevocably decided, indeed, already accomplished.'[63] A figure lurks in the shadows here, unobserved by Morson (who never, I think, mentions him in his book), but who looks to the sheepish Strawson, on the three occasions he refers to him in his essay, devilishly like a Diachronic, namely Martin Heidegger, though 'I do not understand his notion of temporality,' he concedes.[64] Well, let's have a go, keeping Yu Tsun in mind as we do.

The key concern of *Being and Time* (*Sein und Zeit*, 1927) is one of the central and long-standing questions of philosophy, ontology: what is *Being*? Heidegger sees himself as part of a philosophical tradition, and sets his discussion of ontology against that of Aristotle in particular. For Heidegger, Being is not something that is separated from its context in time and place. A hammer has being, and has properties that he calls 'present-to-hand' (*vorhanden*) – light or heavy, and so on – but, more importantly, is an object in use – *too* light, *too* heavy, more or less fit for the purposes *we* might put it to, *possible* uses and *possible* ways for it to be. And when things are 'ready-to-hand' (*zuhanden*) in this sense, we don't pause to contemplate their properties, but just get on with using them in the broader environment in which we situate them in relation to ourselves (unless they aren't 'to hand', or don't work, when, rather than get on with using them, we are led to think about them – regard them as 'present-to-hand' and contemplate the properties they do or do not have). Heidegger's habitual example of such a broader environment is the cobbler's workshop, with its hammers, nails and leather, but anyone who works with books will be familiar with the experience of how one treats them as 'ready-to-hand', picks them up and opens them at the page one needs without further thought – or suffers a minor existential crisis when they, or what one thought one would find in them, are not there. So also with the tools of our mental environment, ideas, which are 'ready-to-hand' when fit for purpose, but when not, oblige us to pause, to halt the temporal flow that is characteristic of the experience of being 'ready-to-hand', and view them as 'present-to-hand'.[65]

The world is full of entities that have being, Heidegger says, but only one being has Being as a concern and frames the question 'What is Being?' That is the human being, and so should be the focus of the study of Being. A hammer can't take charge of its being but a human being is whatever it has decided to be. However, the human being is not disembodied from its context, and its power to decide is not unlimited. Heidegger habitually refers to the human being as Dasein (from the verb *dasein*, 'to be there/here'). 'There/here' in time as well as place: Dasein doesn't choose whether to be born, or where, or when, but is 'thrown' into the world, and then is, given its circumstances (to which it can respond), its possible ways of being. However, Dasein's choices can be limited not simply by the circumstances into which it is thrown but by what 'they' (*das Man*) think and do. Fashion, peer pressure, the authority of tradition or whatever – most human beings do what they do most of the time simply because it is the done thing, a condition Heidegger calls 'fallenness'. In this state of fallenness, 'inauthentic' Dasein does what it does simply because 'they' do it, whereas 'authentic' (*eigentlich*) Dasein makes up its *own* (cf. *eigen*) mind. Dasein is 'constantly "more" than it factually is',[66] always contemplating possibilities, always up to something, even though our usual condition is one of fallenness and inauthenticity. The basic state of Dasein is what Heidegger calls 'care' (*Sorge*), making Dasein ahead of itself, thinking about what to do next, and it is this care that invests the entities around us with significance. The cobbler's broader environment, his workshop, is not an inert assemblage of things; rather, in relation to the cobbler's care in completing a pair of shoes, ready-to-hand (and so not the object of his direct contemplation) *this* hammer is good *for* driving in *these* nails. In a broader environment infused with significance by Dasein's care, those entities may be fellow human beings. Recall Yu Tsun, first on his bed helpless and bewildered:

bereft of care, he is locked in the present, and the 'countless men in the air, on the face of the earth and the sea' engaged in a terrible war are entities without Being for him. By contrast, later, when he has a plan and is acting on it, each of the passengers he observes on the train is to him a fellow Dasein, up to something as he himself most definitely is, however impassive they, and he, may seem to be in the course of the train journey. And he sees them in terms of their temporality, as human beings in time, with memories, hopes and expectations.

For Heidegger, temporality is of central concern to ontology: 'We shall point to *temporality* as the meaning of the Being which we call "Dasein".'[67] It is more important when rather than where we are thrown into the world, for we can move from one part of the world to another, as Yu Tsun has done, but we cannot live in the fifth century BC, say, rather than the twentieth or twenty-first AD. But for Heidegger, temporality (*Zeitlichkeit*), time as experienced by such a being pitched into its existence, is primary, and time in the abstract (*Zeit*), the time of physical processes, and intersubjective phenomena such as clocks, calendars or chronologies (what Heidegger calls 'world-time', *Weltzeit*) are derivative of it, however much they impinge on us in what we are up to. Recall Yu Tsun's escape from Madden. The 'eight-fifty train' presumably ran in accordance with the timetable every day, but the *eight-fifty* train has significance, or *Being*, for Yu Tsun in respect of his plan to evade Madden and kill Albert before he himself is apprehended. In his Introduction to *Being in Time*, Heidegger sets out his purpose:

> Dasein *is* in such a way as to be something which understands something like Being. Keeping this interconnection in mind, we shall show that whenever Dasein tacitly understands and interprets something like Being, it does so with *time* as its standpoint. Time must be brought to light – and genuinely conceived – as the horizon for all understanding of Being, and for any way of interpreting it. In order for us to discern this, *time* needs to be *explicated primordially as the horizon for the understanding of Being, and in terms of temporality as the Being of Dasein, which understands Being.*[68]

To do so necessitates a reappraisal of 'the way in which [time] is ordinarily understood … the traditional concept of time, which has persisted from

Aristotle to Bergson and even later.'[69] By this traditional concept of time, Heidegger means Aristotle's explanation of time as a succession of 'nows', and the alternative he proposes has some affinities with Augustine's notion of the mind's *distentio*, though needs to be carefully distinguished from it.

If Dasein is moved by 'care' to look to possibilities for action, death marks an end to those possibilities. It need not be felt to be imminent, as it does for Yu Tsun, first in his aporetic state when he helplessly awaits it,[70] but then as the event that threatens the fulfilment of the plot he has devised. But what Yu Tsun has done in his new-found resolution is, precisely, to emplot the rest of his life, and then insert himself as the protagonist *within* that plot. A general awareness of death, that at *some* stage we will no longer *be*, the attitude that Heidegger calls 'being towards death', exerts pressure upon us not to postpone our choices indefinitely, but also, and especially in the case of 'authentic' Dasein, informs those choices. Dasein's awareness of time is not restricted to the present moment, and the immediate choice of what to do next. The attitude of being towards death can prompt a broader review in terms of what one *chooses* to do with one's life as a whole. Heidegger envisages Dasein as looking ahead to the future, to the moment of not-being, and *from there* reaching back through the present to the past. But what choices are to be made in terms of one's existence as a whole? There are plenty of pre-ordained narrative patterns, ethical codes, careers and so on that one can take off the shelf, as it were, and insert one's self into (as Madame Bovary and Anna Karenina do);[71] is the cobbler a cobbler just because his father and grandfather were cobblers before him? But for Heidegger, that is what *das Man* does, and is inauthentic as a result.

Authentic Dasein must become 'resolute' (*entschlossen*, 'dis- or 'unclosed'), shunning the 'talk' (*Rede*) of the 'they' to survey its life from death to birth in an effort to disclose the possibilities not envisaged by *das Man*. Of all the possibilities that lie open for Dasein, the roads that might be taken, one is chosen, and for resolute Dasein, it is the road not taken by others. Dasein is therefore to make its life resemble a plot, but not just any old plot, rather one in the course of which it discloses or uncovers, for better or for worse, its authentic ('own') self. Recall Yu

Tsun once more: he emplots a future for himself that only he can fulfil, and in the course of working out his plot experiences a process of self-disclosure, of who he *is*. The conversions of Paul and Augustine inform Heidegger's thinking, and serve to illustrate his notion of *Augenblick*, the moment of vision which marks the decision of resolute Dasein (though of course, neither Paul nor Augustine themselves would see their future as *self*-imposed). One might point to Livy, who sets himself to be the historian of Rome's rise to power from its foundation to his own times, as (already but not yet) an example of resolute Dasein. In his moment of vision at the outset, he wonders whether he will have done something worthwhile if he shall have completed writing the history of Rome; the future perfect, the completed future, is the characteristic mode of resolute Dasein. Livy professes not to know, but embarks on a future filled with anticipation, and in which the choices then made take on the sense of being fated or necessary – as they are, in the sense of being already determined in the moment of vision. Yu Tsun's plot is, he knows from the prospect of its fulfilment, villainous, but he attests to this sense in his advice: *The author of an atrocious undertaking ought to imagine that he has already accomplished it, ought to impose upon himself a future as irrevocable as the past.* For resolute Dasein, its life's work is mapped out, and it determinedly seeks to follow it through to the end, come what may. Within Heideggerian autobiography and the temporality it constructs, the narrated self is represented as, in the most crucial aspects which 'disclose' who one is, in the future of the narrating self rather than in its past, a reversal of Augustine's autobiographical temporal modality.

Dasein's temporality has three aspects or 'ecstases' ('standing outside' or 'displacement'), which cannot straightforwardly be mapped on to conventional notions of past, present and future, or on to Augustine's three-fold present.[72] These conventional ideas are effectively what 'they' say about temporality and written into the language we habitually use, so Heidegger plays about with the familiar German vocabulary of time so as to distance himself from it. What 'they' call past, present and future do not exist clearly distinguished in and of themselves. For Heidegger, the future is the primary ecstasis: time is time *for* doing something (recall the connotations of *zuhanden*), so Dasein rushes ahead towards death, but then bounces back towards itself (*Zu-kunft*, the 'future' as 'coming towards'),[73] a rebound that takes it back also into the past (for which Heidegger's preferred term is *Gewesenheit*, 'having been-ness') – not the past *per se*, as having happened once and for all, and gone away (*Vergangenheit*, 'having gone away-ness'), but the *past that is relevant to the choices that 'makes' a moment feel 'present'*. To see the past as *vergangen*, 'gone away', is to regard it as irrevocable, not subject to being called back for re-interpretation, and so under the shadow of necessity, an imposition we can only submit to; to see it as *gewesen*, 'having been', is to regard it as open to our interpretation and decision. Recall my configuration of Herennius Pontius's advice to the Samnites, which in the version he prefers, rebounds to a past in which the Romans were not (destined to be) enemies but were (potential) friends-to-be.[74] The German *Gegenwart*, 'present', etymologically suggests 'waiting towards', the mark, for Heidegger, of irresolute Dasein, in contrast to the resolute Dasein's *Augenblick*. Resolute Dasein's address of the choices open to it render particular configurations of elements (and not necessarily of the same elements) of the past significant in the light of those choices, and endow them with *being* in the past, with 'having been-ness', but as a having-been that *still* 'presents' itself to us as the possibility of deciding freely. So for Dasein, as well as there *being* forking possible futures, we must also think of there *being* forking possible pasts. In the moment of *Augenblick*, resolute Dasein chooses one of the paths ahead, which links with one of those possible pasts to form a highway from birth to death. Its life is mapped out, and the map can be consulted for the route, to see en route where one has been as well as where one will have been.

For Heidegger, then, the temporality of Dasein is primary, and other notions of time (the World-time of clocks and chronology) secondary and derivative of it. That is not to say that World-time is illusory or unimportant. Livy adopts it (along with its heavy load of metaphysical baggage) as the structure of his history of Rome. It matters crucially to Yu Tsun that he knows he has precisely 40 minutes' start once Madden misses the train, and when in Albert's study, he sits facing a tall circular clock: 'I calculated that my pursuer, Richard Madden, could not arrive for at least an hour. My irrevocable determination could wait.' He has time to engage with Albert in which he can satisfy the curiosity that Albert has inspired in him, and still complete his plot. The cobbler may keep one eye on the clock so as to finish a repair for a customer in time for it to be picked up, a writer, like Livy, may observe the passage of the years so that he can complete his projected task within the span of life that prospectively remains to him, but still give up a little time to indulge in counterfactual speculation. Chronology also helps us to understand why Heidegger mentions Aristotle, but Aristotle never mentions Heidegger.

Secondary and derivative also in Heidegger's eyes is Aristotle's notion of time as a succession of 'nows', which, shorn of existential significance, form the basis of no more than units of measurement:

> Ever since Aristotle all discussions of the concept of time have clung *in principle* to the Aristotelian definitions; that is, in taking time as their theme, they have taken it as it shows itself in circumspective concern. Time is what is 'counted'; that is to say, it is what is expressed and what we have in view, even if unthematically, when the *travelling* pointer (or the shadow) is made present. When one makes present that which is moved in its movement, one says 'now here, now here, and so on'. The 'nows' are what get counted. And these show themselves 'in every "now"' as "nows" which will 'forthwith be no-longer-now' and now which have 'just been not-yet-now'. The world-time which is 'sighted' in this manner in the use of clocks, we call the '*now-time*' [*Jetzt-Zeit*].[75]

It is not that Aristotle got it *wrong*. Rather, in making actuality logically prior to potentiality in accordance with a theory of time that emphasises the 'now', he got his priorities precisely the wrong way around – though understandably so, for 'temporality ensnares itself in the Present, which, in making present, says pre-eminently "Now! Now!"'[76] This is crucial to our ability to plan. If we imagine Livy as saying 'One day I shall be dead; I must complete my history of Rome by then', *then* is 'not-yet-now' within a succession of nows, just as 'I have finished nine books of my history since I began then', *then* is 'no-longer-now' within that succession. The problem Heidegger has with Aristotle is the way he makes this successions of 'nows', with its focus on the present, the basis for his theory of time *in principle*, and thus as the basis of his metaphysics.

Counterfactual history, with its emphasis not on what happened but on what might have happened, the possibilities that were open to or confronted historical agents, reflects Heidegger's orientation towards the future (although his writings reflect an ongoing struggle not to do so *in principle*, and by so doing endow his own notions with universalising metaphysical pretensions).[77] And this orientation towards the future has consequences for his reading of texts from the past. Heidegger's own determination to be a great philosopher does not involve him trouncing his predecessors, refuting their arguments conclusively and so relegating them to oblivion. Rather, the texts of past thinkers like Aristotle are to be read with an eye to their possibilities, the possibilities rejected or overlooked as well as the possibilities chosen. Heidegger's emphasis on the future is again, in these terms, neither right nor wrong, but, in bringing into view what Aristotle overlooked, offers a field of potentiality for subsequent students of time – and, as we know, sets in motion a critique of the dominance in the Western philosophical tradition of the present as the privileged point of perspective and of the metaphysical weight attributed to 'presence'.

For Strawson, the world is a place where there *are* 'Episodics' and 'Diachronics', for Heidegger, it is a place where, like Yu Tsun, you *can be* 'episodically' or 'diachronically' as the case may be. Heidegger's philosophy may be intimidatingly abstract, and unenlivened by the narratives you find in (the also often intimidatingly abstract) Plato, but *Being and Time* is spectacularly rich in *narrativity*, for this lies at the heart of Dasein's sense of self. Practically, the aspiration of resolute Dasein is to be, or more precisely, to *have been*, a Diachronic. Save that Dasein, being towards death, will never be in the position to pass the absolute, definitive judgement that Strawson passes on himself, since at the point at which such a judgement could be made Dasein will no longer be. And a future Dasein (at any rate, an 'authentic' one, orientated towards the future) may see that earlier Dasein not in terms of absolute failure or success, but, as with Heidegger on Aristotle, as a field of possibilities chosen, rejected or overlooked, one who, in the light of the decisions the future Dasein makes, and the potential worlds thereby brought into being, may turn out a friend or an enemy. And so on, *ad infinitum*. It is this recession to infinity of an ultimate conclusion that makes Heidegger's metaphysics of time so uncomfortable: one is forever 'within' time. The (quasi-)providential – the self, reason, truth – is forever provisional, generated out of an experience of time that looks to narrative to give that experience shape and meaning.

Many philosophers are prepared, even content, to see themselves within time, and their discourse as a historical, and historically contingent, one, amongst them many of those Strawson classes as Diachronics. Insofar as it searches for a transcendent, timeless truth, philosophy must nevertheless negotiate the manifestations of narrativity. Plato does so by embedding his speculations within the elaborately developed settings he gives to his dialogues and through the *dramatis personae* who engage with each other, so as to present philosophising as going on 'within' time, coming to no definitive conclusions and breaking off, to be resumed another day. Though philosophical works may not contain formal narratives, and narrativity may be effaced in certain kinds of philosophical writing,[78] we need to be on our guard against the idea that it is eliminated entirely. For Richard Rorty, philosophy is 'a kind of writing'.[79] Even in its most austere manifestations, it is telling some kind of story, and on the whole philosophers, Rorty suggests, do not make good storytellers: 'When we do tell stories, they tend to be bad ones, like the stories that Hegel and Heidegger told the Germans about themselves.'[80] And it can often be their narrativity that persists long after the imperfections of the arguments (in the sense of their lack of completeness) become obtrusive. W.G. Runciman has recently wondered why texts of political theory such as the *Republic* of Plato, the *Leviathan* of Hobbes or *The Communist Manifesto* of Marx and Engels have remained canonical and profoundly influential even as their arguments are contested and found wanting. There are no timeless concepts in the Western tradition of political thought, he suggests, but (in a formulation subtly inflected by a Heideggerian critique of the metaphysics of presence) 'concern about the potential for conflict and disorder which is inherent in all known human societies *is* timeless'.[81] He expresses the durability of these texts in terms of grammatical modality. If their theory is found wanting in the indicative ('This is what is going to come about') or the imperative ('This is what ought to come about'), they still speak to us in the optative mood ('If only this *were* to come about, how much better a place the world would be!').[82] It is not simply as discourses of knowledge, but as discourses of desire, for the end, that these texts continue to speak to us. Strawson would, I reckon, be quick to brand Runciman a Diachronic.

In 'Against Narrativity', Strawson (in optative mood) would like to eliminate this element. In seeking a final or definitive answer to the question of the self and narrativity, Strawson sets up his terms of reference: 'I will use "I*" to represent: that which I *now* experience myself to be when I'm apprehending myself specifically as an inner mental *presence* or self.'[83] By reducing temporality to a 'now' divorced from past and future (a problematic notion already for Aristotle) in pursuit of immediate self-presence, Strawson tries to reduce narrativity towards zero, putting an 'end' to time either by stopping the succession of 'nows' or by transcending their potential infinity.[84] But only *towards* zero: the 'self' he 'presents' is caught up in a process of re-present-ation ('I will use "I*" to *represent*'), and remains a self divided into narrating and narrated; 'I' has stepped outside 'I*' and its temporality so as to circumscribe it. Representation involves *making* rather than *being* 'present', the bind of the metaphysics of presence that so exercised Plato. And 'I*' is so circumscribed by 'I' *for the sake of* argument, the play of desire in which the future obtrudes on the present and the past. Strawson's Episodic 'self' can be, precisely, represented as no less temporal, and textual, than Augustine's or Heidegger's.

Inadvertently or otherwise (that issue of the essential surplus of knowledge once more), Strawson puts his finger on this when he talks of '*styles* of temporal being'. Genre is another aspect of being in time. The mimetic drama *Oedipus* can create effects which would be difficult in a heterodiegetic epic or novel, or in philosophy, and other types of writing have been developed which look to highlight the abstract, the conceptual, the logical, and to occlude the writer and his or her desire. Part of the appeal of genres is that they are to some degree predictable: when a work is assigned to a particular genre (drama, philosophy, history and so on), the structure associated with that genre 'provides' a 'sense of the ending' against which we read that work – which any particular work can question no less than affirm. That teleological aspect of genre, at the level of form, looks to what Derrida called a predictable, calculable, programmable future, in life and literature alike. Such a future is a modality of the present, but *l'avenir* may surprise by the content we encounter – the monstrous *arrivant* which may be the Sphinx at Thebes, the undead Alexander fetching up on the shores of Italy, or Yu Tsun, the figure of Heidegger's resolute Dasein, at Stephen Albert's door in a book blandly entitled *Antiquity and the Meanings of Time*. Like the boy reading Tacitus's *Annals*, we all ought to have something sensational to re-read (and re-live) on the train.

5

TIME, KNOWLEDGE
AND TRUTH

A number of themes and questions about human temporality and interpretation explored in previous chapters come together here as we consider the issue of time and the knowledge of 'nature'. 'The world is not unexplained, since it is told like a story,' according to Roland Barthes, and behind intelligible narrative of the world lurks a 'demiurge', who has given that world its form. Accounts which seek to make the physical world intelligible are haunted by the figure of the Author-God and the problem of what to do with him. Assume the existence of this unseen being as the creator of a world that is seen as a text in the sense that it is, in itself, intelligible in terms of its unity and design? If so, human accounts of the world will seek to represent that prior design, but like the interpretations of a text will be ever partial and accommodated to the circumstances in which the interpretation is produced. Seek to deny the existence of such a figure? If so, the 'author-function' must be taken on by the human enquirer, with all the challenges to total knowledge that human situatedness in time poses, faced by what Barthes called a world 'that has been sent sprawling before us' on to which humans impose what discursive order they might.[1]

Within time and history, these two antagonistic views are locked into an uneasy and ongoing dialogue that generates our discourses of knowledge and truth. The first section considers the responses of, in turn, Augustine, Aristotle and the Epicurean atomist tradition, particularly Lucretius, which posits a universe infinite in time as well as space, and so without a beginning or an end – and *a fortiori* without a creator. Lucretius seeks to transcend the human time-bounded perspective by what I argue is a subtle exploitation, in his representation of the figure of Epicurus, of the Aristotelian distinction between actual and potential infinity, framed in a narrative that condenses the concept of a *reason* that can, theoretically, embrace all phenomena, whatever time and whatever place. For all that Lucretius seeks to eschew explanation in terms of the supernatural, he still has recourse to imagery of the divine in his representation of Epicurean reason. You may seek to drive out God and his hypostases, reason, science, the law, as Barthes puts it, but the greater the claim to intelligibility, the more they inhabit the argument, albeit often covertly. In the second section, I track how the intellectual achievement of Epicurus in attaining what Lucretius represents as *universal* knowledge is legitimated in a narrative form that is structurally similar to the narrative associated with the project of universal empire explored earlier (Chapter 2 above). Both narratives seek to point to a truth that exists outside time, but from a perspective within time, they illustrate a traffic that flows both ways between knowledge and sociopolitical authority. Claims to truth, whether epistemological or historical/political, are subject to be seen as superseded over time, and the third section examines how the linked narratives of empire and knowledge were re-deployed by Francis Bacon in the service of his project to inaugurate a new intellectual beginning, and have contributed to the emergent sense of 'modernity' as a (contested) modality of experience that consigns earlier thought to 'antiquity'. In seeking to draw together a number of the strands of the argument in this chapter and earlier in the book, the fourth section returns to a theme that has featured throughout it, that of the Book of Nature, to consider how responses to the question of what 'language' the Book is written in shape both realist and anti-realist traditions of interpretation.

Augustine's favoured imagery for his relationship to God is textual; he is, as it were, a character within the text of which God is the author. The text is not simply the story of his life, but 'the total history of the sons of men', which God can grasp as a whole, its beginning, its middle and its end, a history, that is, of God's creation which, like the world itself, was created, along with time itself, at a moment in the past and will end on the Day of Judgement. In trying to understand his part in this creation and his place within time in the last three books of the *Confessions*, Augustine is moved by the sheer enormity of these issues to consider the text which recounts God's act of creation, the Book of Genesis: 'In the beginning, God created the heavens and the earth...' It is foolish, he says, to ask what God was doing before he created the world, for he is eternal, and time was created along with the world. God made the world, but not in the way humans make things (11.5.7): 'You were not like a craftsman who makes one physical object out of another by an act of personal choice in his mind, which has the power to impose the form which by an inner eye it can see within itself.' The human craftsman, himself God's creation, imposes form on what already exists, and using the materials that God created. Moreover, the craftsman creates in sequence and over time; but 'you spoke and they were made, and by your word you made them.' This involves Augustine in the perplexing notion that something can come from nothing, and he cannot get beyond the notion that God's act of creation involves the imposition of form. Taking Genesis 1:2 as his basic text ('the earth was invisible and disorganized, and darkness was above the abyss'), he struggles in *Confessions* 12.6.6 towards a definition of the abyss as 'a nothing something' (*nihil aliquid*) and 'a being which is non-being' (*est non est*), and concludes, 'Nevertheless it must have had some kind of prior existence to be able to receive the visible and ordered forms.'[2] Although Genesis is not that creation itself but a narrative of that act of creation, written in human language by the human Moses (11.3.5), Augustine simultaneously subscribes to the common image of the world itself *as* text, a text created by God, and so 'readable', at least in accordance with limited human understanding.[3] Nonetheless, Augustine is careful to distinguish this *as* an image, a human attempt to grasp what is, in the fullest sense, *ineffable*, not capable of being spoken.

Augustine's interests look towards the theological, and an understanding of the 'nature' of the physical world is not the focus of his attention. The cosmos is ordered and beautiful, he believes, but we cannot fully appreciate this, for we cannot see it as God does, as a whole: 'We, for our part, can see no beauty in this pattern to give us delight; and the reason is that we are involved in a section of it, under our condition of mortality, and so we cannot observe the whole design.' If we were immortal, and had an infinity of time in which to observe *every* detail, we could, but given that we are not, we must simply accept God's providence (*City of God* 12.4):

> Hence the right course for us, when faced with things in which we are ill-equipped to contemplate God's providential design, is to obey the command to believe in the Creator's providence. We must not, in the rashness of human folly, allow ourselves to find fault, in any particular, with the work of that great Artificer who created all things.

To show interest in the natural world, as Augustine says he finds himself sometimes doing, is a sinful distraction he calls *curiositas* (*Confessions* 10.35.57):

> When I am sitting at home, a lizard catching flies or a spider entrapping them as they rush into its web often fascinates me... The sight leads me on to praise you, the marvellous Creator and orderer of all things... When my heart becomes the receptacle of distractions of this nature and the container for a mass of empty thoughts, then too my prayers are often interrupted and distracted.

Aristotle feels no such theological constraint on his interest in the natural world. He does not use the metaphor of the world *as* text or book, but a number of his terms and images suggest the boundedness and unity of his object of study, and overlap intriguingly with those of the textual artefact. A retrospective historicising glance, one might say, sees traces of the textualisation of 'nature' already operative at this point en route along the royal road that issues forth in the later image of the Book of Nature. Here he is in the very opening sentences of his *Physics*, thinking at once about the methodology of the study of nature (1.1, 184a10–16):

Since in all approaches [*methodous*] that involve beginnings [*archai*] or causes [*aitia*] or elements [*stoicheia*], it is acquaintance with these that constitutes knowledge [*to eidenai*] and understanding [*to epistasthai*] – for then we think ourselves to know each phenomenon when we are acquainted with its first causes [*ta aitia … ta prōta*] and its first beginnings [*tas archas tas prōtas*] and have got right down to its elements [*mechri tōn stoicheiōn*] – it is clear that in knowledge concerning nature [*tēs peri physeōs epistēmēs*] also we must first try to define [*diorizesthai*] the matter of beginnings [*ta peri tas archas*].

A chain of necessary or plausible causation is also what interested the Aristotle of the *Poetics* about plot, as did the issue of the beginning, which he defined there as that which does not come after something else of necessity (*Poetics* 1450b27–8). Is the overlap of approach and terminology a 'coincidence', of no philosophical interest? The word translated as 'element' here (*stoicheion*) crops up in the discussion of verbal style (*lexis*, one of the six 'parts' of tragedy), where it refers to an 'indivisible sound' (*phōnē adiairetos*, *Poetics* 1456b22) – not just any sound, but the irreducibly smallest one from which a compound sound like a word can arise. However, most significant of all is the word I have translated as 'beginnings', for this would often be translated nowadays by the term 'principles': to understanding something, we must cordon off or put a boundary around or define (*diorizesthai*) that before which there is nothing, the thing in first place, the ultimate starting point. The study of poetics also has its 'approach' (*methodos*, *Poetics* 1447a12), which begins – 'naturally' (*kata physin*, after the manner of 'nature') – 'first of all from first things' (*prōton apo tōn prōtōn*, *Poetics* 1447a12–13).

Physics thus does not have its own 'final vocabulary', to recall Richard Rorty's phrase,[4] which is wholly peculiar to its own object of study. Within time, we interpret 'nature' as we go along, and cannot view it or describe it from the privileged position of the end. Nonetheless, this remains the dream of the discipline of physics; the end or goal, the *telos*, of physics is a 'final theory' or a 'theory of everything', but for the moment, it must bide its time; the *study* of the physical world involves, like a plot, a beginning, a middle[5] and an end. Aristotle does not deploy the image of a book to give unity to what he studies, but he does have a *concept* which embraces the phenomena of the world even more economically and effectively – 'nature' (*physis*). His assertion that the study of poetics has an approach that begins 'after the manner of nature' (*kata physin*) from first principles is already indicative of the way that physics, the study of 'nature', would like to see itself as the model for *all* explanation, to be itself the principle of explanation.

For all that their 'approaches' diverge, Aristotle and Augustine are equally fixated on the issue of 'first beginnings'. Although they have taken different directions, and each believes he has taken the direct route to the truth, this is the fork in the road to which they both look back methodologically. Plots, of course, have authors: no problem for Augustine, or for the Aristotle of the *Poetics*, though for the Aristotle of the *Physics* it is the source of some concern. Aristotle has no difficulty with the idea that the world has always existed and there is no divine oversight of its workings, but *conceptually*, he feels, in terms of a valid *method* of physical explanation, physical processes must have some ultimate 'beginnings'. However, to posit some *super*natural force as setting things in motion attributes to a physical process a non-physical cause, something 'above' or 'beyond' the concept one has striven so carefully to demarcate and define, 'nature', and that just won't do. Such a craftsman-creator or 'Demiurge' appears influentially in Plato's *Timaeus*.[6] Part of Aristotle's project is thus to try to demarcate physics (*ta physika*, 'the things to do with nature') from metaphysics (*ta metaphysica*, 'the things that come after [*meta*] the things to do with nature' – for physics, as we have seen, likes to think of itself as occupying first place) through his own distinct 'books', the *Physics* and the *Metaphysics*. However, Aristotle owes much to this Platonic heritage. As David Sedley puts it,

> His momentous innovation on that heritage lies in his theologically motivated decision to insulate god from any requirement to intervene in nature, either as creator or administrator. The result is that, while Aristotle's world retains all the positive values – both functional and other – that Plato had associated with divine craftsmanship, these are now explained by on the one hand phasing out the divine craftsman as moving cause, and on the other representing nature as so closely isomorphic with craft in its structure as to be capable of producing its results even in the absence of a controlling intelligence.[7]

Thus, 'Nature', the *concept* which he uses to circumscribe and define the processes which are the object of his study, comes close to being anthropomorphised as a craftsman.

This comes through in his discussion of the four different kinds of 'causes' in *Physics* 2.3, the material, the formal, the efficient or moving, and the final or end-related. Aristotle offers a number of examples as he goes along. Thus, if we talk of a statue, the material cause is bronze, the formal cause the shape the sculptor gives to it, the sculptor is the efficient cause, and the final is the purpose for which it was created. This is readily understandable in the case of human artefacts or activities, but more elusive (though it can be productive to think with) in respect of natural processes, especially where efficient and final causes are concerned, where the question of agency and purpose become very tricky.[8] Although Aristotle uses the example of a sculptor or a silversmith rather than a writer, this model of the human artefact swings the *Physics* in the direction of the *Poetics*, and its programmatic statement of its approach (*methodos*), in terms of the craft (*technē*) particular to *poiēsis*, how plots should be constructed so as to stand together or form a unity (*pōs dei sunistasthai tous muthous*, 1447a9). For all Aristotle's efforts neatly to distribute and demarcate different objects of study across his different texts, overlaps remain. Pursue this line of thinking, and the priority and authority granted to physics starts to look like the product of a moment of methodological decision. It is not hard to imagine a parallel universe in which Aristotle, at the fork in the road marked 'first beginnings', took the other turn and decided he should call what we know as his *Physics* the *Metapoetics*. Now that is an intriguing 'what if...' question.[9]

However, back in the world we are familiar with, instead of putting a *super*natural force like Plato's Demiurge 'above' or 'beyond' the crucial point of beginning and so problematically make it 'start things off', the Aristotle of the *Physics* deals with this by relegating it to the end, the *telos*, as the 'unmoved mover' towards which all physical processes teleologically strive.[10] You could be forgiven for feeling that Aristotle has simply put off or postponed the problem conceptually by this manoeuvre, and that certainly seems to have been the reaction of some of his philosophical successors.[11] In particular Epicurus (whose traditional dates are 340–270 BC) wondered whether you couldn't get rid of the supernatural from your approach to 'nature' from the very beginning, *in principle*. He took over and developed the theories of the fifth-century thinker, Democritus, who held that the world was made up of minute, indivisible particles of matter – atoms (from the adjective *atomos*, that which cannot be cut up, indivisible), whose only properties are size, shape, weight and movement, and which come together randomly to form the visible objects of the world and dissolve again into their constituent *elements* (Epicurus often uses the term *stoicheion* of these atoms). This effectively gets rid of the problems of agency and purpose from Aristotle's theory of causes. The efficient cause is the random movement of the atoms which leads them to collide and interlock. This movement has no purpose whatsoever, but produces the universe we see around us.

Crucial to the Epicurean view of the world was the abolition of any ultimate beginnings and ends: the universe has always existed and will always exist, and so what need is there of any creator figure or unmoved mover? The universe is boundless in space as well, infinite in all directions. The supernatural is abolished by leaving no 'outside' for it to inhabit; Epicurus's 'gods' are brought inside the system and have a shadowy and ineffectual existence in the spaces between the innumerable worlds in the universe, where they can get up to no harm – or good, for that matter. Epicureanism posed the greatest philosophical challenge in antiquity and beyond to theological worldviews such as Augustine's. In one sense, Epicurus abolishes time along with the supernatural. Time becomes purely a matter of the human perception of physical motion and rest. As Lucretius, whose Latin poem *On the Nature of Things* (*De rerum natura*) is the greatest testament to the power of Epicurean thinking, puts it, 'Time also does not exist of itself' (*tempus item per se non est*, 1.459); rather, 'from things themselves there follows the sense of what has been done in the past, then what is present to us, and further what is to follow thereafter; nor should we admit that anyone has a sense of time in itself separated from the movement of things and their quiet calm' (1.459–63). Any such sense is a purely human abstraction, not a feature of things themselves.

The masterstroke of the atomist tradition was arguably not the theory of matter for which it is perhaps best known today, but its dazzling exploitation of the concept of the infinite. Aristotle had also believed that the universe is infinite in time and space, but his unmoved mover is evidence of the problems posed by the need for any human *account* of that universe to be finite, bounded by a beginning and an end, and by the way that features of that account (particularly the figure of the author/craftsman) migrate into the phenomenon it purports to describe. The formal imposition associated with human authorship and the anthropocentric character of language, which continue to make agency and intention fiendishly difficult to distinguish in language, play devilish tricks. Thus the full title of Darwin's book on the theory of evolution was *On the Origin of Species by Means of Natural Selection, or the Preservation of Favoured Races in the Struggle for Life*, but while the theory requires that the language Darwin uses of this 'efficient cause' be purged of reference to intention or purpose, *selection* could be taken to imply a selector and *preservation* a preserver; *favoured* races might suggest to the unguarded that there is one who is providentially conferring advantages on these races to some end or other.[12] *Origin* could also mislead in the context of a work that effectively deconstructs any absolute divisions of animals into 'natural' kinds, and denies that one could point to any one particular moment as marking the beginning of such a 'kind'.[13] The Epicurean tradition could not escape this bind either, but Lucretius casts a very keen eye on the issues raised in this chapter so far.

Lucretius makes the figure of Epicurus himself a key element in the explanations *On the Nature of Things* presents. In 1.62–79, Lucretius presents Epicurus in extravagantly heroic terms.[14] The human race is depicted as lying grovelling under the weight of an appropriately personified figure of Religion or Superstition (*religio*, 63), 'which showed its face from the regions of the sky, standing over (*super...instans*, 65)[15] mortals with horrible appearance'. Throughout the poem, Lucretius rejects any description of the universe that would make the divine responsible for creating it or controlling what goes on in it; such explanations are seen to keep the human race subdued by irrational fears. Epicurus is figured as the champion of humankind, and overthrows the oppressor. He does so through intellectual rather than military feats, first by raising his eyes to observe (1.66–71):

primum Graius homo mortalis tollere contra
est oculos ausus primusque obsistere contra,
quem neque fama deum nec fulmina nec minitanti
murmure compressit caelum, sed eo magis acrem
inritat animi virtutem, effringere ut arta
naturae primus portarum claustra cupiret.

A Greek man was the first to dare to lift up mortal eyes against it, the first to make a stand against it. Neither the fables of the gods nor thunderbolts subdued him, nor the sky with its menacing roar, but all the more provoked the eager courage of his mind to desire to be the first to break through the confining bolts of nature's gates.

Ignorance of how the world really works confines the human race as if in a city under siege, and Epicurus's intellectual achievement is presented in terms of a military leader, unintimidated by the 'threats' of the heavens (symbolised by the thunderbolt), who breaks the siege and sallies forth (1.72–77):

ergo vivida vis animi pervicit, et extra
processit longe flammantia moenia mundi
atque omne immensum peragravit mente animoque,
unde refert nobis victor quid possit oriri,
quid nequeat, finita potestas denique cuique
quanam sit ratione atque alte terminus haerens.

The lively vigour of his mind prevailed, and he marched out beyond the flaming ramparts of the world and traversed in mind and imagination the measureless universe, from where as victor he reports back to us what can come into being and what cannot, in short the way in which the power of each thing is limited and has a boundary-stone deep set.

Epicurus's sally carries him – in his mind and imagination (*mente animoque*, 74) – beyond the flaming ramparts of the world (our planet and the stars we see above us in the sky) and across the whole universe (*omne immensum*, 74),[16] and he brings home reports about the regions he has conquered (Julius Caesar's commentaries on the conquest of Gaul, written in the 50s BC, about the same time as Lucretius's poem, come to mind) in the form of an explanation of what can, and what cannot, happen in the universe. His victory reverses the earlier situation (1.78–79):

quare religio pedibus subiecta vicissim
obteritur, nos exaequat victoria caelo.

Therefore religion in its turn lies crushed beneath his feet, while his victory lifts us level with the heavens.

Thanks to Epicurus, who celebrates his victory with a traditional gesture of humiliation of his enemy, the human race is now in the position traditionally associated with the gods.

The first thing to notice in this passage is its claim to universal truth. The human race is to have confidence in Epicurean physics because it can explain *everything*. The power or potentiality of each and every phenomenon in the universe is set within limits (*finita potestas ... cuique*, 76), its boundary-stone, which defines what we would call its *properties*, deeply set (*alte terminus haerens*, 77) and so not liable to be uprooted and moved. What can and cannot happen is thus strictly *defined*, that is, set within its own limits (Latin *fines*). Epicurus has brought everything under intellectual control, and this is conveyed through the characteristically Roman image of surveying: to maintain physical control of territory, you need intellectual control of it as well.[17] The universe, everything there is (*omne*) may be immeasurable (that is the sense conveyed by *immensum*, an adjective formed from the verb *metior*, 'to measure'), yet measure it is precisely what Epicurus is represented as doing. Paradoxical, but the claim to universal truth involves such paradoxes, and this passage is dramatically representing them. Epicurus is emphatically a human being here. He is the 'Greek *man*' who dared to raise '*mortal* eyes' against religion (66–67), yet he somehow manages the task of traversing the 'immeasurable everything' (74), which would take not only one lifetime, but, strictly speaking, an infinite number of lifetimes. The boundlessness of the universe in space and time is crucial to Epicurean theory,[18] and particularly to its rejection of the idea of a divine figure who created the universe and controls its workings. Infinity allows the self-organisation of the atoms to produce every *possible* permutation somewhere at some stage – past, present or future – in the universe, in such a way that, though the emergence of complex and reflective organisms such as human beings may seem to be a fluke in a universe formed by the chance collision of miniscule pieces of indivisible matter, such a development was inevitable somewhere, some time.[19] A universe without boundaries of space and time conversely underpins the claim of that theory to universality: no matter where you look, no matter when you look, Epicurean theory can explain *anything* you observe.

Epicurus does not have an infinite number of lifetimes to carry out this task. In fact, he is represented as having completed it within his single life's span. The representation of Epicurus here touches on the philosophical question, to which Aristotle repeatedly returns,[20] of whether infinity can ever be traversed. Aristotle was much exercised by Zeno's paradox of half-distances famously posed by the story of the race between Achilles (in Homer, frequently described as 'swift-footed') and the tortoise. Achilles (in Homer, frequently described as 'big-hearted') gives his opponent a start, but by the time he has traversed half the intervening distance, the tortoise has moved on from where it started. By the time Achilles has once more traversed half the intervening distance, the tortoise has moved on a little further, and so on, and so on; on this basis, Achilles will never catch the tortoise. Absurd, of course, but that is one of the problems posed by infinity: the halves get ever smaller and smaller, but there is no end to them. Wrestling with this problem, Aristotle draws a distinction between actual and potential infinity (*Physics* 8.8, 263b3–6):

> So, the reply we have to make to the question whether it is possible to traverse infinitely many parts (whether these are parts of time or of distance) is that there is a sense in which it is possible and a sense in which it is not. If they exist actually, it is impossible, but if they exist potentially, it is possible.

In the case of Achilles and the tortoise, the halves make up a potential infinity, and so Achilles can traverse them and win the race. This is the philosophical point that underlies *mente animoque* ('in his mind and imagination') in Lucretius 1.74. Epicurus does not *physically* traverse the infinite universe and does not give an explanation of every *actual* phenomenon (Lucretius's poem would then be an endless text), but offers a *ratio* (cf. 1.77), a rationale from which, theoretically, any phenomenon at any time or any place, past, present or future, *can* (potentially) be explained.

The journey then is a conceptual one, a journey that one can imagine as having been completed. John Locke put it thus in his discussion of infinity in *An Essay Concerning Human Understanding* (2.17.7, my emphasis):

> I think it is not an insignificant subtilty [*sic*], if I say, that we are carefully to distinguish between the idea of the infinity of space, and the idea of a space infinite. The first is nothing but a supposed endless progression of the mind, over what repeated ideas of space it pleases; but to have actually in the mind the idea of a space infinite, is to suppose *the mind already passed over, and actually to have a view of* all those repeated ideas of space which an endless repetition can never totally represent to it; which carries in it a plain contradiction.

Lucretius's depiction of Epicurus suggests that the poet gave some careful thought to this problem, which bears upon his own attempt to represent Epicurus's universal truth in his poem. One of the features of his Epicurus is that 'neither the fables of the gods nor thunderbolts subdued him, nor the sky with its menacing roar, but all the more provoked the eager courage of his mind...' (1.68–70). Unexplained meteorological phenomena were *par excellence* the symbol of irrational and superstitious fear, the thunderbolt being traditionally the weapon of Jupiter with which he punished those who displeased him. Thus Lucretius feels obliged to expound the Epicurean explanation of thunder and lightning in atomist terms at considerable length in 6.219–378. He rounds off his account with these lines (6.379–82):

> *hoc est igniferi naturam fulminis ipsam*
> *perspicere et qua vi faciat rem quamque videre,*
> *non Tyrrhena retro volventem carmina frustra*
> *indicia occultae divum perquirere mentis...*

It is by this means it is possible to understand the very nature of the fiery thunderbolt and to see by what power it achieves each of its effects – not by unrolling scrolls of Etruscan incantations, vainly to seek out signs of the hidden mind of the gods...

The Etruscans were famed for their expertise in divination, and Lucretius pictures the superstitious unrolling scrolls containing their *carmina*, a word that covers spells, incantations and prophecies, and wasting their time by poring over them in a vain attempt to work out the intentions of the gods. The description of Jupiter metaphorically going through the same action in the *Aeneid* as he foretells the future to Venus draws on the same tradition. But *carmina*, in the sense of 'poems', are also the medium Lucretius is using to expound Epicurean doctrine.[21] The unstated implication is that it is better to unroll the scrolls of his poem and pore over what it says – you won't be wasting your time. Lucretius's discretion, if such it was, in not making this explicit is noteworthy, but it is precisely by making of the universe a text that the infinite can be brought within finite bounds and made comprehensible, just as the endless succession of times is brought within bounds and the significance of each event within it made manifest in the Virgilian Jupiter's prophecy. The fittingness of the designation of Lucretius's text as a *carmen* is doubly determined in that it too has a prophetic aspect, in the sense that, containing universal truth, the form of its explanation is just as applicable to things in the future as to those in the present and the past.

Narratives, as we have seen, can be condensed into a concept. What Epicurus 'reports back to us' from his journey across the universe is a *ratio*, a *theory* of the universe. At the macroscopic level, the infinity or boundlessness of the universe is a crucial philosophical aspect of the Epicurean theory of the universe.[22] It is also an important element in thinking about the problem of what it means to explain something. At the human level, or even more so at the microscopic level of the atom, the explanatory power of Epicureanism depends on the 'way in which the power or potentiality [*potestas*] of each thing is limited [*finita*, set within boundaries, 1.76]': not everything whatsoever can happen, but is limited by what atoms can, and equally importantly, cannot do. All the objects in the visible and sensible world are compounds of atoms, which have only size, shape, weight and movement, and, as their name suggests, they cannot be cut up (*a-tomos*) into smaller units. The notion of infinity thus does not go all the way down. Everything in the universe that can be said to exist is a compound made up of these atoms, so defined. The movement and interlocking shapes of these atoms lead to the formation of those compounds, which are subject to eventual dissolution into their constituent atoms once more under constant atomic bombardment.[23]

But the atoms themselves survive: they were never created and will never perish, and are distributed across the universe. If, at the largest scale, the universe has no boundaries, at the smallest, there is a boundary, the indivisibility of the atom, and this is philosophically no less crucial to Epicurean theory.[24] Every phenomenon in the universe can be referred back to it and its (limited) properties, and so within the structure of the explanation it occupies first place, the 'beginning'.

The Epicurean atom is too small for the eye to see, but what it lacks in terms of visibility, it more than makes up in a quality that is philosophically far more important, its finality: the atom provides a definitive point of explanatory closure. There is an infinity of actual atoms in the universe, but everywhere you look for an explanation, you start out with the *atom* and you end up with the *atom*. If individual atoms can be located in space and time, the *concept* of the atom transcends them, and 'embodies' ultimate truth.[25] It is on this conceptual level, 'in his mind and spirit', that Epicurus achieves his feat, transcending his own human situatedness to bring back to mankind a theory the validity of which is not limited by time or place. A true theory may, for those who subscribe to it, be 'outside' time, but even its most faithful adherents, even the deviser and embodiment of that truth, exist 'within' time and circumstance. Epicurean truth may not be subject to time or place, but its remarkable irruption into history is associated by Lucretius (6.1–8) with a very specific time and place, Athens in the lifetime of Epicurus in the late fourth and early third centuries BC.

EMPIRES OF KNOWLEDGE

Epicurus is represented by Lucretius in military terms as a hero who declares war on religion,[26] conquers its territory, imposes his terms on it, and returns home triumphantly. If the shape of scientific explanation is not necessarily narrative,[27] the legitimation of such explanation usually is.[28] For Jean-François Lyotard this can be traced back at least to the allegory of the cave in Books 6 and 7 of Plato's *Republic*, which emphatically illustrates the way such narratives generate a traffic between knowledge and sociopolitical authority. The philosopher who has exited the cave and discovered the truth returns to inform those who remain there, and it is to such holders of eternal truth that Plato entrusts autocratic political power. 'Within' time, knowledge and power are inextricably intertwined. Lyotard further remarks that the use of narrative to legitimate knowledge can theoretically take two routes, 'depending on whether it represents the subject of the narrative as cognitive or practical, as a hero of knowledge or a hero of liberty'.[29] In practice, Plato's philosopher, who emerges from the cave to discover truth and then returns to enlighten the dwellers therein, and Lucretius's Epicurus, who traverses the universe and similarly returns to report to humankind the nature of things and so free it from irrational fears, combine these roles.[30] Lucretius's narrative is framed in terms of Roman imperial conquest, with Epicurus surveying conquered territory as a general would. Epicurus returns to us from his foray across the immeasurable universe bringing back as victor to us (*refert nobis victor*, 1.75) a prize of war, a comprehensive theory of the nature of things, in a gesture that specifically recalls a Roman general exhibiting his spoils when celebrating a formal triumph.[31] This ceremony glorified not just the journey outwards, but the return home to the point from which one started out. An actual infinite universe has no centre,[32] but Epicurus's 'journey' across the potential infinite exploits the capacity of narrative form, which joins beginnings and ends purposively,[33] to establish our world at the 'centre' of that universe, just as the triumph ceremony marks out Rome as the centre even of a 'universal' empire 'without boundaries of time or space'.[34]

Lucretius's representation of Epicurus has its roots in the heroisation of great thinkers in the earlier philosophical tradition, and even in Epicurus's own lifetime the foundations for what we find in Lucretius were already being laid.[35] This image of Epicurus was developed in the context of the conquests of his older contemporary Alexander the Great, who in mid-career was already being eulogised as subduing not simply the *oikoumenē*, the known 'inhabited' world, but beyond as well. The Athenian orator Aeschines in his speech *Against Ctesiphon*, delivered in 330 BC, remarks of Alexander that he 'had departed for lands that lie beyond the Great Bear, and not far short beyond the boundaries of the whole inhabited world' (165).[36] In Lucretius's time, this Alexander imagery was current of both Pompey (nicknamed *Magnus* 'the Great' in emulation of Alexander) and Julius Caesar.[37] In the Roman declamatory schools, Alexander's conquests were favourite themes for the *suasoria*, including an exercise[38] which involved taking on the role of Alexander deliberating with himself whether he should set sail on the Ocean which was thought to surround the *oikoumenē*: a recurrent topic is whether he would find land on the other side.[39]

Much more suggestive for my purposes is the anecdote preserved in Plutarch (*De tranquillitate animi*, 466 D). It involves the philosopher Anaxarchus of Abdera, who accompanied Alexander on his campaigns. Crucially, Anaxarchus was a follower of the early atomist Democritus, also from Abdera, who claimed that there are infinitely many worlds:[40]

> Alexander wept when he heard from Anaxarchus that there was an infinite number of worlds. When his friends asked him if any accident had befallen him, he answered: 'Do you not think it is a matter worthy of lamentation that when there is such a vast multitude of them, we have not yet conquered one?'

Lucretius's Epicurus trumps Alexander in submitting the whole universe to his intellectual dominion. Moreover, while Alexander weeps at the prospect of a task hardly begun and with no hope of completion, Epicurus returns in triumph, mission already accomplished. Again, Aristotle's distinction between actual and potential infinity is crucial for discerning the differences between the two figures. To return once more to Jupiter's promise to the Romans of an empire without boundaries of time and space, the Romans 'within' the history that Jupiter foretells are like Alexander confronted by an actual infinity that is an endless task, while the god views the same sequence from 'outside', a potential infinity that he has traversed. Virgil's narrative combines and distributes the two notions with enormous subtlety, allowing his readers to occupy both subject positions simultaneously, and so get the best of both worldviews. In historical terms, Lucretius helped to prepare for this.

Lucretius' 'imperialist' Epicurus can help us to consider further the issues of time, knowledge and truth, and the traffic between knowledge and sociopolitical authority. Since the 1970s, the discipline that has come to be known as science studies has grappled with the challenge of bringing 'within' history the 'universal truth' claimed by the natural sciences. Science studies distances itself from the traditional legitimating narrative that the truth (it is characteristically singular in this narrative), always already there though hitherto unrecognised, is *discovered* in favour of one that suggests that truths (plural) are painstakingly *made*, within time and circumstance. The two narratives can be seen to complement each other,[41] but science studies seeks to challenge the hegemony of those narratives of scientific knowledge that treat discovery as a concept by viewing it instead as a metaphor. The starting point of science studies, its principle, is that no final distinction can be drawn between the political and the epistemological. The attempt to forge dynamic theoretical links between these two domains has been a central concern of the work of, most notably, Steven Shapin and Simon Schaffer,[42] Bruno Latour,[43] and Reviel Netz,[44] and has been attended by heated controversy, in a scholarly episode often called the 'science wars'.[45] Latour coined the phrase 'political epistemology' as a shorthand for the way in which knowledge and politics can be seen to go hand in hand from a perspective 'within history': any shift in epistemology obliges us to rethink politics, and vice versa, without granting either category the autonomy from, or hegemony over, the other which it craves. Political epistemology does not set out to explain science or knowledge in terms of politics or social context as though these were clearly demarcated 'natural kinds' or were in possession of their own 'final vocabulary' – indeed, political epistemology asks us as part of its agenda to problematise precisely that way of thinking, as it seeks to negotiate overlapping vocabularies, without recourse to a final explanation of one discipline *in terms of* the other.

One result of this intellectual movement has been an upsurge of interest in the conceptual connections between knowledge and empire, both within classical studies and beyond.[46] Thus, for example, Trevor Murphy subtitles his study of the Elder Pliny's *Natural History*, a monumental compilation in 37 books dedicated to the Emperor Titus, *The Empire in the Encyclopaedia*.[47] In their Introduction to a collection of essays on a number of early imperial writers, *Ordering Knowledge in the Roman Empire*, Jason König and Tim Whitmarsh encapsulate the characteristic approach of these studies well: 'we explore the possibility that the Roman Empire brought with it distinctive forms of knowledge, and, in particular, distinctive ways of ordering knowledge in textual form'; their principal interest, they say, 'is in texts that follow a broadly "compilatory" aesthetic, accumulating information in often enormous bulk'.[48] However, Lucretius's spare six-book poem feels a very different sort of text to Pliny's gargantuan *Natural History*, although both appeal to empire as a way of characterising the knowledge they contain. Empire is concerned with accumulation, to be sure, with pushing back the boundaries of territory or, as it might be, knowledge, but that's not the only possible conceptualisation of empire. Accumulation is a Wikipedia model of knowledge: issues of truth and accuracy circulate, sometimes very energetically, around individual details, but there's nothing to stop anybody adding more and more articles – *ad infinitum*, just as Alexander aspired to conquer ever more worlds.

Rather different is a text that claims to offer you not truths but *the* truth. One critic has encapsulated what he calls the 'ambition' of Lucretius's poem thus: it 'transcends limitations of space and time: rooted in the understanding of the eternal workings of nature, Epicureanism aspires to be a lesson for all people in all ages.'[49] Conceptually underlying this ambition is Lucretius's representation of the achievement of Epicurus, who has traversed the whole universe and reports back not on each and every phenomenon, but on the rationale (*quanam...ratione*, 1.77) by which each phenomenon can be explained, whenever, wherever. That is what Lucretius promises in his work, whose title *On the **Nature** of Things* suggests that the 'things' that are explained have a *nature*, a rationale that lies hidden, but a nature, as always already there, that awaits our *discovery* of it. The different conceptualisations of empire can once more be mapped on to Aristotle's distinction between actual and potential infinity, and the capacity of the latter, but not the former, to be traversed. To repeat: Epicurus's journey offers not a serial explanation, unending, of every phenomenon, but a theory according to which any phenomenon can, potentially, be explained. These principles and concepts, it is suggested, hold good at any time and at any place, and so escape the bounds of time and history. This is emphatically not a *Natural History*, after the fashion of the Elder Pliny's.

Opposed to a model of *accumulation*, then, is one of *compression*, as John Barrow explains:[50]

We might define science to be the search for compressions. We observe the world in all possible ways and gather facts about it; but this is not science. We are not content, like crazed historians, simply to gather up a record of everything that has ever happened. Instead we look for patterns in these facts, compressions of the information on offer, and these patterns we have come to call the laws of Nature. The search for a Theory of Everything is the quest for an ultimate compression of the world.

As Barrow's reference to a Theory of Everything suggests, compression underlies the notion of a *final* explanation, a notion prominent in Lucretius's poem and which finds its basis in the concept of the atom.[51] Compression also underlies reductionism, the belief that, for all their apparent differences, biology may be reducible to chemistry and chemistry to physics in such a way that the sciences (plural) are ultimately unified as science (singular).[52] A reductionist impulse is evident in Lucretius's designation of atoms as 'primary' particles (*corpora prima, rerum primordia*), most significantly in his use of the term *principium*, 'the thing that occupies first place', of both a primary particle (as in 1.484) and the premise or starting point (what Aristotle called 'beginnings', *archai*) of an argument (as in 1.149), for in Epicurean terms the atom, not subject to division or further analysis, is both.[53]

Epicurean atomism also provides a paradigm of realism, and, for all that it famously leaves room for free will at the human level through the notion of atomic swerve,[54] for determinism as well. What we see in the world is the result of atoms that move mechanically of their own accord, and through their collision and interlocking form compounds. Realist modes of thinking rely upon the notion that ultimately, somewhere back along the chain of causation that has resulted in what you see before you, you can get back to some 'thing' (the *res* that is in the title of Lucretius's poem) that is self-evident, requiring no analysis (that is, no 'breaking up'), just as, when this theory is applied to matter, there is an ultimate limit to division in a primary particle that cannot be divided further, an atom. But a realist/reductionist syndrome operates also, and often in an occluded manner, across a range of disciplines. For example, in those discussions of the relationship of, say, knowledge and power which treat one phenomenon as simple and fundamental and the other as complex and in need of explanation, and which then privilege one term over the other by explaining one *in terms* of the other, allowing it to occupy 'first place' in the argument.

Lucretius's description of Epicurus's journey thus offers a legitimating narrative of the knowledge he has gained in terms not just of an empire project, but of a *universal* empire project. Knowledge and empire can be linked in terms of the ever-greater accumulation of information and skills, but when this association is seen in terms of universal empire, a distinctive note enters, as in the notion of universal history, which is not the same thing as a history of the universe; nor is it an encyclopaedic account of everything that is known in the style of the Elder Pliny's huge work. Rather, as we saw in Chapter 2, it is an attempt to find a *meaningful pattern* in the development of human society in terms of a narrative structured by a beginning, a middle and an end, which similarly involves compression by being structured around a concept such as *power*. The narrative of Epicurus's universal empire project is structured around the concept not of power, but of *truth*. Virgil's Jupiter holds out for the Romans the prospect of an empire without boundaries of space or time, tantalisingly a prospect of universal empire, seen from the viewpoint not of those within the flow of the events of history, for whom the explanation for any particular event may be painfully unclear, but of one who can see that or any other event in its full and incontrovertible significance in relation to the pattern as a whole. Crucially, the narrative structure involved is one that lies beyond 'human' powers of narration within history, and so is given a divine imprimatur. Jupiter and Epicurus occupy equivalent positions in relation to humankind.

Within such legitimating narratives – ancient and modern alike – the truth stands outside time, and its final and total achievement remains only a prospect for those within it. However firmly they believe themselves to have achieved progress in respect of certain particulars and to be directed teleologically towards the end, those within time nevertheless must await the day when the whole story will have been unfolded. Practically, this is forever, for, as with Alexander, there is an infinity of worlds to conquer; but we can glimpse also the potential infinity in which this overarching project will have been achieved. As Stephen Hawking famously put in at the climax of *A Brief History of*

Time, 'if we do discover [*sic*] a complete theory … it would be the ultimate triumph of human reason – for then we would know the mind of God.'[55] Hawking writes as one still working towards this *telos*, but confident that the pattern as a whole exists, could he but descry it in full. Epicurus, albeit he is a mortal man, is unusual in *already* having achieved the truth, and, however averse Lucretius is to invoking the divine in any conventional sense, it provides the imagery in which he feels obliged to characterise Epicurus's achievement. His 'theory' is 'sprung from his divine mind' (*ratio…/…divina mente coorta*, 3.14–15), and 'he was a god, a god, it has to be said…who first found out that theory of life which is now called wisdom' (*dicendum est, deus ille fuit, deus…/qui princeps vitae rationem invenit eam quae/nunc appellatur sapientia*, 5.8–10). The truth stands outside time, and yet is now, Lucretius avers, *fully* available to those who exist within time, if only they master the wisdom. Lucretius's narrative is of the *revelation* of this 'theory of everything' at a particular point within time and history, and takes the form of a curiously familiar narrative structure that satisfies this temporal logic: a story of incarnation, not in Bethlehem on the first Christmas day, but in Athens in the fourth century BC when the city '*gave birth* to a *man* endowed with such great genius who *at a point in the past* set forth *everything* from his *truth-telling* lips' (*cum **genuere virum** tali cum corde repertum/**omnia veridico** qui **quondam** ex ore profudit*, 6.5–6).

While paying due attention to the epistemological dimensions of this argument, let us not overlook the political. Lucretius's description of Epicurus as *princeps* in 5.9 (cited above) refers of course to his role as the one who was the 'first' to discover the theory with which his name is associated. The infinite universe of Epicurean theory, without boundaries of time and space, finds its explanatory closure in the indivisible atom, which Lucretius calls *principium*, the thing that occupies first place. A similarly unbounded universal empire a generation after Lucretius finds its rationale in the figure of an 'individual' – not a particular individual, however eminent (for Augustus, as it may be, is no less a figure within history and no less subject to death than Epicurus himself, for Lucretius the greatest of all men),[56] but one who adopted as his preferred appellation the term *princeps* and who similarly occupies first place in the system.[57] The homology is striking,[58] and carries on in the leadership of the Catholic Church, which inherited the tropes of universal empire.

Common to all these ideologies is the belief that, though their humanity means that their access to knowledge is inevitably partial, ultimately the truth is in some sense already there and on their side. Ready as they are to concede its metaphoricity, neither Virgil nor Augustine has any problem with the notion that this truth has an 'author' (Latin *auctor*) and that the associated 'text' has 'authority'. Augustine, indeed, can point to a material book, the Bible, that embodies that truth and is the proper object of study, though it needs endless exegesis, commentary and allegory if that eternal truth is to be accessed, however imperfectly, in the here-and-now. Lucretius's solution to knowing the truth was to enclose 'nature' within poetic form, the infinite *re*presented in the (seemingly) finite closural control of an author omniscient thanks to knowing the rationale for everything that can happen. Lucretius is happy to deploy the image of the book explicitly in relation to wrong-headed ideas when he represents the Etruscan seers as poring over their scrolls in a vain attempt to understand thunder and lightning in 'authoritative' theological terms. However, he is hesitant about deploying the image in relation to Epicurean theory, though he can't avoid it entirely when talking of his own poem. For Lucretius, a realist all the way down, the rationale is, emphatically, *there* in the world, and *nobody put it there*. So, while Lucretius is happy to 'textualise' nature, most famously by making the letters of the alphabet that combine to form words an analogy for the differently shaped atoms that combine to form the compounds we see around us, you will look in vain for a fully explicit image of the Book of Nature in his work. Not so Augustine, for whom the heavens and the earth are God's creation. In his commentary on Psalm 45:6–7, he says, 'Let God's written page be a book to you, so that you may hear these things; let the world be a book to you, so that you may see these things. In those codices, only those who know their ABCs read them; but in the world as a whole, even the uneducated can read' (*liber tibi sit pagina divina, ut haec audias; liber tibi sit orbis terrarum, ut haec videas in istis codicibus non ea legunt, nisi qui litteras noverunt; in toto mundo legat et idiota*).[59] Side by side with the Book of Scripture is the Book of the World, which is open to everyone. However, the notion that truth inheres literally or metaphorically in a text and can be accessed by study or observation of that text is a problematic one, as we shall see when we revisit the issues raised here from the perspective of a millennium-and-a-half and more later.

A NEW WORLD?

Narratives of knowledge as an empire project give us a model of endless accumulation; narratives of knowledge as a *universal* empire project subtly combine endless expansion over time with the compression into concepts and theories that translate that knowledge into eternal truth that can be pointed towards in the here-and-now. These narratives touch, in the words of Hans-Jörg Rheinberger, 'the roots of the occidental *episteme*. What is at stake,' he continues, 'is the fissure between knowledge and truth, the fragmentation of the unity of knowledge through the sciences themselves, in space and time.'[60] Rheinberger's observations touch on two interlocking mythic and ideological narratives which structure the history and philosophy of knowledge and play on a distinction between Science, capital S in the singular, and sciences, lower case, in the plural. The first (most memorably represented in the biblical story of the Tower of Babel) is a narrative which sees a prelapsarian originary and unified truth fragmented into multiple and conflicting discourses, the second a teleological narrative that would see these multiple and conflicting discourses united in peace as the provinces of a single unit.

The legitimating narratives of Science for those 'within' time have this characteristic teleological shape, whether one positions oneself as looking back on the moment of fulfilment, like Lucretius, or as looking forward to it, like Stephen Hawking. These narratives operate with a distinction of truth on the one side, and ignorance, superstition or myth on the other. The distinction is a moving one, serving at any one moment to differentiate what is regarded as secure knowledge from unfounded or erroneous belief, and it is often linked to the theme of progress: the borders of mumbo-jumbo (that hallowed term of imperialist epistemology) have been pushed back, or, in the case of Epicurus and his enemy religion, comprehensively abolished by scientific reason – reason being the conceptual term precipitated out from this narrative as the capacity to see the picture as a whole. Lucretius believed that Epicurus had said the final word on the nature of things, but time has taken its toll of his doctrines. The atom of the twenty-first-century physicist is a far cry from that of Epicurus. Lucretius's text, it may be felt, in many respects has had its day, and is of antiquarian interest only, definitively superseded and comprehensively consigned to the past. However, that too is a totalising narrative of knowledge and truth, and is open to sceptical scrutiny.[61] In order to open out the argument further, let us turn to one of the masters of such narratives, and the figure often seen as a prime source for the legitimating narrative of a 'modernity' that has consigned 'antiquity' to the past in just this way, Francis Bacon.

The title of Bacon's utopian fantasy of 1626, *New Atlantis*, takes its cue from the myth of the island of Atlantis told in Plato's 'creationist' dialogue, *Timaeus* (24d–25d), and its continuation, *Critias* (108e–121c). In the myth, Atlantis is imagined to have existed beyond the Pillars of Hercules, the Straits of Gibraltar, which marked the start of Ocean and the limits of the world known to the ancients. The travellers to Bacon's island (now re-located to the south seas of the Pacific) encounter the director of a research institute called Salomon's House, or the College of the Six Days Work, who declares as its mission statement that the '*End* of our Foundation is the knowledge of Causes, and the secret motions of things, and the *enlarging of the bounds of Human Empire*, to the effecting of *all things possible*'.[62] The aspiration towards totality is expressed by Bacon in terms of empire at a historical moment when the Virgilian associations had been exercising a particularly powerful sociopolitical influence for more than a century.[63] Jupiter's prophecy had come to function as a way of asserting historical affiliation and continuity, even in the face of apparent rupture, the demise of the Roman empire, by way of the doctrine of *translatio imperii* and the associated idea of *translatio studii*, which 'translate' power and knowledge, 'carrying' them 'across' any historical boundary that would seek to separate past and present. This doctrine could be especially potent at moments when the achievements of the Romans of old could be felt to have been bettered. In particular, there was now a definite answer to the question posed by Alexander in the old declamatory exercise of whether there was land on the other side of the Ocean that bounded the *oikoumenē*. At the beginning of the sixteenth century, the territories of the Hapsburg Holy Roman Emperor Charles V encompassed not only more of Europe than the Romans had ruled, but also lands in the New World that the Romans had never known about. This allowed Charles to boast on his device, dating from 1516, that there was 'more beyond' (*plus oultre*) the Pillars of Hercules depicted there. In the greater sweep of history, Jupiter's prophecy of empire could be seen as one step closer to fulfilment than it had been in the times of the Romans.

Territorial aggrandisement was only one aspect of the boast. The origins and exact meaning of the phrase *plus oultre* (which in Latin would be *plus ultra*) remain obscure. It is not an ancient motto, but Dante in the *Inferno* attests to a tradition that the pillars themselves were 'where Hercules left his warning that Man should not go *further beyond*' (*dov'Ercule segnò li suoi riguardi,/acciòche l'uom **più oltre** non si metta*, Canto 26, 107–8). The implied negative (*non*) *plus ultra* would suggest simply a statement that there was 'nothing beyond', and so it would be pointless to venture further. But a theological sanction may also be felt. The alternative (*ne*) *plus ultra* would be an injunction to curb not simply human ambition but human curiosity as well, which was seen in the Christian tradition as a vice. Augustine in *Confessions* 5.3 had used his own experience to warn against the presumption associated with mankind's cognitive abilities, its *curiositas*. Curiosity about the future is the most presumptive, and precise predictive knowledge is Augustine's particular target. He takes as his exemplary model the capacity of astronomy to make exact prognoses of the future (for example, of eclipses) in respect of what were regarded as the most exalted objects in the universe, the stars in the heavens. Therein, he thought, lay a temptation for man to an irreligious pride in the power of his intellect, whose origin he ascribes to himself rather than seeing it as the creation and gift of his Maker. His path to God is thus blocked: 'By the proud you are not found, not even if their curiosity and skill number the stars and the sand, measure the constellations, and trace the paths of the stars' (5.3.3).[64]

The discovery of the New World and that there was indeed 'more beyond' helped to loosen this bond on curiosity. As Earl Rosenthal has put it in his investigation of Charles's slogan,

> It...embodied the excitement and the sense of man's enhanced power experienced by the informed courtiers and humanists of Europe who eagerly awaited news of the latest discoveries in the previously unknown hemisphere. Understood in this context, [Charles's] motto *Plus Oultre* was not simply a chiding reversal of a restrictive Herculean proverb but, rather, a new slogan that expressed, quite literally, a new vision of the world.[65]

As Rosenthal suggests, the excitement came from the prospect not simply of territorial acquisition but of increased knowledge, which together offered 'quite literally, a new vision' of the world – a new overarching narrative within which to place these advances. What was at stake was not just an increased body of knowledge but a changed attitude towards what constituted knowledge. Rosenthal's reference to a new *vision* captures the rhetoric of an emerging distinction between an 'ancient' and a 'modern' world, a break that is not purely temporal but epistemological as well, and is associated with a legitimating narrative that, even though it has come under sceptical scrutiny, as we shall see, remains a modality of experience inhabited by many 'moderns'.

It is such a vision that underlies Francis Bacon's project for a Great Instauration (*Instauratio Magna*), the covering term for the uncompleted miscellany of writings that occupied the final six years of his life (1620–26) and helped to develop this narrative. *Instauratio* is a term steeped in religious associations. It is the word used in the Latin Vulgate Bible of Solomon's renovation of the Temple of the Jews.[66] The classical roots of the term associate it with the repetition of a ritual that has had to be abandoned. Historically, this can serve to suggest the efforts of the past as abortive, with the consequent need for a fresh start if, specifically, a *sacred* task is to be properly fulfilled. The magnificent title page of Bacon's *Instauratio Magna*, with its depiction of ships sailing beyond the Pillars of Hercules, encapsulates Bacon's project. Its vision of the expanding horizons of knowledge combines the imagery of Roman imperialism with the biblical prophetic tradition in its use as a motto of an adaptation of a quotation from the Book of Daniel (12:4), 'many shall pass through and knowledge shall be increased' (*multi pertransibunt & augebitur scientia*). However, even as it evokes the past, there is a much more powerful orientation towards the future. This is a vision that, like Jupiter's in the *Aeneid*, invites its readers not simply to look forwards, but to look towards the end, towards the divine order within which humankind exists. The Book of Daniel is to the Old Testament what the Revelation of St John is to the New, a prophetic book that describes what will happen before the world comes to an end. The inscription therefore looks to the completion of time and the end of history, within Bacon's Christian worldview, the Second Coming and the Last Judgement. As with Jupiter's prophecy in the *Aeneid*, some of this has already come to pass, for Bacon in the voyages of discovery and the circumnavigation of the globe, and, again as with Jupiter's prophecy, the orientation towards the end endows the present moment with a providential significance and urgency.[67]

The Pillars of Hercules symbolise an epistemological barrier, even a prohibitive sanction, now overcome. Just as the voyages of discovery had gone beyond what the ancients had achieved historically in terms of worldly dominion, so their epistemological authority was now open to challenge. In the Preface to the *Instauratio Magna*, Bacon remarks of 'the received arts' of antiquity,

> In my view men properly appraise neither their assets nor their strength, but place too much faith in the former and too little in the latter. The consequence of wildly overvaluing the received arts is that men do not look beyond them; the consequence of undervaluing their own strength is that they waste it on trivia and do not try to test it on business of real weight. These things are then like baleful pillars set up against the sciences, as men are not encouraged by the desire or hope of getting beyond them.[68]

'Baleful pillars' translates *Columnae, tanquam fatales*, which does not adequately capture the sense that people mistakenly regard these barriers as *fated*, their actions and their very intellectual horizons *determined* by the story thus told. However, Bacon uses the tropes of this story so as to sketch out a fresh orientation towards the future. In one of the aphorisms (97) that make up the *Instauratio Magna*, he takes on the role of Alexander the Great:

> …human reason in its present condition is just a farrago and mass made up of a good deal of faith, a lot of accident, and a fair few infantile notions which we swallowed when young.
>
> But if someone in the prime of life, with senses unimpaired and a mind washed clean, applies himself anew to experience and particulars we should hope for better things from him. And here I promise myself the fortune of *Alexander* the Great, but let no one accuse me of vanity until he has heard me out, for my words aim at the exposure of all vanity.
>
> For this is how *Aeschines* spoke of *Alexander* and his deeds: *We surely do not live a mortal life, but were born for posterity to tell and proclaim the wonders of us* [*Against Ctesiphon* 132]; as if he took *Alexander's* deeds for miracles.
>
> But in a later age *Titus Livius* thought better and more incisively about the matter, and said something like this about *Alexander*: that *he had nothing other than the nerve to despise foolish fears* [*eum non aliud quam bene ausum vana contemnere*, 9.17.16]. And I think that future ages will bring in a similar verdict on me: that *I did nothing great, but only made less of things thought to be great.*[69]

In looking towards a fresh future, Bacon reconfigures the past, seeing Alexander not as some miracle-worker, but as a very human figure operating within his world, though special in not being bound by received dogma. In proposing a *Novum Organum*, a new 'instrument' or methodology, Bacon was looking to supersede the old *Organon* of Aristotelian logic, which he saw as restricting humankind's capacity for knowledge. The Bible might be the revelation of God's purpose and the source of an ultimate authority, but endless speculation based on human texts as if they contained a definitive method or world-picture, the *modus operandi* of the Aristotelianism he rejects, was a dead end. 'From these Greek philosophies,' he complains in another aphorism (73) in the *Novum Organum*, 'one can scarcely adduce after all this time a single experiment that tends to help and alleviate the human condition, and that can, properly understood, be truly credited to the speculations and dogmas of philosophy.'[70] The opposition between experiment and speculation signals a willingness not simply to *observe* and *represent* (as

Aristotle had) but to *intervene* in the course of nature.[71] The role of the natural philosopher for Bacon is to advance knowledge in practical ways through experiment so as to enhance the welfare of humankind. The Alexander whom Bacon fashions as a precursor is one with innumerable worlds to conquer, and who, far from being daunted, is fired by the prospect. Bacon's vision is an unashamedly imperial and providential one – there *is* an overarching pattern to all of nature's phenomena – but he aligns himself with the human viewpoint from within the project, not God's outside it.

In the third part of the *Instauratio Magna*, the *Historia Naturalis et Experimentalis*, Bacon resumes his attack on the 'wrong-headed philosophies' which attempt to read off explanations of the world from the principles set out in Aristotle's texts rather than observe the world and seek to discover the truth there:

> …if there be humility towards the Creator, if there be reverence or willingness to magnify his works, if there be charity in men and eagerness to relieve human necessities and afflictions, if there be any love of truth in nature, hatred of shadows, and desire to purify the intellect, we should beg men again and again to set aside for a while or at least discard these fickle and wrong-headed philosophies, which have put theses before hypotheses, led experience captive, and exulted over God's works; and to read through with due humility and reverence the volume of creatures [*summisse, & cum veneratione quâdam, ad Volumen Creaturarum evolvendum accedant*], and dwell and reflect on it, and, purged of opinions, to study it with a pure and honest mind. This is that speech and language which went out to the ends of the earth, and did not suffer the confusion of Babel; let men learn this thoroughly and, becoming childlike, return to infancy again and deign to take its abecedaria into their hands. They should spare no effort in interpreting and unravelling it, but advance energetically, and stick at it until death.[72]

Two associated ideas dominate this extract. The first is the Fall. For Bacon, the advancement of knowledge is the means by which mankind can reverse the damage caused by the Fall and the confusion of tongues associated with building the Tower of Babel. In a work of 1603, *Valerius Terminus*, Bacon defines what the 'true ends of knowledge' must be: 'it is a restitution and reinvesting (in great part) of man to the sovereignty and power (for whensoever he shall be able to call the creatures by their true names he shall again command them) which he had in his first state of creation.'[73] The Adamic language of calling creatures by their true names was lost in the Fall, but Bacon hopes that the loss can be made good by the new methodology. Adam not only named the creatures but commanded them as well; nature is to be controlled as well as understood. The second important idea is the Book of Nature, and Bacon enjoins his readers, as it were, to return to childhood and learn the ABCs of it. Though the originary language and understanding of Adam was lost forever, the hard work of observation and experiment could allow us 'humbly and with due reverence to turn to unrolling the volume of the creatures'.

Bacon's reference to *'unrolling* the volume of the creatures', with its associations of the papyrus scroll used in antiquity, is eye-catching in an author for whom the printing press, along with gunpowder and the magnetic compass, 'unknown to the ancients', were the defining inventions of recent times (*Aphorism* 129).[74] Bacon's language of unrolling, which evokes above all the metaphorical scroll which marks Jupiter's divine authoring of history in Virgil's *Aeneid*, suggests an ancient genealogy for an image which he is going to use to make a fresh and very bold claim. Although the topos of the Book of Nature is not classical and only begins to emerge with Augustine's book of the world (*orbis terrarum*), we have seen that the trope of the world as 'readable' extends back beyond Lucretius's analogy of atoms and letters of the alphabet to Aristotle, includes Bacon's abecedarium of nature, and continues in the current image of the genetic 'code'.[75]

That the world, or aspects of it, might be thought of as a *book* has particular entailments, and the fleeting metaphor of Jupiter's book of Fate hardly more than hints at the philosophical and theological dimensions of the image, let alone the scrutiny to which the image would be subjected. In his critique of what he calls the 'logocentrism' of the West in *Of Grammatology*, Jacques Derrida tracks what he calls a 'fundamental continuity' that 'systematically contrasts divine or natural writing and the human and laborious, finite and artificial inscription',[76] a continuity that can be tracked through Plato's 'writing the truth in the soul' (*Phaedrus* 274c–276a), and the symbolism of the book in pagan and Christian antiquity through the Middle Ages to the present.[77]

Beyond the plethora of words, shifting and uncertain in meaning, lay something stable and eternal, figured as the Logos or Word. Within this metaphorical economy of words and the Word, the idea of the book, 'which always refers to a natural totality, is profoundly alien to the sense of writing', which is seen as sequential and time-bound.[78] Writing is enmeshed in human circumstance, open and disruptive, while the book has structure, closure and a sense of totality. The theological dimension of the Word, expressed in the opening words of St John's Gospel ('In the beginning was the Word, and the Word was with God, and the Word was God'), ensured a central place for the dynamic of word and Word in any Christian thinking.

Another vital development was the invention of the codex book which superseded the papyrus scroll, and with it the emergence of one specific book that gathered together under the sign of authority – the supreme authority – disparate writings of different provenance into a unity, the Bible. Beyond the multiplicity of its contents, all of them limited and incomplete, all bearing the signature of human authorship, lay the perfect Book, comprehensive and authorised by God's Word. However, the Word of God was available to mankind only in human language, and so in need of the fallible and time-bound processes of reading and interpretation to gain access to its eternal wisdom and truth. On the analogy of the Bible, Nature too in the late Middle Ages comes to be frequently figured as a book[79] that, like the Bible, contained signs and meanings which the reader had to subject to processes of interpretation: 'The Word as *verbum Dei* signified the Bible; the Word also authored, through its originative creative power, God's Works – the world and creatures.'[80] God's plan for the world could be *read* not only in the Scripture, but in the Book of Nature as well. But if Nature was a Book, what language was it written in? Bacon's answer, the language of Adam, was not to be long-lived, but his mobilisation of the topos had profound effects.

The Book of Nature was a persistent topos, but to describe it *as* a topos works to isolate it from the movement of history and to mask how it was differently deployed in a variety of polemical contexts, never more intensively than in the early seventeenth century, when the issue of the authority vested in texts was under particular scrutiny. In a superb study, Mario Biagioli has analysed how Bacon's contemporary, Galileo, used a range of configurations of the book over a decade or so in a number of different debates 'to legitimize his brand of natural philosophy by casting nature as a material inscription of God's logos – a "text" that was simultaneously opposed to the Aristotelian corpus and complementary to the Scripture'.[81] As he puts it, 'the topos of the book of nature did not emerge as an abstract methodological reflection, but as a context-specific response to critics who had invoked the absolute authority of another book: the Scripture.'[82] Galileo's brilliant appropriation of the image to consider the 'language' in which the Book of Nature is written will be considered in the next section, but Bacon's is no less audacious.

Bacon had expressed in his image of the Book the aspiration to make good the loss of the Adamic language after the Fall, but was equally eager to escape the constraints of the received attitude towards the Aristotelian corpus and Scripture, which believed that ever more detailed poring over the minutiae of texts was a path to the truth. This was a methodology, as we have seen, that Lucretius was already keen to distance himself from, associating such practices with the superstition of Etruscan divination. However, Bacon was constrained by a force of religious belief that Lucretius was happy to debunk. Bacon's rhetorical strategy and manipulation of imperial imagery effect two additions to the canon: the old *Organon* of Aristotelianism is supplemented by his own *New Organon*, and the authority of the Book of Scripture is supplemented (as Augustine had sanctioned) by that of the Book of Nature. The key mechanism for this supplementarity is typological reading: Alexander the Great and Aristotle are both retrospectively prefigured as types to which Bacon presents himself as the antitype who supersedes them. As we saw in Chapter 2, this typologising is nowhere felt so strongly as in Christian biblical interpretation which figures events or personalities in the Old Testament in the light of the New, but also is characteristic of the notion of *translatio imperii*, the transfer of power that takes place when the old order of things is superseded by and subsumed within the new. Gary Saul Morson formulates this aspect of typologising reading well: 'Prefiguration is one way in which a later book may supersede an earlier one and vitiate its integrity while claiming to preserve its sacred status', and he adds, 'Religions are defined by the *latest* book they acknowledge as sacred.'[83] Morson also remarks (my emphasis),

A *straight line* drawn between an earlier and a later testament or key eliminates readings that *lead in other directions*. Among other things, Christian prefiguration destroys the possibility of seeing events in the Hebrew Bible as prefiguring events in Jewish history, which in its own turn overwrites *possibilities imaginable* at the time the books were written.

This recalls the way in which the past is tidied up by what we might term, after Heidegger, *resolute* interpretation. At a stroke, Bacon can reconfigure as dead ends traditions of interpretation that had long been pursued with the utmost earnestness. We are no longer constrained by what 'they' say.

To appreciate Bacon's contribution, it is important to emphasise what he was *not* rejecting. He was not rejecting the importance the ancients had attached to observation of the world, nor was he rejecting the idea that the world was God's creation. Rather, with his advocacy of experiment and the manipulation of nature, he was supplementing *both* the empiricism and painstaking observation associated with Aristotle and the atomists, *and* the sense of a hidden reality that lies behind appearances that is associated with the theological creationism of Plato. The latter issues forth from the theological perspective that the world is imagined in the mind of the divine figure who created it as having a form, in the way a picture or a statue is the product of the craftsman, or a text is the product of the author. God the craftsman *invents* or *constructs* according to his vision outside time, but the human experimenter within time *discovers* what was there all along could we but discern it, what the ancients still prompt us to call the *nature* of things. Recall that the competing claims of the terms *discovery* and *invention* make up the turf disputed in the science wars between those who would make the latter ('realists') and those who would make the former ('constructivists') their methodological first principle in looking for a final answer to the question of what science *is*.

Bacon's theoretical emphasis on experiment was one important step in this reconfiguration of ancient ideas, but, as Shapin and Schaffer suggest in their discussion of the development of the air pump, it was Boyle later in the seventeenth century who invented the experimental method still current in scientific practice so as to distinguish *matters* of fact from the *interpretation* of fact.[84] Bruno Latour picks out three salient features from Shapin and Schaffer's analysis. First, the rejection on the part of this experimental method of what he calls 'the certainties of apodeictic reasoning', reasoning that seeks to *demonstrate* something on the basis of some first principle (in the manner of Aristotle or Lucretius), 'in favour of a doxa':

> Instead of seeking to ground his work in logic, mathematics or rhetoric, Boyle relied on a parajudicial metaphor: credible, trustworthy, well-to-do witnesses gathered at the scene of the action can attest to the existence of a fact, the matter of fact, even if they do not know its true nature... Boyle did not seek these gentlemen's opinion, but rather their observation of a phenomenon produced in the closed and protected space of a laboratory.

This shifts the emphasis from the *truth* of the fact to its *reliability*: the formal experiment can be reproduced over and over again with the same result, as witnesses can attest. Second, these facts are, precisely, constructed:

> Ironically, the key question of the constructivists – are facts thoroughly constructed in the laboratory? – is precisely the question Boyle raised and resolved. Yes, the facts are indeed constructed in the new installation of the laboratory and through the artificial intermediary of the air pump... But are the facts that have been constructed by man artifactual for that reason? No: for Boyle... extends God's 'constructivism' to man. God knows things because He creates them... We know the nature of the facts because we have developed them in circumstances that are under our complete control.

Facts are, as the derivation from the perfect passive participle of the Latin verb *facere* might suggest, 'things made'. Third, the limitations of these facts must be observed; they don't 'tell' us about anything other than themselves:

> Our weakness becomes a strength, provided that we limit knowledge to the instrumentalized nature of the facts and leave aside the interpretation of causes. Once again, Boyle turns a flaw – we produce only matters of fact that are created in laboratories and have only local value – into a decisive advantage: these facts will never be modified, whatever may happen elsewhere in theory, metaphysics, religion, politics or logic.[85]

The experimental fact is produced at a certain time and a certain place, under precisely defined conditions, but, as Latour suggests, that is what is so special about it. The experiment which produces this fact can be replicated times innumerable at any time and at any place so as to reproduce the fact, which can thereby become *universal*, whatever the social, historical or philosophical circumstances that happen to prevail at any one time. And, if it turns out it cannot be replicated, then it is not the universal it has claimed to be. It can become as true (but only in and of itself) as anything can be, and that is what is so impressive about it: it seems to be not the product of our labour, which dissolves in our mind, but 'there' in the world. And if it is 'there' now, it must have been 'there' in the past (had we but known it), and will be no less 'there' in the future.[86] The artefact of the mind, the concept, so distressingly slippery and subject to change over time and circumstance, so subject to what Derrida calls *différance*, so readily historicised as reflecting the circumstances of its context and use, comes to seem so much less universal than the experimental artefact, an engine of revelation to which witnesses can point again and again (whenever they want to) and say 'there'. But, as Latour cautions, once this 'timeless' fact is related to other elements and inserted within some larger structure of interpretation (Latour's list of 'theory, metaphysics, religion, politics or logic' is but indicative), it is taken 'within' time and mobilized towards the end of that form of interpretation. A fact that has been so painstakingly taken out of time and stabilised is returned to the movement of history.

Latour's approach has its constructivist sympathies, but contrary to the criticisms often made of his work, he is not in the business of denying what we may call 'reality' or 'truth'. It is rather that the production of any knowledge that can aspire to those names cannot, in his account, be captured as the revelation of what was there all along in a flash of genius as narratives predicated on *discovery* would have us believe,[87] but very hard work indeed – which is another legitimating narrative, of course, though to the end of a different understanding of knowledge and truth. Put another way, though he asks us to historicise relentlessly by seeing science as a human practice, he does not let history have the final word. We have learnt to construct the timeless, perhaps the greatest of all human achievements, but we need also to appreciate the limits of what we have done. Latour's work can caution us against swallowing whole the imperialistic teleological myth that we are coasting ever closer to knowing the mind of God, the foundation myth of the *discovery* metaphor. His work is a caution too against internalising the rhetoric of the 'Scientific Revolution' and 'modernity' (or, indeed, 'antiquity'): the title of the book from which we having been quoting is *We Have Never Been Modern*.[88] These are, after the manner of Koselleck, concepts with a history, and modalities we inhabit and invest in, rather than objective descriptions of our circumstances.[89]

A narrative of modernity that (fore-)sees its end in knowing the mind of God maps itself on to the teleological narrative of Christian theology, where our fallen state and confusion of tongues is part of a forward movement that ends on Resurrection Day. Latour's account deconstructs this myth: he dispenses with the idea that knowledge had any Tower of Babel moment when originary unity was fragmented, and, in contrast to the Bible's pessimistic view of our fallenness, offers a resolutely upbeat version of the myth[90] to underpin his confidence and delight in humankind's potentially *endless* capacity for construction and invention. This orientation towards what-is-to-come (Derrida's *l'avenir*) not only looks forward to future knowledge that is predictable but welcomes the unexpected and unforeseen knowledge that will come upon us as an *arrivant* and could oblige us to re-narrativise what we think we are doing. This is a perspective on knowledge that seeks to supplement an imperfect metaphysics of presence with a Heideggerian emphasis on potentiality. Hans-Jörg Rheinberger calls the objects of scientific research 'epistemic things', and explains (my emphasis),

> They are material entities or processes – physical structures, chemical reactions, biological functions – that constitute the objects of inquiry. As epistemic objects, they *present* themselves in a characteristic, irreducible vagueness. This vagueness is inevitable, because, paradoxically, epistemic things embody *what one does not yet know*.[91]

He might be speaking of texts.

THE END OF LANGUAGE AND THE END OF THE BOOK?

We left hanging the question of the 'language' in which the Book of Nature is 'written'. The notion that once upon a time there existed a language in which everything could be expressed perfectly and without ambiguity is not restricted to the story of the Garden of Eden and the Fall of Man to which Bacon referred. Plato's dialogue *Cratylus* conjures up the figure of a 'nomothete', who gave names to things, rather as Adam gave names to the animals in Genesis. Cratylus suggests that the sounds were chosen according to the objects' nature (*physis*), while Hermogenes argues that they were assigned by human convention (*nomos*). Socrates, however, would like to abolish the mediation of language altogether: knowledge is not based on our relation to the names of things, but to the things themselves, or more precisely to our ideas of the things, the Forms. In *The Search for the Perfect Language*, Umberto Eco has tracked in detail the extraordinary range of responses to this perceived dilemma from the Middle Ages to his own times, his emphasis being on the frequently bizarre practical proposals suggested.[92] Nostalgically, Hebrew, Greek or Latin were variously proposed as that perfect language. This impulse can still be strongly felt in Heidegger, who spent the latter half of his life seeking to get back, beyond an Aristotelian philosophical terminology he felt to be under the dominion of a Latin-language reception, to the presocratic Greek of Parmenides and Anaximander. The search for the perfect language can take the form of a historical quest, but a favoured alternative strategy is, as Plato's Socrates does, to seek to transcend language in some way. Three examples from authors with very different agendas, and then we shall return to Plato via the mathematicians he so admired.

For Augustine, Creation is pictured as the performative speech act narrated in Genesis: 'God said, "Let there be light" and there was light.' God is not only the arch-constructivist, he is the supreme nomothete ('And God called the light Day, and the darkness He called Night'), and delegates this power to Adam before the Fall in the naming of the animals in the Garden of Eden. Although *word* is a metaphor through which Augustine seeks to understand his relationship with God, his writings are marked by an impatience to move beyond the temporal constraints he feels it imposes. As Eric Jager puts it, 'The *Confessions* as a whole contains an autobiographical version of the hermeneutics of the Fall that Augustine bequeathed to the Middle Ages.'[93] The garden scene in Milan, with its tempting voices, the fig tree and other imagery from Genesis, is a typological reprise of the Fall, and the performance of the *sortes biblicae*, with its moment of revelation, figures Redemption.[94] In that moment of redemptive reading, Augustine needed to go no further than the end of the sentence (*finis*, 8.12.29), and he closed the book (*codicem clausi*, 8.12.30). This temporal end to reading looks forward to the end of time. Near the end of his own book, Augustine contemplates the temporal limits of scripture itself: 'Your scripture is "stretched out" over the peoples to the end of the age' (13.15.18). God's *written word* was inscribed by mortal men for mortal men, but God's *scripture* is a 'solid firmament of authority over us', for '"the heaven will fold up like a book" (Isa. 34:4), and "now like a skin it is stretched out" above us (Ps. 103:2)' (13.15.16).[95] As Jager puts it, 'The end of Scripture envisioned here is part of a totalising scheme of language, history, and cosmos.'[96] At the end of time and of the cosmos, we will be able to 'read' the 'face' of God, as the angels do (13.15.18):

> They have no need to look up to this firmament and to read so as to know your word. They ever 'see your face' (Matt. 18:10) and there, without syllables requiring time to pronounce, they read what your eternal will intends. They ever read, and what they read never passes away... Their codex is never closed [*non clauditur codex eorum*], nor is their book ever folded shut. For you yourself are a book to them and you are 'for eternity' (Ps. 47:15).

The perfect language is no language at all, and it exists outside, not within, time.

Lucretius sees his task as precisely having to work within the constraints of language, though his project aspires to transcend them. Lucretius believes that universal truth was revealed to humankind by the 'Greek man', Epicurus, in Athens in the fourth century BC. His task, a difficult one as he sees it, is to bring that revelation to a Roman readership, as he says to his patron (1.136–45):

nec me animi fallit Graiorum obscura reperta
difficile inlustrare Latinis versibus esse,
multa novis verbis praesertim cum sit agendum
propter egestatem linguae et rerum novitatem;
sed tua me virtus tamen et sperata voluptas　　　　　　　　　140

suavis amicitiae quemvis efferre laborem
suadet, et inducit noctes vigilare serenas
quaerentem dictis quibus et quo carmine demum
clara tuae possim praepandere lumina menti,
res quibus occultas penitus convisere possis.　　　　　　　　145

Nor does it escape me in my mind that it is difficult to cast light in
Latin verses on the obscure discoveries of the Greeks, especially since
we must deal with many things by means of new words because of the
poverty [*egestatem*] of the language and the novelty of the matter. But
your merit and the hoped-for pleasure of your friendship persuade me
to undergo any effort and induce me to stay wakeful through the calm
nights seeking by what words and what poetry I may be able to spread
forth before [*praepandere*] your mind the clear light by which you may
see right into matters that are hidden.

Lucretius needs to render Epicurus's discoveries into a language in
which there is a lack of established terms for the things he wants to talk
about – in that sense he presents himself as within time, a constructivist
inventing new words – but along with that admission, there is a subtle
effacement of language in this passage. The imagery of light and dark
encourages the reader to concentrate not on the language but on 'seeing'
the 'things' themselves (cf. 1.144–45). It's a pity an atom is too small to
see, but you are to get beyond worrying about *atomi* (a transliteration
from the Greek Lucretius eschews throughout his poem) or *genitalia
corpora rebus* or *semina rerum* or *corpora prima* or *primordia rerum*
– the proliferation of rebarbative phrases just underscores that they all
point to the same (simple) *thing*. *Praepandere* (1.144) perhaps uses the
image of unrolling a scroll, but what you will see in that scroll aren't
words, but *things* (*res*, 1.145). The phenomena of the visible world have,
in the imagery of 1.77 examined earlier, their 'boundary stone deep set'
(*alte terminus haerens*), but the implication of Lucretius's realism is
that, though the 'terms' in which the theory is described may appear to

shift in their translation from Greek to Latin, the truth resides not in the shifting words, but in the deeply rooted 'things'.

He lays emphasis on the 'poverty' of his language (1.139),[97] though it has been argued that he is playfully asserting the superiority of Latin as a medium for expressing Epicurean ideas,[98] and this is a notion that can be readily entertained within the broader context of the reception of the imperial imagery deployed in the poem. The notions of universal truth and universal empire are complicit in Lucretius's representation of Epicurus, and the dream of a universal language may be no less so. As Joseph Farrell has argued, 'the Virgilian model of universal extension and absolute potency' gives rise to a Latin culture that 'tends to imagine itself and its language as universal and powerful beyond all competitors'.[99] Epicurus's truth may stand outside time and any version that is offered of it, but Lucretius makes a pitch that within time and history *his* version can claim to be definitive. His act of linguistic translation from Greek to Latin thus enacts *translatio imperii*. This 'carrying across' is the process that seems to point towards such universality in acknowledging the historicity of linguistic boundaries while claiming that the truth transcends them and is, universally, translatable.[100] Lucretius's dream may not be so much for a perfect language, rather that the universality of the truth he conveys renders the language that expresses it – Greek, Latin or any other – invisible.

For the third example, we return to the Book of Nature. As briefly touched on in the previous section, Mario Biagioli has analysed how Bacon's contemporary Galileo used a range of configurations of the book over a decade or so in a number of different debates 'to legitimize his brand of natural philosophy by casting nature as a material inscription of God's logos – a "text" that was simultaneously opposed to the Aristotelian corpus and complementary to the Scripture'.[101] The scarequotes Biagioli places around 'text' suggest for him its metaphoricity. Bacon had expressed in his image of the Book the aspiration to make good the loss of the Adamic language after the Fall. However, much the most famous of all invocations of the Book was made by Galileo in his dialogue *The Assayer* (1623).[102] In response to his Scholastic opponent, Galileo suggests that philosophy, the true knowledge of nature, is not a book like the *Iliad* or *Orlando Furioso* written by some human author. No, philosophy is 'written in the language of mathematics':

Philosophy is written in this grand book, the universe, which stands continually open to our gaze. But it cannot be understood unless one first learns to comprehend the language and recognize the letters in which it is composed. It is written in the language of mathematics, and its characters are triangles, circles and other geometric figures without which it is humanly impossible to understand a single word of it. Without these, one wanders about in a dark labyrinth.[103]

Galileo effects a brilliant sleight of hand here, as he seeks to efface the textuality associated with the Book of Nature: the 'grand book' here *is* the universe, and once one has grasped that its 'language' is the geometrical relationship of things one to another, one need not look beyond the surface of these geometric figures, as one does with language, for some deeper or hidden meaning: the forms are all. In his critique of logocentrism, Derrida locates Galileo's book within his contrast of a metaphorical 'natural and universal writing, intelligible and nontemporal' and a writing that is 'sensible, finite... on the side of culture, technique and artifice'.[104] However, Galileo deftly casts geometrical figures as configurations that are there, in the world, and contrasts them with the 'letters' and 'characters' like those of the alphabet which define human writing, and are of necessity a mediation between human understanding and the divine Word or Logos. Biagioli suggests that Derrida falls short in placing Galileo's Book of Nature on a par with scripture as an example of 'natural writing', which is to overlook a further level of metaphoricity in Galileo's 'book' above and beyond that of scripture. Galileo's 'book of nature was *neither* a book written by humans (like the Aristotelian corpus) *nor* a metaphorical book (like the Scripture),' he says, where access to the Logos was mediated through actual letters and characters and interpretation was required: 'Galileo's topos showed itself to be more of a logocentric construct than Scripture itself in that it claimed an immediate coexistence with the logos.'[105] In Galileo's use of the topos in *The Assayer*, God did not *write* the Book of Nature or even draw geometrical shapes in it, but is figured rather as an architect who gave geometrical shape to his creation – a demiurge whose creation is equated with the imposition of *form*.

Galileo stretches the metaphor of the book almost to the point where it falls apart, but he does not explicitly erase it. As in the case of

Jupiter's 'book' in Virgil's *Aeneid*, when the metaphor has done its work in suggesting a truth *beyond* words, it is quietly allowed to fade away – before the paradoxes become too obtrusive. If humans were to try to read Jupiter's 'book', their task would be one that went on forever as they followed the story of 'empire without end'. Galileo uses the image of the book to suggest a notion of truth as form, and as something self-evident; but its contents are likewise infinite.[106] There is no limit to the number of nature's laws, but there are constraints of time on the human observer, and the discovery of that complete truth is endlessly deferred. In spite of the paradoxes, the image of the book carries with it some powerful compensatory associations:

> Galileo's book of nature provides a very evocative image for those who think of knowledge as *already achieved* – as a well-organized, unambiguous map of a terrain that has been fully measured and triangulated. The book of nature conveys an image of totality, a magisterial image of knowledge like that of an encyclopedia or, even better, the Scripture – a book whose characters were all already known, without the possibility of adding new ones.[107]

The sense of something transcendent already achieved that the image of the book brings with it (even if the task of reading remains to be completed, and is endless) evokes also Virgil's characterisation of empire: its *presence* seems palpable, even if on reflection what is yet to be achieved is likewise endless. Lucretius presents the truth of Epicureanism as a *totality* already achieved, but while he is prepared to see his own project in terms of textual inscription, it is noticeable how he seeks to eschew this in relation to Epicurus's achievement. Although he has surveyed the infinite universe in his journey across it, he does not return, in Biagioli's words, with a 'well-organized, unambiguous map of a terrain that has been fully measured and triangulated'. Even a diagram is taboo. Epicurus *reports* back to us (*refert nobis*, 1.75) 'how each thing has its potentiality set within boundaries and its deep-set boundary mark' (1.76–77). Against one isolated reference to Epicurus's writings (3.10), Lucretius prefers to use the metaphor of 'speech' to refer to Epicurus's thought.

Nonetheless, as Derrida's discussion of the opposition of speech and writing can remind us, for all that speech is often taken to be a guarantor of presence, even the spoken word is a form of mediation that seems to keep 'the world itself' at one remove.[108] Galileo's solution to this dilemma is a subtle one: the 'language of mathematics' is actually no language at all, but *out there* in the geometrical patterns in which the Creator formed nature. For mathematical realists, geometrical shapes or numbers are not constructs of the human mind, as language is. As Roger Penrose memorably puts it, 'Like Everest, the Mandelbrot set is just there.'[109] So believed the Pythagoreans, and Plato too. This outlook was succinctly expressed by Manilius, the late Augustan poet of astrological determinism, who in his didactic poem the *Astronomica*, celebrates the power of mathematical calculation to reveal the movements of the heavens. The heavens *are* mathematical, and so the positions of the constellations, past, present and future, are calculable. He regrets that words, even the rhythms of poetry, can never capture this without the risk of diminishing it (4.430–35), but expresses the hope that 'as I report through my poetry the jurisdiction of destiny and the sacred motions of heaven, my words must conform with its dictates: it is not granted to me to fabricate, only to point out, the pattern' (4.436–38):

sed mihi per carmen fatalia iura ferenti
et sacros caeli motus ad iussa loquendum est:
nec fingenda datur, tantum monstranda figura.

In the climactic line 438, Manilius plays on *figura* and *fingenda*, which are etymologically linked: the pattern (*figura*) is not, as the word might seem to suggest, something that is to be dreamed up or constructed (*fingenda*). It is *monstranda, there* in the movements of the constellations *to be pointed out*. He goes on to say 'nor is it right for the world to be dependent on words; in the reality it will be greater' (*nec fas est verbis suspendere mundum:/rebus erit maior*, 4.441–42). The word *fas*, here translated by 'right' and cognate with the verb 'to speak', connotes a religious or ritualistic permission or prohibition on speaking. The suggestion of ineffability is piquantly associated with the idea Manilius rejects that the universe is somehow dependent on *words*. The invocation of *res*, 'things', makes Manilius a realist, and for realists, mathematical form, thus theologically inflected, is *discovered* rather than invented by the human mind.[110]

Mathematical entities appear to be independent of space and time, in that relationships like '2+2=4' seem true regardless of where or when they are invoked, as Winston Smith sought to convince O'Brien in *Nineteen Eighty-Four*. But where, or in what sense, can these 'things' be said to exist? For mathematical realists like Manilius, the answer is obvious: in the mind of God. In 4.439–40, he glosses his assertion that it is *not granted* to fabricate, only to point out the pattern (*nec fingenda datur, tantum monstranda figura*), with what he takes that to entail: *'to have indicated* the deity is more than enough; he himself *will grant* to himself authority' (**ostendisse** *deum nimis est:* **dabit** *ipse sibimet/ pondera*).[111] Mathematics are 'divine arts' (*divinas artes*), as he refers to them in the opening line of his poem, brought down from the heavens. For Augustine, the test case is infinity (*City of God* 12.19). Rejecting the 'blasphemy' that God does not know all the numbers, Augustine ridicules the notion that God's knowledge extends only to a certain sum. He refers to Plato's *Timaeus* (35b–36d) for the argument that God constructed the world by the use of numbers, 'while we have the authority of Scripture, where God is thus addressed, "You have set in order all things by measure, number, and weight" [Matt. 10:30].' Still, the result feels paradoxical,[112] and Augustine too resorts to the trope of ineffability:

> Never let us doubt, then, that every number is known to him 'whose understanding cannot be numbered' [Ps. 147:5]. Although the infinite series of numbers cannot be numbered, this infinity of numbers is not outside of the comprehension of him 'whose understanding cannot be numbered'. And so, if what is comprehended in knowledge is bounded within the embrace of that knowledge, and thus is finite, it must follow that every infinity is, in a way we cannot express, made finite to God because it cannot be beyond the embrace of his knowledge [*profecto et omnis infinitas quodam ineffabili modo Deo finita est, quia scientiae ipsius inconprehensibilis non est*].

Like other varieties of realism, the mathematical finds some kind of recourse to the notion of the divine irresistible (Penrose, for example, avers that 'There is something absolute and "God given" about mathematical truth'[113]), even if those defenders of realism resistant to theism place God within scare-quotes or hasten to describe their expression as 'metaphorical' – their version of the ineffability topos.

Galileo, in a move that is characteristic of proponents of realism, appeals to a 'language' that is not a language, in the sense that he asserts that there is no mediation involved. For their part, critics of realism characteristically bring the discussion back to what they see as the irreducible textuality of knowledge, its mediation through various forms of representation, diagrams, graphs, models and formulae as well as language. Both camps have their take on infinity. For a realist like Lucretius, there is nothing outside the universe, but for a critic of logocentrism like Derrida, there is nothing outside the text, no outside-text (*il n'y a pas de hors-texte*). Each has its characteristic way of configuring through a legitimating narrative how timeless knowledge and truth make their appearance in history, the realist through the miraculous *discovery* of something that has been there all along, had we but known it, the anti-realist through the painstaking *construction* or *invention* of something that can claim to be universal, though it didn't exist before. Mathematics is no less susceptible of an anti-realist account that would see it as the painstaking construction of human textualising effort. Observe the Greek mathematicians in Reviel Netz's account, toiling away as they develop technologies of representation[114] through which they can generate compelling modes of argument:

> I will argue that the two main tools for the shaping of deduction were the diagram, on the one hand, and the mathematical language on the other hand. Diagrams – in the specific way they are used in Greek mathematics – are the Greek mathematical way of tapping human visual cognitive resources. Greek mathematical language is a way of tapping human linguistic resources. These tools are then combined in specific ways. The tools, and their modes of combination, are the cognitive method.
>
> But note that there is *nothing universal* about the precise shape of such cognitive methods. They are not neural; they are a *historical construct*. They change slowly, and over relatively long periods they may seem to be constant. But they are still not a biological constant... They can only be studied as historical phenomena, valid for their period and place.[115]

Rather than start from the assumption that an ideal world of mathematics exists eternally (in the mind of God), waiting patiently for a genius within history to access it, Netz sees the emergence of Greek mathematical thinking as intimately connected with the development of some very practical 'tools' out of already existing visual and linguistic 'resources', the lettered diagram and a very restricted vocabulary: he notes that 'the entire Archimedean corpus is made up of 851 words',[116] and that typically a large corpus of mathematical writings will have 'around 100–200 words used repetitively, responsible for 95% or more of the corpus (most often the article, prepositions and the pseudo-word "letters")'.[117] It is through the scrupulous development of these technologies that Netz's mathematicians found themselves able to track equivalences and transitive relations through successive stages of argument in a way not possible in the messy empirical world.

Geometric proof involves a mode of 'translation' where *exact* equivalences can be 'carried across' to the next stage of the argument, as against linguistic discourse, where equivalences (e.g. *imperium* and *power*, or the *Aeneid* and *Nineteen Eighty-Four*) are at best only crude approximations on either side of an 'equation' that involves the continuing negotiation over time of differences and similarities. So for Netz it is not *beyond* but *in* the textual that Greek mathematics achieves its success in bringing together the finite and the universal:

> Greek geometric propositions are not about universal, infinite space. As is well-known, lines and planes in Greek mathematics are always finite sections of the infinite line and plane which we project. They are, it is true, indefinitely extendable, yet they are finite. Each geometrical proposition sets up its own universe – which is its diagram.[118]

Each diagram is structured and finite, but is *demonstrably* true for the specific 'universe' it 'sets up'. As in Shapin and Schaffer's analysis of experiment, the human mathematicians mimic God's constructivism. Netz devises metaphors in keeping with his emphasis on mathematics as a practical skill: the proofs generated go into the 'tool-box', ready to be brought out to construct another demonstration (just as Boyle's air pump is a piece of kit that can be deployed in the context of fresh experiments).[119] But this tool-box is good for Greek mathematics *and nothing else*. Netz is at pains to fashion an account that does not have recourse to universalist assumptions about human 'nature', for example, that deduction is somehow biologically hard-wired into the human brain. His specifically *Greek* mathematicians are doing something that is 'valid for their period and place', and he emphasises the point in a footnote: 'What I study is not "deduction" as such; what I study is a specific form, namely the way in which Greek mathematicians argued for their results.'[120] Nonetheless, thanks to the diagrams and the particular uses of vocabulary they have developed, their techniques can then be transmitted across time and space.

This sets Netz directly at odds with Plato, who in a famous and influential scene in the *Meno* (81e–86b) uses a set of exchanges about geometry between Socrates and a slave to suggest that there is no such thing as learning, only a remembering of knowledge that was always already there in our immortal souls before our birth. For Netz, these techniques are not a hard-wired feature of human brains, and so people who are not Greek mathematicians can nonetheless *learn* how to use them. They become *transferable* skills, skills that can be 'carried across' time and space: Pythagoras's theorem can be proved beyond the borders of Greece at any time and any place – so long as the networks of transmission that carry the techniques associated with the proof are not broken. Once more, *translation* offers a model of continuity, save that in this case it is one of continuity absolutely without change. These skills are transferable, Netz emphasises, *only* within the discursive limits as narrowly defined by the mathematicians. At a historical moment when the potentialities of *epi*deictic persuasion and rhetoric are being explored by the sophists within various contexts of public debate, the Greek mathematicians were developing a mode of *apo*deictic proof, which would, in its own terms, be binding, and could convince rather than just persuade.[121] They did so by rigorously limiting themselves to the study of forms, and eschewing all discussion of content. Greek mathematics was about Greek mathematics and nothing else.[122] He emphasises how austere and isolated Greek mathematicians were, a tiny circle of devotees focused inwards to the elaboration of the very specific, very specialised object of study they had fashioned.

The work of these few Greek mathematicians might have remained marginalised had it not come to the notice of the Platonic-Aristotelian tradition.[123] But this reception proved crucial to the later perception of mathematics:

> [W]e all know the fate of a book which suddenly becomes a bestseller after being turned into a film – in the version 'according to the film'. This process originated in south Italy in the late fifth century BC, but it was Plato who turned 'Mathematics: The Movie' into a compelling vision. This vision remained to haunt western culture, sending it back again and again to 'The Book according to the Film' – the numerology associated with Pythagoreanism and Neoplatonism.[124]

But it also proved crucial to the later perception of philosophy. Latour is not as polite as Netz, and sees what Plato did with mathematics in terms of an appropriation, or even a hijacking. Characteristically, he reserves his greatest scorn for what he sees as the attempted Platonic elision of the textual:

> The major scandal for philosophers in antiquity, a scandal that is still with us today, is that no two philosophers agree with one another. Was the Platonic philosophy a real emulation of geometers' practices that produced conviction around the collective inspection of lettered diagrams, sticking to the conclusions that forms, and only forms, could lead to? Of course not, since they did not use diagrams to begin with. Philosophy did not carefully limit itself to forms, as geometers did…but instead claimed to be talking about *contents*: the Good Life, the proper way of searching for Truth, the Laws of the City, etc. It is as though Plato extracted no more than a style of conviction from geometry and added to it a totally unrelated content; it is as though the type of persuasion mathematicians obtained at great pains (because they limited themselves to forms) could nonetheless be reached, at almost no demonstrative cost, by philosophers with regards to what they saw as the only relevant content! A mimicry of mathematics, just sufficient to boot the Sophists out of philosophy.[125]

Plato is a more sophisticated rhetorician than Latour will here allow. In the Vatican fresco, Raphael represents Plato as pointing to transcendent truth in the heavens rather than grasping it, just as in the dialogues when human time presses in, Socrates leaves the discussions to be resumed. Yet, Latour is spot on when he suggests how Plato's philosophy is entangled in his historical context.[126] Latour's approach directs attention to the consequences of this appropriation at the level of political epistemology, that any shift in epistemology obliges us to rethink politics, and vice versa. In Plato's *Gorgias* (508a), one of Socrates's put-downs is that Callicles neglects the study of geometry (*geometrias gar ameleis*), *and so* has no idea of fair shares or just deserts in social terms. Latour points to the spell that the myth of the Cave in the *Republic* continues to cast, with its relationship between true knowledge and the social world. The philosopher (or, as it might be, the scientist) 'once equipped with laws not made by human hands that he has just contemplated because he has succeeded in freeing himself from the prison of the social world, can go back into the Cave so as to bring order to it with incontestable findings that will silence the endless chatter of the ignorant mob'.[127] In its presumptive appropriation of 'timeless' knowledge for its own ends within time, the myth of the Cave holds out for Latour a political epistemology that is not only a negation of democracy but a waste of so much human potential.

We may look to an answer to these questions, but the shadows are lengthening and the end of this book beckons. Translation has been a recurrent theme of *Antiquity and the Meanings of Time*: translations of language, power, knowledge and skills, with consequences – good or bad – that within the temporal sphere of our existence we will continue to debate to different ends, not all of them foreseen. That theme touches upon the exhilarations, the dangers, the challenges of reading. We can never wholly grasp the traces of the past in the present, but on one issue Latour and Netz have got it about as right I currently think they could. We will not even be able to point to those traces that interest us, those moments of enlightenment that make us realise, if only temporarily, our human potential if the networks of transmission that carry the techniques and skills we need to do so are broken. One of the greatest pleasures of writing this book is that I have come to read books I never expected to read. A new day will dawn, and a new book will be opened. That book may well be one I have opened many times before, but never read like *this*. I look forward to moments of fresh enlightenment. The time one thinks one is right is the time to think again.

NOTES

PREFACE

1   Ricoeur (1984), 52; emphasis Ricoeur's.
2   Ricoeur (1984), 7: 'We may deplore the fact if we like, but the phenomenology of time emerges out of an ontological question: quid est enim tempus? ("What, then, is time?" [11.14.17]).'
3   Cf. Ricoeur (1988), 12.
4   Ricoeur (1984), 6; emphasis mine.
5   Ricoeur (1984), 3.
6   I have found both Lloyd (1993) and Currie (2007) perceptive and sympathetic in their approaches to Ricoeur.
7   Lloyd (1993), 172.
8   Morson (1994), 1.

CHAPTER 1

1   See Vance (1973) and (1984); Rothfield (1981).
2   I have used Chadwick (1991) for translations from the *Confessions*.
3   The doctrine of incarnation means that God also exists within time. We shall return to this in Chapter 5.
4   Wills (2011), 100.
5   On the 'inward turn' in Augustine, see e.g. *De vera religione* 39.72: 'Do not go outwards, return within yourself. In the inward man dwells truth' (*noli foras ire, in teipsum redi. in interiore homine habitat veritas*) and Taylor (1989), 127–43, who speaks of 'a certainty of self-presence: Augustine was the inventor of the argument we know as the "cogito", because Augustine was the first to make the first-person standpoint fundamental to our search for the truth' (133). See further Nightingale (2011), 123–28.

6   Cf. Austin (1962).

7   For all that, O'Donnell (2005a), 213 notes that 'Augustine's narrative, artfully constructed of self-accusation and excuse, has proven impermeable to assault. The only piece of narrative that has ever undergone assault on grounds of truthfulness is the fragment of time in the garden in Milan when he hears the child's (or the angel's?) voice urging him to "take up and read". For an autobiographical narrative with heavy theological undertone, written by a man with a suspect past and enemies of several sorts, that gullibility – the word is not too strong – is astonishing.' He notes that Peter Brown's classic biography of Augustine in the chapter that covers the 'conversion' (2000, 99–102) does no more than present without further comment an abridged translation of the garden scene in *Confessions* 8.

8   O'Donnell (1992), 3.56.

9   Chadwick (2001), 44.

10   Chadwick (1991), xxv.

11   Cf. Jager (2000), 29.

12   See Wills (2011), 58–63 and Nightingale (2011), 150–51 on the renunciation of sex; O'Donnell (2005b), 59–61 on the importance of formally undertaking the rituals of the Christian Church.

13   This was written shortly after the death of Antony in 356, and translated into Latin by Evagrius of Antioch in the 370s. Antony renounced the world for a life of asceticism after wandering into a church and hearing the priest reading Matthew 19:21: 'If you would be perfect, go, sell what you possess, and give to the poor, and you will have treasure in heaven.'

14   Wilcox (1987), 129.

15   Derrida (2008), 2.129.

16   Fludernik (2005), 611; she cites as examples J.M. Coetzee's *Waiting for the Barbarians*, Margaret Atwood's *Surfacing* and Eva Figes's *Ghosts*. A complex example is Martin Amis's *Time's Arrow*, which tells the story of a Nazi doctor's life backwards from death to birth. Its narrator (the soul?) is obliged to adopt the reflector mode. Such experiments are not confined to fiction. Derrida frames his 'Circumfession' (Bennington and Derrida [1993]) as 'fifty-nine periods and periphrases' that use constant allusion to Augustine's *Confessions* to reflect upon his life and beliefs, and adopts the present tense as its default mode. On this work, see the collection of essays in Caputo and Scanlon (2005); Gersh (2010).

17 O'Donnell (1992), 1.xviii.
18 Chadwick (1991), xxi puts this nicely: 'Decisions made with no element of Christian motive, without any questing for God or truth, brought him to where his Maker wanted him to be.'
19 As O'Donnell (1992), 3.38 observes.
20 Stock (1996), 78. Cf. Wills (2011), 73: 'The whole scene with Alypius has a witness, a very credible one, the lawyer-bishop of Tagaste, with whom Augustine was in constant communication in the period when he wrote *Confessions*.' Alypius had been born in the same North African town as Augustine, had accompanied him when he travelled to Italy in 383 and returned with him to Africa after the events narrated in the *Confessions*.
21 By contrast, the fig tree is just one of the details of the scene packed with biblical significance; cf. Jager (1993), 91–95 and (briefly, but effectively) Wills (2011), 72–77. On Augustine's extravagant and expressive 'body language' in the conversion scene, see Nightingale (2011), 153–56.
22 Cf. Wills (2011), 9 on the way in which the rhetorical structure of the Psalms influences the style of the *Confessions*. Augustine's *Expositions of the Psalms (Enarrationes in Psalmos)* was in process at the time.
23 O'Donnell (1992), 2.29 and 3.37.
24 Sizoo (1958), 104–6 suggests that *tolle, lege* was an Italian harvest chant ('lift, sort'), and that Augustine, as a fairly recent arrival from Africa, could have been unfamiliar with it. If so, his misinterpretation of the phrase would be, for his narrating self, another sign of divine providence.
25 O'Donnell (1992), 3.61.
26 See Jager (2000), 36, who draws attention to how the codex form of the book facilitates this.
27 Jager (1993), 95 and n.120. Note also the intensifier *–ce* added to the demonstrative *huius*, which, in the words of Lewis and Short's *Latin Dictionary* (s.v. *hic, haec, hoc*) 'points to something near or present, or which is conceived of as present': the temporal perspectives of narrated and narrating selves are impossible to disentangle in this word.
28 Courcelle (1963), 194–95 believes that the codex opens here not by chance or through the performance of the *sortes* but because Augustine had reached this point in his reading when the earlier visit of Ponticianus had interrupted him, prompting Ponticianus's comments then on Antony and asceticism. In his concern to establish the historical credentials of the incident, Courcelle seeks to rationalise the scene as far as he can, emphasising that Alypius lights upon the verse which strikes him

so forcibly '*par des voies naturelles*, et non par un hazard merveilleux' (emphasis Courcelle's), namely 'the finger or some other mark' Augustine had placed in the text after he had consulted it. In an earlier discussion of this scene, Courcelle (1950), 199 similarly suggests that Augustine had resumed reading at the point where he had been interrupted, but leaves open the possibility that from the perspective of what we have called the narrated self, the effect is comparable to that of the *sortes*: 'Le premier verset qui lui tombe sous les yeux prend pour lui valeur d'oracle et décide de sa vie.'

29 O'Donnell (1992), 3.68–69.

30 Chadwick (1991), xxiii.

31 As Wills (2011), 74 remarks, 'Alypius' change of heart is a real conversion, a change of religion, as opposed to Augustine's response to an ascetical vocation. Augustine had already been convinced, before he ever reached the garden, of the doctrines he took to be the essence of Christianity. Alypius was not. He had no issue with virginity, it was his natural bent. But he did not, till the moment in the garden, accept the truth of Christianity. His lawyer's mind was resisting. This is why he took Paul's words…as aimed at him personally.'

32 The evidence is presented in Courcelle (1950), 200 n. 1.

33 Trans. King (1995), 136–37.

34 On Augustine's 'extromission' theory of vision, 'whereby the "rays" of the eyes flow outward into the world: the rays "shine through the eyes and touch whatever we see"', see Nightingale (2011), 111–12 (who is quoting Augustine's *De Trinitate* 9.3.3 here), and the further bibliography she cites.

35 According to Aristotle in the *Metaphysics* 1010a7–15, the historical Cratylus took the dictum of Heraclitus, that you can't step into the same river twice, further to suggest that you can't step into the same river once. As Sedley (2003), 19 comments, 'This is clearly a Cratylus who has come to believe that things change so rapidly that you cannot engage with them, either by naming them or by stepping into them, in any way that takes any time at all: during the time taken, however short, they have become something else. So the only way to engage with them is one that is complete at an instant: just point your finger.'

36 A critique of *Confessions* 1.6.8 forms the starting point of Wittgenstein's *Philosophical Investigations*. For Augustine's critique of ostensive definition see Burnyeat (1987); Kirwan (1989), 52–53; Stock (1996), 155; and, in general, Tallis (2010), 69–86.

37 Tallis (2010), 9.

38 Tallis (2010), 11.

39 Tallis (2010), 11; emphasis original.

40 Tallis (2010), 28.

41 Tallis (2010), 132.

42 Tallis (2010), 133.

43 Tallis (2010), 73; emphasis original.

44 Recall too O'Donnell's characterisation of *ecce* as a 'verbal punctuation mark', *punctuation* being another term derived from the Latin *pungere*, to point.

45 Tallis (2010), 86.

46 Tallis (2010), 128.

47 Tallis (2010), 119.

48 The Latin verb *dicere*, to say, was in an earlier form *deicere*, and is cognate with the Greek *deiknumi*, to point out.

49 Sherman (2008), 29 describes the care with which they are drawn: 'some are clothed in the simplest of sleeves and others emerge from billowing cuffs with pendant jewels; some suggest the merest outline of a hand while others capture the sinews, joints, and even nails with a precision that rivals the most artful anatomical study.' For a witty review of Sherman's book well worth reading, see Price (2008).

50 One older term (which has in recent times undergone an unfortunate shift in meaning to which Sherman quite properly does not allude), 'bishop's fist', seems, in the present context, too good to be true. Cf. Sherman (2008), 34: 'it may not be desirable to lose the history of associations preserved in terms like "bishop's fist" and "mutton fist" – even if we can no longer imagine what a pointing hand has to do with either clergymen or sheep or why a hand with an extended finger would be described as a fist.'

51 Sherman (2008), 37.

52 Translation from Mitchell (2008), 153.

53 Vladimir Nabokov (1964), 3.102–3 in his commentary on this passage notes wistfully, 'The art is a lost one today.'

54 The classic treatment is Auerbach (1959), 9–76; see also Kermode (1983), 89–90 and Dawson (2002). Jager (1993), 23–142 explores typology in Augustine, including the garden scene.

55 Cf. Vessey (2005), 251–52, in the wake of the detailed analysis of Fredriksen (1986).

56 Cf. Stock (1996), 16: 'He knows that the life is not a revision of events; it is a revision of his interpretation of them... He sees the person who writes in 397 engaging in a process of self-redefinition rather than setting down a definitive version of the life. Final publication, to extend the metaphor, is endlessly postponed.'

57 Stock (1996), 400 n. 131.

58 On Augustine's knowledge of Plotinus, see Majumdar (2007), 38–39.

59 O'Daly (1987), 152.

60 Stock (1996), 236.

61 Study of Genesis provides the framework for Augustine's thinking throughout his life after his conversion, the earliest being *On Genesis against the Manichaeans* from 388–89. Apart from *Confessions* 11–13, he also wrote an unfinished commentary *The Literal Interpretation of Genesis (De Genesi ad litteram imperfectus liber)* between 401 and 414, and repeatedly adverts to it in *City of God* 413–27. We shall be returning to his thoughts on Creation in Chapter 5 below.

62 Consciousness for Augustine is bound up with language, as is evident from his fascination in the *Confessions* with his own infant self, the time when he was a 'non-speaker' (*infans*) and had to learn rudimentary ways of communicating his desires 1.6.7–8: '...at that time I knew nothing more than how to suck and to be quietened by bodily delights, and to weep when I was physically uncomfortable. Afterwards I began to smile, first in my sleep, then when awake. That at least is what I was told, and I believed it since that is what we see other infants doing. I do not actually remember what I then did.'

63 Chadwick (1991), xxii; cf. 225 n. 11. The reference to Plotinus is *Enneads* 5.3.17.24.

64 O'Donnell (1992), 3.250; emphasis original.

65 O'Donnell (1992), 3.250.

66 Cf. Bettini (1991), 164. The word *coram* articulates the concern with presence-to-God of the *Confessions*. In writing of the metaphor of the 'inscribed heart' Augustine develops for the self, Eric Jager comments (2000), 31–32: 'Augustine often treats memory or recollection as synonymous with the heart by employing the term *recordatio* (and its cognate verb, *recordari*), sometimes using wordplay to emphasise the link between memory and the heart, as when he declares to God, "My heart and my memory are open before you" (*coram te cor meum et recordatio mea* [*Confessions* 5.6.11]).'

67 This is itself an instance of apostrophe, of course.

68 Culler (1981), 139.

69 Culler (1981), 142.

70 Culler (1981), 146.

71 J.L. Austin's distinction between performative and constative discourse is relevant here, though note also Derrida (2005), 152: 'A performative produces an event only by securing for itself, in the first-person singular or plural, in the present, and with the guarantee offered by conventions or legitimated fictions, the power that an ipseity gives itself to produce the event of which it speaks – the event that it neutralizes forthwith insofar as it appropriates for itself a calculable mastery over it. If an event worthy of this name is to arrive or happen, it must, beyond all mastery, affect a passivity.'

72 Culler (1981), 148.

73 Culler (1981), 150.

74 Culler (1981), 152–53.

75 Augustine is clearly familiar with Aristotle's arguments, but probably encountered them in a Latin translation rather than the original Greek, a language he never felt at home with. Important recent treatments of Aristotle on time are Annas (1975), Derrida (1982), 29–67, Coope (2005) and Roark (2011); also the commentary of Hussey (1983). For the *Physics*, I use the translation of Waterfield (1996).

76 Cf. Coope (2005), 13: 'for Aristotle, indivisible things like points or instants exist only in so far as they are boundaries, divisions, or potential divisions of a continuum.' Annas (1975), 109–10 notes, however, that on three occasions 'the now seems to be compared rather to the unit of number and appears to have the logic of a period rather than a durationless instant marking off a period.' For ancient debates on indivisible 'atoms' of time, which necessarily have a minimal size and extension, cf. Sorabji (1983), 17–21 and 365–83.

77 Bostock (2006), 150.

78 Who these previous thinkers were is not clear. Coope (2005), 32 n. 5 associates the idea with Plato's Academy, but does not think it was Plato's considered view. Cf. Augustine, *Confessions* 11.23.29: 'I have heard a learned person say that the movements of sun, moon, and stars in themselves constitute time.'

79 On what Aristotle means by this see Coope (2005), 85–92. Beyond the philosophical niceties, Aristotle here seems to be struggling to express a need that was only to be adequately satisfied with the development of the mechanical clock in the late Middle Ages.

80 See the discussion of Coope (2005), 159–72.

81 Cf. O'Daly (1987), 153: 'His famous description of time as a *distentio animi* cannot be a definition, but is, rather, a metaphor that evokes whatever accompanies or follows upon the cognitive act of measuring time. It is a colourful and highly novel metaphor, to be translated not so much by the term "extension" as by "tension" or "distraction causing anxiety".' Nightingale (2011) puts forward the stimulating argument that in Augustine's corpus more generally the human being, as she puts it (22) 'dwells in two different time zones: while the body changes in earthly time, the mind stretches away from the present in psychic time.' A focus on what Augustine says about time in *Confessions* 11 leads to a concentration on the metaphysics of presence, which is obviously a matter of abiding concern for both Augustine and his commentators; but Nightingale's contrast of earthly time, in which the body changes, experiences appetites, decays and dies, with the psychic time of the mind leads to a fruitful shift of focus towards the physics of presence. This allows for a very powerful take on *distentio* (2011, 8): 'For Augustine, the human mind distends outward from the present moment into the past and the future. It therefore has no grasp on the present. Ontologically and psychologically, it always has memory and expectation, and is thus distended into different temporal periods. This has significant psychological ramifications. First, the distended mind cannot experience divine presence in spite of its drive toward the metaphysics of presence. And, second, the mind cannot dwell in the here and now of the body – what I call the *physics of presence*.'

82 Note the apostrophe here in the closural moment of this argument, as the mind grasps itself in a moment of self-presence. For the rational self-reflection so characteristic of Augustine's writings, in which the mind looks at the mind, see Nightingale (2011), 115–23.

83 9.12.32; the other occasions are 4.10.15 and 10.34.52.

84 See Jager (2000), 1–27; the citation is from Jager (2000), xx.

85 See Jager (2000), 27–43 for an excellent account.

86 It is three times referred to as such in *Confessions* 8.12.29. On the historical shift from scroll to codex and the change in book metaphors that accompanies this technological shift see Jager (2000), 34–38.

87 Jager (2000), 36.

88 See Jager (2000), 9.

89 See especially Olson (1997); also Olson (2006) and Dawson (2009).

90 Sternberg (1978), 255, cited by Culler (2007), 185–86.

91   Cited by Olson (1997), 51.

92   Fowles (1971), 86.

93   Fowles (1971), 86.

94   Culler (2007), 190.

95   Culler (2007), 185 and 201.

96   For an overview see Riffaterre (1981).

97   See Kermode (1983).

98   Thus Homer, *Iliad* 1.1 or Virgil, *Aeneid* 1.1. We shall be considering the 'prophetic' aspect of literature over the next two chapters.

99   And yet, other things 'easily come forward under the direction of the mind familiar with them' (10.11.18) – as is the case with the hymns and psalms which he knows.

100 For helpful commentary on this phrase see Nightingale (2011), 96–97.

101 Barthes (1967), 32; emphasis original.

102 Barthes (1967), 30; emphasis mine.

103 Barthes (1967), 30; emphasis mine. These considerations will be the subject of Chapter 5.

104 A prominent recent example is Steiner (1989). He says of his book that (1989, 3): 'It proposes that any coherent understanding of what language is and how language performs, that any coherent account of the capacity of human speech to communicate meaning is, in the final analysis, underwritten by the assumption of God's presence.'

105 Barthes (1986), 52; emphasis original.

106 Barthes (1986), 52–53.

107 Students of intertextuality and allusion in literature often, after Conte (1986), trope the process as 'memory', and see it thematised within literature as an act of memory; cf. Hinds (1998), 3–5.

108 Barthes (1986), 54.

109 Prickett (2002), 220.

110 Augustine, *De Trinitate* 10.11.18.

CHAPTER 2

1   Kermode (1966), 5. The imagery of light and shadow plays with knowledge and its lack. From the privileged position of knowing the end or outcome, earlier events can 'foreshadow' later, but from a perspective in the midst of time their significance can seem cloaked in darkness.

2　The translation of this difficult phrase is that of Feeney (1991), 137, who confesses to not knowing what 'the end' refers to. Mitchell-Boyask (1996), 293 refers it to the end promised by Aeneas in 1.199, 'which, indeed, quickly occurs', although he concedes that we are not told that Jupiter is responsible for it. Austin (1971), 87 calls it 'a transition-formula... referring not so much to the particular scene of mourning as to the whole episode from 157 onwards: one chapter of the Trojans' affairs is over, a new development is to begin at 305; and at this turn of events important matters are being settled by the gods.'

3　Feeney (1991), 137.

4　Well analysed by Culler (1981), 169–87. 'Characteristically' of course lifts us out of the particular into the (would-be) timeless world of theory, though narratologists use a plethora of terms to articulate the distinction Culler points to.

5　The narratological distinction thus makes the story logically prior to the discourse, though, as Culler shows, the story can no less be seen as the effect of the discourse.

6　Cf. Mack (1978), 48–54; Fowler (1997), 259.

7　Genette (1980), 36.

8　The phrase *in medias res* comes from Horace's *Ars poetica*, where Horace advises the aspiring epic poet not to stick grimly to the chronological order, citing the opening of the *Odyssey* as exemplary (141–42); 'nor does he begin the return of Diomedes from the death of Meleager, or the Trojan War from the twin eggs [*gemino... ab ovo*, i.e. from the conception of Helen]: always to the outcome he hastens, and snatches his listener into the middle of events [*in medias res*], assuming them as known' (146–49). Horace is enjoining a principle of selection (i.e. 'the wrath of Achilles' rather than the whole Trojan war), but since the Renaissance, his words have been applied to a principle of narrative ordering, as Genette takes it. Cf. Sternberg (1978), 36–40. The opening 'from the egg' (*ab ovo*) is memorably sent up in Sterne's *Tristram Shandy*, where Tristram meticulously begins the narrative of his life from the moment of his conception, though immediately needs to flashback to explain those circumstances.

9　Barthes (1967), 30.

10　Cf. Genette (1980), 67–79.

11　Genette (1980), 69; for the term 'homodiegetic' (1980), 245.

12　The Horse is the 'fatal gift of Minerva' (*donum exitiale Minervae*) in 2.31, the adjective playing on the sense of *exitium* as both 'outcome' and 'death'.

13 Genette (1980), 244–45 gives as his prime example Homer in the *Iliad*.

14 See Halliwell (1987), 100. We will return to the issue of unity of *praxis* towards the end of this section.

15 Chatman (2009), 32.

16 Barthes (1967), 30–31.

17 The phrase *altae moenia Romae* in 1.7 is a bit difficult to render (perhaps 'the walls of lofty Rome'), but seems to suggest the city in its achieved pomp. Austin (1971), 31 has a good note.

18 The verb Virgil uses here, *volvere*, is extraordinary, but it is one with connotations of reading a scroll he plays on as *Aeneid* 1 itself unfolds. My translation suggests that Aeneas has read the Book of Misfortunes from beginning to end.

19 He turns over 'such' cares in his heart (*talis iactantem pectore curas*, 1.227).

20 The perfect tense *pollicitus* (1.237) lacks the normal auxiliary part of the verb 'to be' that would make the identity of the agent clear. Austin (1971), 90 comments, 'sc. *es* ("You *promised*", says Venus to her father, like any disappointed daughter)'. Yes indeed, but we should not overlook the way the poet has not made this entirely explicit. Nonetheless, the tense makes Venus's reference analeptic, a point to which I shall return shortly.

21 O'Hara (1990), 133, who goes on to show in detail (133–63) how Jupiter's speech emphasises for Venus's sake the positive aspects of the 'future' and downplays the negative; summarised in O'Hara (2007), 78–82. Cf. also Mack (1978), 68–69. That Jupiter is highly adept at 'tailoring' his utterances to his different audiences was noted by Virgil's fourth-century commentator, Servius, in his note on 1.261; cf. Thilo-Hagen (1923), 1.97. See also Lyne (1987), 80–81, for whom Jupiter 'packages' his revelations of the future 'in a manner designed to afford [Venus] the maximum of comfort'.

22 As Feeney (1991), 139 remarks, 'a mere seven words concern the action of the poem: *bellum ingens geret Italia populosque ferocis/contundet* ("he will wage a huge war in Italy, and crush fierce peoples", 263–64).' Jupiter is the Barthesian Author *par excellence*.

23 Cf. 1.286–88: *nascetur pulchra Troianus origine Caesar/imperium Oceano, famam qui terminet astris,/Iulius, a magno demissum nomen a Iulo* ('from this noble lineage will be born Trojan Caesar, so as to bound dominion by the Ocean and reputation by the stars, Julius, a name descended from great Iulus'). The identity of this Caesar (Julius and/or Augustus?) has been the focus of much inconclusive debate; cf. Austin (1971), 108–10, O'Hara (1990), 155–63, Kraggerud (1992), Dobbin (1995), Hedjuk (2009), 290–91.

Willis (2010), 86 perceptively comments, '*Imperium* is coextensive with the earth, but also with history: Caesar is not, in this passage, a specific living individual whose historical accomplishments originate in his unique character or his achievements; he is a *nomen*, transmitted and received from great Iulus, from Troy.' The name 'Caesar' thus takes on the mark of sovereign succession, and the construction *qui* plus the subjunctive *terminet* sets out not any one individual's achievement but the goal of that sovereignty.

24 Willis (2010), 83–104 offers a superb analysis of these issues, both in Jupiter's speech and elsewhere in the *Aeneid*. My account is complementary to hers.

25 The paradoxical transcendence of infinity will be a major theme in Chapter 5 below.

26 Feeney (1991), 153.

27 Heinze (1993), 237–38 (295 in 1915 edn).

28 See now Hedjuk (2009), a systematic examination of Jupiter's actions in the *Aeneid*, which persuasively sees them as centrally concerned with issues of power (*imperium*) and adulation (*fama*).

29 Feeney (1991), 155.

30 Servius (on *Aeneid* 10.628) can't quite make up his mind: 'if the voice of Jupiter is Fate, he is able to change the course of Fate by saying something else' (*nam si vox enim Iovis fatum est, potest aliud fando fati ordinem commutare*); Thilo-Hagen (1923), 2.445. Commager (1981) presents the etymological evidence, and catalogues the numerous word-plays on *fari* in the *Aeneid*; cf. also Lyne (1987), 73–74 and O'Hara (1996), 121.

31 See the elegant discussion in Willis (2010), 93–96 of how Mercury 'translates' the atemporal commands of Jupiter/Fate into the 'actual situation of address in the encounter with Aeneas' in *Aeneid* 4.265–76.

32 Bettini (2008), 314. The same phrase *dehinc talia fatur* was used in 1.131 to introduce Neptune's outburst on observing the effects of the storm instigated by Juno.

33 Bettini (2008), 315.

34 Cf. Bettini (2008), 315: 'Spoken by the authoritative voice of Jupiter, the prophetic act of *fari* corresponds directly to the realization of the god's statement: *fari*, that is, implies a powerful way of speaking in the sense that it reveals events that are still unknown and directly brings about their realization.' Bettini elsewhere notes (2008, 334) that Varro (*De lingua Latina* 6.53) describes how the compound verb *effari* was used by augurs

marking out spaces for observing celestial signs: 'From this (i.e. from *fari*) comes the expression "spoken things" (*effata*), referring to the formulas with which the augurs have marked out the boundaries of the fields outside the city for observing celestial omens. From this, areas marked out for augury are also said to be "defined with a word" (*effari*), and the augurs declare (*effantur*) their boundaries (*fines*).' This verb, as Bettini says, blurs the distinction between 'saying' and 'delimiting' or 'defining', but it could be added that traces of this ritualistic behaviour may be felt in Jupiter's speech to Venus in which he 'defines' the (non-)boundaries of the Roman dominion (*his ego nec metas rerum nec tempora pono:/imperium sine fine dedi*, 1.278–79).

35 *Sermon* 105.7.10, cited in O'Hara (1990), 126–27.

36 Cf. Austin (1971), 101–2. That *volvens* may mean 'rolling in the mind' is rejected by Henry (1873), 562–64, who adduces a number of parallels to suggest that it means 'rolling, turning over with the speech, i.e. in words'. With his characteristically reductive vigour, Henry wishes *volvens fatorum arcana movebo* to be 'only another less usual way of saying "fatorum arcana canam [I shall sing the secrets of Fate]"'. However, Conington (1876), 2.59 cites Cicero *Brutus* 298, *volvendi sunt libri cum aliorum tum inprimis Catonis* ('you should unroll the books of other authors, but especially Cato's').

37 Bettini (2008), 326 n. 20.

38 Conington (1876), 2.59.

39 It is worth recalling that this is the verb also used of the Parcae in 1.22 (*sic volvere Parcas*), when Juno alludes to her knowledge of Fate. According to Servius in his note on this line, the metaphor comes either from spinning a thread or from unrolling a scroll (*aut a filo traxit 'volvere' aut a libro*). He goes on to say that, of the three Parcae, 'one speaks, the second writes, and the other spins threads' (*una enim loquitur, altera scribit, alia fila deduxit*); Thilo-Hagen (1923), 1.20. The verb can connote the actions of all three, and all attempt to capture an action that is outside time.

40 See the passages cited by Austin (1971), 102, and add Horace *Odes* 3.7.20, *fallax historias movet*, used of a crafty adulteress 'packaging' mythological stories in an effort to seduce the virtuous Gyges. The term *moment* tropes time through movement (the Latin *momentum* is derived from **movimentum*; cf. *Oxford Latin Dictionary* s.v. 5a); contrast *punctum*, which seeks to point the finger at that fleeting moment.

41 Culler (1981), 171.

42 Barthes (1967), 30.

43 Derrida and Ferraris (2001), 20; emphasis mine.

44 Royle (2003), 110–12 has helpful comments on Derrida's notion of the *arrivant*, and the etymological association of the language of *arrival* with the Latin *ad*, 'to', and *ripa*, the 'bank' of a river or the 'shore' of the sea. The *arrivant* is something that comes upon us for which we are not prepared. As Royle (2003), 111 puts it, 'The question of the ... arrivant is a question of the border or threshold, of who or what comes to shore or turns up at the door.' To thematise the distinction Derrida is asking us to consider, recall how the *Aeneid* treats what might be seen as the (monstrous) 'arrival' of the Trojans in Italy as their 'fated homecoming'.

45 Derrida (1992), 51.

46 Quint (1993), 30.

47 Fukuyama (1992), 55.

48 Quint (1993), 33.

49 Cf. Walbank (1970), 1.43, ad loc.

50 Fukuyama (1989), 3; emphasis original.

51 Derrida (1995), 386–87.

52 Verbs of pointing or showing (*ostendo* is a compound of *tendo*, 'to stretch', with the prepositional prefix *ob*, 'in front of') are here associated with Fate's predictable future, but also provide the vocabulary for Derrida's monstrous (cf. *monstro*, 'show') *arrivant*: *portentum*, *ostentum*. These are pointed to not out of recognition but of want of knowledge.

53 Within the poem's perspective, this is how a Roman – of any epoch – should be treated. Dido initially welcomes the man who washes up on her shore, but after falling in love with him loses the historical 'vision' she previously had and re-narrativises him when he announces he is leaving as a monstrous *arrivant* she was mad to take in. Cf. her speech in 4.365–87, especially 365–67: '*nec tibi diva parens generis nec Dardanus auctor,/ perfide, sed duris genuit te cautibus horrens/Caucasus Hyrcanaeque admorunt ubera tigres*' ('neither was a goddess the mother of your family nor Dardanus its ancestor, traitor, but the freezing Caucasus gave birth to you on its harsh crags and Hyrcanian tigresses gave you suck') and 373–74, '*eiectum litore, egentem/excepi et regni demens in parte locavi*' ('a castaway on the shore and in need I rescued you, and, mad that I was, gave you a share of my kingdom').

54 Recall Aeneas's use of *olim* in 1.203, which there unambiguously refers to the future. The ambiguity of *olim* in 8.348 was remarked upon by

James Zetzel in his 1993 Jackson Knight Memorial Lecture at the University of Exeter; see Edwards (1996), 31 and Martindale (1997), 5. For its past and future orientation, see the *Oxford Latin Dictionary* s.v. 1 and 3 respectively.

55 Wood (2001), 369.

56 Gibbon (1994), 3.1062.

57 Richardson (2009), 132 with note 65 for the passages: Horace, *Odes* 3.5.4; 4.15.14; Propertius 1.6.34; 3.1.16; Virgil, *Aeneid* 1.279, 1.287, 6.782, 6.795, 6.851.

58 The phrase *aeterna urbs* first appears in Tibullus 2.5.23, in a poem that dates to 19 BC, and, like the *Aeneid*, is built around the theme of prophecies of Rome's destiny.

59 MacCormack (1998), 188; see further Paschoud (1967), 169–274.

60 Cf. Paschoud (1967), 224–27; O'Daly (1999), 20–21.

61 *Letter* 126.2.2, cited by O'Donnell (2005b), 228; also Paschoud (1967), 218–21. Cf. also O'Daly (1999), 28: 'Jerome compared Rome's fall with the Babylonian destruction of Jerusalem and – as Augustine was to do in Book 1 of the *City of God* – with the Greek sack of Troy (Jerome, *Letter* 123.15–16, 127.12).' For Augustine's rather more dispassionate response to the sack of Rome as he viewed events from Hippo in North Africa see Paschoud (1967), 239–45, MacCormack (1998), 188–204, O'Daly (1999), 28–30, Brown (2000), 285–96, O'Donnell (2005b), 227–34.

62 The passage is adduced in another context by O'Hara (1990), 126–27, whose translation I have adopted.

63 As O'Daly (1999), 246 observes, Augustine cites *Aeneid* 6.847–53 again (together with *Aeneid* 1.279–85 and 8.646–48) in *City of God* 5.12 more positively as part of an argument that Rome's imperial achievements are God's reward for Roman virtue. For *City of God*, I use the translation of Bettinson (2003).

64 Cf. Morson (1994), 1: 'Images of utopia typically derive not just from a thirst for social justice but also from a hunger for the end of time as we have known it; for the time when (as the Book of Revelation promises) "there shall be time no longer." At the end of history, the anachronising of beliefs is over. At last, we shall no longer need to fear that our present opinions and beliefs will be outdated; for at the end, what is outdated is outdating itself. Thus, utopian temporality satisfies a hunger for certainty, which the various forms of historical time do not.'

65   For the philosophical roots of Augustine's identification of 'City' with 'Empire', see Pagden (1995), 17–18. The play on the words *urbs* ('city') and *orbis* ('world'), common from the late Republican period onwards and still surviving in papal addresses *Urbi et Orbi* ('to the city and the world') cemented the association; Jerome, in the preface to his first book on Ezekiel, could look back on the sack of Rome with the words *in una urbe totus orbis interiit* ('in this one city [Rome] the whole world perished'). O'Daly (1999), 23, in his discussion of 'Cities Real and Desired', notes that 'literary discourse about society and religion in the fourth century often took the form of exploring the theme of the city, and of Rome in particular.'

66   Augustine himself called it 'a huge work' (*City of God* 22.30), and O'Donnell (n.d.) describes it as 'the longest single work presenting a sustained argument around a coherent single theme to survive from Greco–Roman antiquity'.

67   Wilcox (1987), 127.

68   Wilcox (1987), 128.

69   Cf. also *City of God* 1.35: 'those two cities are interwoven and intermixed in this era [*in hoc saeculo*], and await separation at the last judgement.' On Augustine's sources for the notion of 'two cities' in Scripture and in earlier Christian writing, see O'Daly (1999), 53–66.

70   Koselleck (2002), 76–77. He offers a fascinating oversight from this perspective of the work of Herodotus, Thucydides, Polybius, Sallust, Tacitus ('someone who was existentially vanquished') and Augustine. Cf. (2002), 78 on Polybius ('taken to Rome as a hostage, [he] had to first experience the absolute estrangement of the vanquished, before he learned to identify himself with the victor to such an extent that he was able to describe its ascent as a world power; but he did so necessarily from a perspective that was both internal and external, one which could never have been available to the victorious Romans'), and (2002), 79 on Augustine ('Through his doctrine of the two worlds, he sought salvation from all history, and insofar as he relativized earthly attempts at self-organization eschatologically, he taught they should be interpreted all the more austerely').

71   On this passage see further MacCormack (1998), 202–3, who notes that, in quoting *Aeneid* 1.278–79, Augustine makes some slight changes to Virgil's text to accommodate his own syntax, substituting *ponit* ('places') for *pono* ('I place') and *dabit* ('will grant') for *dedi* ('I have given').

72 The translation is taken from Green (1997), 56.

73 Koselleck (2004), 100.

74 Kermode (1983), 29–33.

75 See Kennedy (1999) for further discussion and examples.

76 Orwell (1969), 199.

77 Orwell (1969), 211–12. Rorty (1989), 169–88 perceptively argues that the last third of *Nineteen Eighty-Four* is not so much about Winston's disintegration as what it is to *be* O'Brien, inhabiting the modality he does.

78 Orwell (1969), 212.

79 Orwell (1969), 41–42: 'Something seemed to tell him with certainty that Tillotson was busy on the same job as himself. There was no way of knowing whose job would finally be adopted, but he felt a profound conviction that it would be his own. Comrade Ogilvy, unimagined an hour ago, was now a fact. It struck him as curious that you could create dead men but not living ones. Comrade Ogilvy, who had never existed in the present, now existed in the past, and when once the act of forgery was forgotten, he would exist just as authentically, and upon the same evidence, as Charlemagne or Julius Caesar.'

80 Cf. Bennington (1990), 121: 'we undoubtedly find narration at the centre of nation: stories of national origin, myths of founding fathers, genealogies of heroes'.

81 Willis (2007), 339.

82 Hardt and Negri (2000), xiv–xv.

83 Hardt and Negri (2000), 11.

84 Hardt and Negri (2000), xiv; emphasis original.

85 Willis (2007).

86 Willis (2007), 343 n. 31; emphasis mine.

87 Cf. Koselleck (2002) and (2004). Hayden White, in his Foreword to Koselleck (2002, ix), describes him as 'the foremost exponent and practitioner of *Begriffsgeschichte*, a methodology of historical studies that focuses on the invention and development of the fundamental concepts (*Begriffe*) underlying and informing a distinctively historical (*geschichtliche*) manner of being in the world.' In science studies, concepts such as the atom or the self are now the object of study of what Lorraine Daston (2000) has termed 'applied metaphysics' or the 'biographies of scientific objects', and Hans-Jörg Rheinberger (1997) 'the history of epistemic things'. Cf. Kennedy (2002), 62.

88 See in general Farrell (2001), 2–6. The perspective is dramatically represented by T.S. Eliot in his famous essay 'What is a Classic?' (1957), 68: 'Thus Virgil acquires the centrality of the unique classic; he is at the centre of European civilization…the Roman Empire and the Latin language were not any empire and any language, but an empire and a language with a unique destiny in relation to ourselves; and the poet in whom that Empire and that language came to consciousness and expression is a poet of unique destiny.' See further Kermode (1983), 15–24.

89 The title of Waquet (2001) is *Latin Or the Empire of a Sign*.

90 Some thought-provoking reflections on this, and on the rise of English in globalisation, in Hösle (2005).

91 Orwell (1969), 251 and 242; emphasis original.

92 Rorty (1989), 73.

93 The Latin term *translatio* 'translaltes' the Greek *metaphora*. In the course of carrying these terms across into English, *translation* has come to refer to the process of carrying meaning *across* the boundaries of a language, *metaphor* carrying meaning across *within* the boundaries of a language.

94 Orwell (1969), 251.

CHAPTER 3

1 Morson (1994), 8.

2 Morson (1994), 44.

3 The translation is that of Lattimore (1999), 170–71. In what follows, I have transliterated the place names in their more conventional Latinised forms.

4 All paraphrase is hazardous, as we will see in the second section below.

5 Morson (1994), 33.

6 Morson (1994), 8.

7 Morson (1994), 8.

8 Morson (1994), 38.

9 Forster (2005), 87. We shall return to this example in the second section below.

10 Danto (1968), 9, cited in Morson (1994), 54; emphasis Danto's.

11 Morson (1994), 63; emphasis original. But it is not only in the phrase 'in order to' but also the verb 'indicate' that the unseen but guiding 'hand' of the author may be detected.

12 Morson (1994), 58–59.

13 Morson (1994), 60.

14 Morson (1994), 289 n. 19; emphasis original.

15 Morson (1994), 61.

16 Morson (1994), 44.

17 Morson (1994), 87.

18 Contrast the methodological approach of Segal (2001), 53 (emphasis original): 'One of the hardest problems in approaching the *Oedipus Tyrannus* is trying to look at it freshly. To do that, one must remove a few layers of misconception; so I have to begin with a few "nots". This is not a play about free will and determinism. The Greeks did not develop a notion of a universal, all-determining Fate before the Stoics in the third century B.C.E.' In legislating for what this play is about, Segal adopts the historicising manoeuvre to which Barthes drew attention, of reducing reality, the reality of this text, to a point in time.

19 Morson (1994), 3.

20 Morson (1994), 5; emphasis mine.

21 Austin (1971), 108 glosses *sic placitum* as 'this is my will and pleasure'.

22 Tolstoy (1957), 1438; emphasis original.

23 For an exploration of what she calls 'the largely neglected history of providence' in both its theological and secular manifestations, and its role in articulating ideas of free will, autonomy and responsibility, see Lloyd (2008).

24 Augustine develops these ideas in philosophical form in a work written after his withdrawal to Cassiacum in 386, *De ordine* ('On Arrangement'), and in *De libero arbitrio voluntatis* ('On the Free Choice of the Will'), which just precedes the composition of the *Confessions*. For discussion of these, see Lloyd (2008), 128–52; also Stump (2001).

25 Augustine signals the difference between his view of providence and that of Virgil in *City of God* 5.1, when he enquires 'why God was willing that the Roman Empire should extend so widely and last so long'. The greatness of the Roman empire was down neither to chance nor destiny: 'without the slightest doubt, the kingdoms of men are established by divine providence. If anyone ascribes this to destiny (*fato*), because he uses the word "destiny" to refer to the will or power of God, then he can keep his opinion, but he should express himself more accurately.'

26 Cited from Danto (2007), 3–4.

27 Hegel (1975), 26–30; emphasis mine.

28   Lloyd (2008), 1. In a recent and fruitful examination, Charles Taylor discusses these changes in terms of ongoing tensions between the interrelated ideas of 'ordinary time, the time which is measured in ages' and 'higher time, God's time, or eternity', which correspond to what I have termed perspectives 'within' time and 'outside' time, or the 'God's-eye view'. He remarks (2007), 716, 'In virtually all pre-modern outlooks, the meaning of the repeated cycles of time was found outside of time, or in higher time or eternity. What is peculiar to the modern world is the rise of an outlook where the single reality giving meaning to the repeatable cycles is a narrative of human self-realization, variously understood as the story of Progress, or Reason and Freedom, or Civilization or Decency or Human Rights; or as the coming to maturity of a nation or culture. The routines of disciplined work over the years, even over lifetimes, the feats of invention, creation, innovation, nation-building, are given a larger meaning through their place in the bigger story.' The key phrase here for my purposes is 'a narrative of human *self-realization*'. Such a narrative is firmly teleological: the future has an end, and with it a form which is already known, even if the details remain to be filled in. In his meditation on history in the last chapter of *War and Peace*, Tolstoy remarks, 'Freedom is the content. Necessity is the form.'

29   Morson (1994), 59.

30   Dawe (2006), 9.

31   Dawe (2006), 15.

32   Hunting improbabilities in *Oedipus* has been a critical sport since the *Poetics*, where Aristotle on three occasions draws attention to how incidents which would offend against his notions of necessity or plausibility are placed, as he says 'outside the dramatic action' (*exō tou dramatos*, *Poetics* 1453b29–32; cf. also 1454b6–8 and 1460a26–30). These incidents are not outside the drama so much as not directly presented within it, rather the matter of narrative report on the part of the characters.

33   As Dawe (2006), 7 points out, Oedipus's immediate reply to Creon in 124 refers to a robber in the singular. Dawe continues, 'When Creon reports the oracle at 107 he uses a plural, and so does Oedipus at 108. The Chorus use plurals at 292, though Oedipus again responds with a singular at 293 – which does not prevent him from using a plural at 308. Oedipus uses the singular here at 124, and again at 139, 225, 230, 236, but at 246–47 he says, "I curse the doer of this deed, whether he be one or acting with several others." At 277 the Chorus use the singular, and at

715f. Jocasta uses the plural. It could hardly be more confusing. And it was meant to be. The simple mathematical proposition of 845 "one cannot be equal to many" must be present to our minds, but kept out of focus, for as long as possible.'

34   Peradotto (1992), 12. In a similar spirit to Morson, he speaks (1992), 2 of his critique of *Oedipus* as 'prompted by the desire to distinguish narratives of emancipation from narratives of enslavement and thereby to promote the autonomy of reading subjects and their society.'

35   Peradotto (1992), 4. Halliwell (1987), 107 suggests that the phrase 'probability or necessity', which Aristotle repeats several times with variations, 'helps to emphasise his requirement of as tight and intelligible a *causal* sequence as possible in the plot-structure of a poem' (emphasis mine).

36   Peradotto (1992), 7; emphasis original. Dawe (2006), 14 remarks of the messenger from Corinth, 'It is the high season for coincidences: this very messenger, it seems, had once been given the infant Oedipus by another herdsman. And who was that herdsman? Why, it was "none other than", as the Chorus ingenuously put it (1052), our elusive friend, the sole survivor [of the attack on Laius].' Dawe refers this to the demands of the convention that all the roles were taken on by three actors only: 'We must accept this piece of dramatic shorthand for what it is, pausing only to note that Sophocles does not take any unfair advantage of it, e.g. by stressing how to the gods no coincidences are too extreme.' Peradotto might counter that Sophocles does indeed take 'unfair advantage' of it, and precisely by *not* stressing how to the gods no coincidences are too extreme.

37   Peradotto (1992), 9.

38   See also Peradotto (1992), 8.

39   Wood (2003), 71.

40   Creon does not mention Delphi explicitly, but the term he uses, *theōros*, is usually taken in the sense of one going to consult the oracle.

41   The Greek is syntactically complex. I have adopted the paraphrase with which Dawe (2006), 81–82 concludes his long note on line 115.

42   Peradotto (1992), 9; emphasis original.

43   Peradotto (1992), 13.

44   And when that authority is Homer, even the sharpest of critics defer to it. Cf. Goldhill (1996), 157 in his review of Ahl (1991), in particular his argument that Oedipus may not have killed Laius, and may not be the son of Jocasta:

'Homer is not just another text in a mythic morass, but a privileged and paradigmatic expression of the past for the fifth century. "The curious act of faith" of which Ahl convicts readers and critics – believing Teiresias – is less curious in the light of Homer and the epic tradition. While there is "room", as Ahl asserts, for even quite radical change within a mythic tradition, it cannot be adequately discussed without a full awareness of the *authority* of past narrative' (emphasis original).

45   Goodhart (1978), 66.

46   Goodhart (1978), 67. Note that by attributing this meaning to *Sophocles*, Goodhart, no less than the tradition of interpretation he distances himself from, divines the absent author's intention. The closural pull of this kind of historicism is a strong one, and Goodhart jumps to its conclusion.

47   Notably Ahl (1991), who 'translates' the play into the terms of fifth-century BC judicial practice. We shall be returning to the issue of such paraphrases shortly.

48   Goodhart (1978), 61; emphasis mine.

49   Morson (1994), 71–81 has an excellent analysis.

50   The classic treatment is Brooks (1984).

51   See Liveley (2008).

52   Goodhart (1978), 61.

53   The only book-length study of *Oedipus* to engage with Goodhart is Ahl (1991); see the review of Goldhill (1996). But Ahl does not broach the larger issues of critical interpretation Goodhart goes on to raise, nor do others. Segal (1995) in his chapter on 'Time and Knowledge in the Tragedy of Oedipus' dismisses Goodhart in a footnote. Rudnytsky (1987), 350–57 offers a critique of Goodhart in an Appendix to his book on *Freud and Oedipus* which attacks 'those critics who have recently called into question the hegemony of the Oedipus myth' (338), including Girard, Deleuze and Guattari, from a position of staunch investment in that myth. He prefaces his critique with the remarks, 'I hope by my work as a whole to have attested in practice to the explanatory power of psychoanalysis and to the *human truth* of the Oedipus myth' (337; emphasis mine).

54   Goodhart (1978), 69.

55   Goodhart (1978), 69.

56   Cf. Cave (1988), 163: 'the interpretation [of *Oedipus* in *The Interpretation of Dreams*] is imperialistic in its claims to say not merely what the myth might possibly mean for modern readers, but what it has always really meant. In its projection backwards, it can and does easily swallow

the *Poetics* whole, deleting at a stroke the dilemma and objections of neoclassical commentators and Victorian critics [on the specific question of Oedipus' guilt].' For further provocative analysis of Freud's approach to *Oedipus* cf. Cave (1988), 162–66.

57 Freud's is not the only system in which the Oedipus of Sophocles's play is universalised as a representative of humankind. This is the reading of Heidegger (2000), 112: 'Oedipus, who at the beginning is the savio[u]r and lord of the state, in the brilliance of glory and the grace of the gods, is hurled out of this seeming. This seeming is not just Oedipus' subjective view of himself, but that within which the appearing of his Dasein happens. In the end, he is unconcealed in his Being as the murderer of his father and the defiler of his mother. The path from this beginning in brilliance to this end in horror is a unique struggle between seeming (concealment and distortion) and unconcealment (Being)...But we should not see Oedipus only as the human being who meets his downfall; in Oedipus we must grasp that form of Greek Dasein in which this Dasein's fundamental passion ventures into what is wildest and most far-flung: the passion for the unveiling of Being – that is, the struggle over Being itself.' For Heidegger, Oedipus's actions involve that process of unconcealment of Being that makes him representative of Dasein. We shall be returning to Heidegger in the next chapter.

58 Cf. Goodhart (1978), 71; I take some details, but supplement them and re-direct them to my own argument's end. For any interpretation which believes itself to have purchase on the truth, the issues at stake are *discovered* or *revealed* as *already* thematised within the play.

59 Goodhart (1978), 68 remarks, 'Substituting the myth for such anti-mythic indications, reading in Sophocles' mythic equivocation ironically the myth itself, repeating Oedipus' mythopoetic gesture – the very Oedipal *méconnaissance* that Sophocles' play already "deconstructs" – criticism succeeds in subduing the profoundly critical nature that it found in literature to begin with, a literature whose very monstrosity – its superimposition of its own mythic conventions upon their arbitrariness – was the source of its uncanny attraction in the first place.' From a Derridan perspective, the monstrous, the uncanny, the *arrivant* throws deterministic thinking out of its comfort zone, though as the reception of Goodhart's own work suggests, deterministic thinking can accommodate the *arrivant* by marginalising and ignoring it.

60 Cf. Goldhill (2009), 22, in the course of a stimulating discussion of the analysis of irony.

61 Cave (1988), 10.

62 Goldhill (2009) is a distinguished recent addition to this long tradition. He notes (2009), 36 'the dark undertow, the sense of necessary failing, which Sophocles' repeated recognition of the misplaced certainties of the human rhetoric of *lusis* should encourage in the critic' and (2009), 37 that *Oedipus* 'constantly suggests that it is the moment that you have a superior knowledge about yourself that you are most vulnerable to self-deception and to self-destructive decisions.'

63 Lucas (1968), 127.

64 Cave (1988), 31 n.8.

65 Velleman (2003), 6; emphasis mine.

66 Velleman (2003), 21.

67 Velleman (2003), 20.

68 Remembering also that the narratives written in the past will also shift them in ways we cannot foresee, as those narratives are re-inscribed and 'translated' into new contexts, as we have seen with *Oedipus*. For studies of causality that treat it as a historical phenomenon see Kern (2004) on the modernist period; and, on postmodern narratives, Heise (1997). In his 'cultural history of causality' from 1830 to the present, Kern (2004) interestingly focuses on the act of murder (mainly as represented in literature), the specific causal factor or motive leading to it, and the sciences (e.g. genetics or neuroscience) and systems of thought (e.g. psychoanalysis, neuroscience) that develop and cluster around each proposed causal factor or motive. Interestingly, this period marks the rise of the 'detective novel', and the trope of Oedipus as detective has been a popular one. The prophet prospectively plots events in advance of their occurrence, the detective retrospectively after they have occurred. Both rely on the logic of repetition for their authority, for prophets that events subsequently map on to their plots, for detectives that their plots subsequently map on to events, and ideally for both that the two respective sequences should converge so as to be the same. The shift in focus from prophet to detective reflects, I suppose, a cultural re-alignment towards a nominally 'historicist' perspective.

69 Goodhart (1978), 66; emphasis mine.

70 Goodhart (1996), 27.

71 See Leonard (2005), 38–47.

72   Vernant and Vidal-Naquet (1988), 89–90.

73   Goodhart (1996), 250. When philosophy is seen to incorporate tragedy, it takes on some of the characteristics associated with it. This is especially the case with Enlightenment philosophies structured teleologically around realisation, which tend to be highly selective in the choice of tragedies they reference. Thus Eagleton (2003), 41 remarks, 'The most renowned tragic teleology is that of Hegel. There is a sense in which one could call his *Phenomenology of Spirit* a tragic text, insisting as it does that philosophy means "looking the negative in the face, and tarrying with it".' More magisterially, Steiner (1986), 2–3: 'The major philosophical systems since the French Revolution have been tragic systems. They have metaphorized the theological premise of the fall of man... To philosophize after Rousseau and Kant, to find a normative, conceptual phrasing for the psychic, social, and historical condition of man, is to think "tragically".' This has precipitated a powerful universalising concept, the *tragic*, in turn historicised by Most (2000), 20: 'we expect a "tragedy" to be "tragic". This expectation may sound self-evident, but in fact this "tragic" ethos is a modern construction, one whose links to the ancient genre of Greek "tragedy" are far more tenuous than its connections to philosophical and social developments over the last two centuries.'

74   Borges (1981), 65. The narrator comments, 'Two texts of unequal value inspired this undertaking. One is that philological fragment by Novalis... which outlines the theme of a *total* identification with a given author. The other is one of those parasitic books which situate Christ on a boulevard, Hamlet on La Cannebière or Don Quixote on Wall Street. Like all men of good taste, Menard abhorred these useless carnivals, fit only – as he would say – to produce the plebeian pleasures of anachronism or (what is worse) to enthral us with the elementary idea that all epochs are the same or are different.'

75   Borges (1981), 69.

76   Cf. Goodhart (1996), 160; also 174 and 194.

77   Goodhart (1996), 263; emphasis mine.

78   Borges (1981), 69.

79   Borges (1981), 66.

CHAPTER 4

1 The question asked by Morley (2000), which is both an elegant example of counterfactual narrative and a probing discussion of the implications of the approach.

2 Ferguson (1997), 1–90.

3 Thus Cowley (2001) is entitled *What If?* and Cowley (2002) *More What If?*; Roberts (2004) *What Might Have Been*. Counterfactual worlds are depressingly full of Nazis, who have become the symbols of this style of history, as the jackets of all these books attest. Counterfactual history (with the Holocaust as its theme) is successfully married with the genres of thriller and police procedural in Robert Harris's *Fatherland*; Ferguson (1997), 7 has some derogatory comments. Fiction that adopts a prophetic mode – utopian or dystopian (e.g. Orwell's *Nineteen Eighty-Four*), or science fiction – implicitly poses the 'what if…?' question and has clear affinities with counterfactual history.

4 Ferguson (1997), 18–19 cites the work of Geoffrey Hawthorn (1991) on 'plausible worlds' as an exception.

5 Ferguson (1997), 19.

6 Ferguson (1997), 53–55.

7 Ferguson (1997), 76–79.

8 See further Kennedy (2002), 120 n. 14.

9 Plutarch's 'parallel lives' (Cicero and Demosthenes, and so on) are the most famous, but reflect a wider tradition known as *synkrisis*, 'judging together'. Alexander became the touchstone for Roman achievement and the object of emulation for prominent Romans in life as well as literature; see Green (1978) and Isager (1993).

10 Helpful analyses of this episode in Suerbaum (1997), Morello (2002) and Oakley (2005).

11 Ferguson (1997), 11.

12 For modern 'takes' on this very counterfactual, see Toynbee (1969), 441–86 and Ober (2001).

13 On the interest of classical historians in chronological synchronicities, see Feeney (2007). The synchronicity here is not quite precise. For a detailed discussion of the episode's introduction by Livy at this precise point, see Morello (2002), 69–74.

14 One of the poems dubiously attributed to Virgil in the *Appendix Vergiliana*, the *Copa*, portrays the eponymous 'hostess' of the poem's

title advertising the delights of her hostelry. Appropriately, the final couplet of her pitch adduces the *carpe diem* motif of taking your pleasures as you may, which fully explains the caution of so resolute a figure as Livy: 'set out the wine and the dice; let him perish who thinks of the cares of tomorrow: Death, plucking at your ear, says "live while you can, I am on my way"' (*pone merum et talos; pereat qui crastina curat:/mors aurem vellens 'vivite' ait, 'venio',* 37–38). The serious historian devoted to deterministic explanation, like Einstein's God, does not play dice.

15   Cf. *Oxford Latin Dictionary* s.v. 1.

16   The events narrated in Book 1 (from the foundation of Rome to the expulsion of the kings) cover over 240 years. The pace slows down the further he goes: Book 9 covers 18 years, and by the time he reaches the crowded year of 43 BC, the start of the civil wars after the assassination of Julius Caesar, he needs five books (118–22) to cover it. For a perceptive analysis of the 'Tristram Shandy' effect in Livy's history – the longer you take to write, the more you have to write – see Henderson (1989).

17   Cf. Livy 9.17.9: 'then great men follow these others, if [Alexander] had occupied himself first with a war against Carthage before one with Rome, and had crossed to Italy as an old man' (*deinceps ingentes sequuntur, si Punicum Romano praevertisset bellum seniorque in Italiam traiecisset*). Ferguson (1997), 9–13 offers some examples of how counterfactual fictions soon become ludicrous if allowed to proliferate or stray beyond very closely defined initial premises.

18   Wood (2003), 73–77 has an excellent discussion of the etymology of *trivial*, from the words for 'three' and 'road', in respect of the Oedipus story.

19   Thus Morello (2002), 62 characterises the Alexander episode as 'a passage which, it so happens, one popular website [http://www.uchronia.net] lists as the first example of the genre'. Oakley (2005), 206 by contrast remarks, 'In general L[ivy] rather enjoys such speculation: note ii.1.3–6 (where he speculates on what would have happened had liberty from the kings come too soon)…how his speeches…and warning figures (see e.g. [9.]3.1–13) often present visions of the future different from what the narrative later records, and that the inverted *ni-* and *cum-*clauses are among his favourite constructions.'

20   Borges (1981), 44–54.

21   Borges's choice of setting in time and place, Britain in the First World War, recalls the classic thrillers of John Buchan and Erskine Childers.

22 Albert says, 'Before unearthing this letter, I had questioned myself about the ways in which a book can be infinite. I could think of nothing other than a cyclic volume, a circular one. A book whose last page was identical to the first, a book which had the possibility of continuing indefinitely' (Borges [1981], 50–51) – a book that sounds like Joyce's *Finnegan's Wake*.

23 Borges (1981), 51; emphasis original.

24 Yu Tsun also creates at the level of his plot, but re-creates his plot in his actions of visiting and killing Albert; both of these processes involve closure, as we will see later.

25 With apologies to the inimitable Gibbon (1994), 3.336. Ober (2001), 52–56 is less prudent in the closing pages of his counterfactual Alexander, though we are mercifully spared the obligatory Nazis.

26 Such a model of time underlies the theory of 'multiple universes' proposed to deal with the paradoxes of quantum physics; see Carroll (2010), 228–56. But this model is every bit as deterministic as the conventional linear model. As Morson (1994), 232–33 comments, 'In a deterministic singular universe, everything that could be is, and so with the plurality of universes. The difference is that multiple-universe determinism applies not to any one universe but to the universe of universes (to the meta-universe)…Choice loses much of its significance insofar as the significance of choice depends on its singularity and on what possibilities were left unactualized.'

27 Derived from the Latin *crux*, a cross. Cf. the definition offered in the *Oxford English Dictionary* s.v. 2: 'That *finally* decides between two rival hypotheses, proving the one and disproving the other; more loosely, relating to, or adapted to lead to such a decision; decisive, critical. Freq. in *trivial* use = "very important"' (emphasis mine).

28 Noted by Morello (2002), 73.

29 The adjective *prudens* is cognate with the verb *providere*, 'to see ahead', 'to have foresight'. But Herennius can be seen as much more than a sage; see next note.

30 The opinions attributed to Herennius here (and, at greater length in the corresponding narratives of Cassius Dio and Appian) preserve a philosophy of 'extreme proportional benefaction' amongst unequals, namely that the hatred of peoples who are in a state of enmity is proportionately equivalent to the love of those same peoples, once they have come into a relationship of friendship (Horky [2011], 133), a theory marked by Peripatetic language and concepts (Horky [2011], 132–40), and so historically plausible for the

late-fourth-century BC setting. Horky argues that our sources 'construct' Herennius as a 'Samnite philosopher', and trace this back to the Peripatetic Aristoxenus of Tarentum, a student of Aristotle, who said that Herennius was an interlocutor of Archytas of Tarentum and of Plato in old age, when he visited Tarentum; cf. Cicero *Cato maior* 41.

31   The verb *parare*, here translated as 'win' or 'acquire', is also used in Latin of 'preparation' for some intended end, and so can take on a weak providential sense of foreseeing that end. Gavius's utterance (*sententia*) would not bring into being the situation he wishes.

32   Oakley (2005), 24; Oakley's discussion has the section heading 'Wise and faulty deliberation and the tragedy of the Samnites' (2005), 23.

33   Ferguson (1997), 67 observes, 'To write history according to the conventions of a novel or a play is … to impose a new kind of determinism on the past: the teleology of the traditional narrative form', though he does concede that 'Literary genres are to some extent predictable; indeed, that is part of their appeal.' 'A *new* kind of determinism' is glossed as 'the teleology of the *traditional* narrative form', suggesting that at best teleology is only occluded in historiography (not least to, and by, its practitioners), and raising the question of whether historiography has ever been or will ever be a completely distinct genre, uncontaminated by other literary forms. Derrida (1980), exploring 'The Law of Genre' ('genres shall not be mixed') from a deconstructive perspective that views the problem from 'within' time, suggests that 'it may be impossible *not* to mix genres'.

34   Suerbaum (1997), 45: 'Der Warner ist der personifizierte Vertreter des alternativen Geschehens.'

35   Ovid does this with his literary heroines in the *Heroides*, which Liveley (2008) shows to be an exemplification of counterfactual thinking.

36   Plutarch, *Life of Pyrrhus* 19, cited by Morello (2002), 65–66, with bibliography on the fame of the speech, the problems of its dating and the authentication of its subject matter.

37   Ferguson (1997), 88.

38   Ferguson (1997), 87; cf. Ferguson (1997), 86: 'We should consider as plausible or probable *only those alternatives which we can show on the basis of contemporary evidence that contemporaries actually considered*' (emphasis original).

39   Morello (2002), 80–83.

40   Oakley (2005), 184 remarks that 'L[ivy] seems to be the first writer to use *destinare* in the sense "mark out".' The verb could be freighted with

more meaning than that, because in the exercise of counterfactual speculation, the argument has a conclusion: for those, whether it be Livy or a contemporary, who 'mark out' Papirius Cursor as the equal of Alexander the Great, if he had turned his forces against Italy, Alexander is *fated* to meet his match. The historian's utterance, like that of Jupiter in the *Aeneid*, sees to that.

41   Cave (1988), 10; cf. Chapter 3 above.

42   Cicero *De legibus* 1.5. For the editors of the *Cambridge Companion to Herodotus*, '[d]espite his shortcomings, flaws and errors, he is manifestly the first historian of the Western tradition': Dewald and Marincola (2006), xiii. Manifestly: etymologically, we can tap him with our hand (*manifestus*) to lay claim to him.

43   Pelling (2006), 108–9; he offers an excellent account of the dynamics of the interchanges in the presence of the tyrant, 109–10.

44   Pelling (2006), 110.

45   Although Herodotus was steeped in the ideas of the Ionian philosophers which were influential in particular for their argument from *to eikos*, the likely or plausible, most scholars see his eventual arrival in Athens and his exposure to its democratic institutions as crucial for the development of his historical thinking; cf. e.g. Dewald and Marincola (2006), 2; Pelling (2006), 116–17.

46   Koselleck (1979).

47   Carr (1987), 198.

48   Carr (1986), 45.

49   Morson (1994), 8.

50   Carr (1987), 198.

51   Strawson (2004), 428, also to be found in (2008), 189.

52   Strawson (2004), 436, also to be found in (2008), 196; cited are Sacks (1985), 110; Taylor (1989), 47 and 52; Ricoeur (1990), 158; all emphases original.

53   Strawson (2004), 429, also to be found in (2008), 190.

54   Strawson (2004), 430, also to be found in (2008), 190.

55   Strawson (2004), 430, also to be found in (2008), 191.

56   Strawson (2004), 433, also to be found in (2008), 194.

57   Strawson (2004), 432 n.7, also to be found in (with some variations) (2008), 193; perhaps it is not so easy after all to classify in this way, or does the passage of time have something to do with it?

58   As a narrating self with the benefit of hindsight after the completion of the plan, and thus beyond its end and 'outside' it, Yu Tsun's memory of

what happened leads him to remark with regret, 'I say it now, now that I have carried to its end a plan whose perilous nature no one can deny. I know its execution was terrible.' His narrating self knows that he killed a man (Stephen Albert) about whom his narrated self knew nothing at the point when he devised the plan, but who, in a conversation lasting 'scarcely an hour', impressed him hugely. Even so, Yu Tsun killed him, the intention attributed to his narrated self at the outset of the plan to make a point to his Chief: 'I wanted to prove to him that a yellow man could save his armies.' All citations from 'The Garden of the Forking Paths' in this and the following paragraph are from Borges (1981), 44–47.

59   These comments of Gillian Beer (2002), 134 on the act of reading are directed towards the reading of fiction, but *mutatis mutandis* apply to a work of history as well, where the outcome may well be (and often is) known, and chime in also with what was said above about counterfactuals: 'The tug of the story is towards ending and the novelist and fiction writer conjure up an extraordinary array of devices to thwart and delay conclusion (and at the same time satisfy the reader) ... The reader must want to know the future, but one of the principal pleasures of reading is the reader's power of imagining multiple alternative outcomes at every moment of the text. The writer spreads out a fan of possibilities. The reader hypothesises the turns of event and feeling. We are pleased to be disappointed as well as pleased to have our hypothesis confirmed. That pleasure depends on fiction's constant tribute to the alternative futures loaded into the reader's imagination. Curiously, these alternative futures can survive even into a second reading...', or, I could add, into the first reading of a work of history where the course of events may be already familiar. See also my analysis in Chapter 3 above of Morson's assertion that even a first reading of *Oedipus* can, for better or worse, partake of the experience of a second reading.

60   The addition of the adjective 'cowardly' to 'felicity' may mark the intrusion of the narrating self's viewpoint in the actual aftermath of Albert's murder.

61   And committing the cardinal sin for Goodhart (Chapter 3 above) of reading the end of literature so as to claim the truth you find there as your own.

62   This traffic can go both ways: as Yu Tsun plots what he *has to* do, he becomes the self that he *is*.

63   Morson (1994), 230.

64   Strawson (2004), 431, 432 and 449, also to be found in (2008), 192, 193 and 206; the last reference is the source of the citation.

65 The hand is significantly involved once more in expressing the experience of temporality; see Derrida's essay on 'Heidegger's Hand', in Derrida (2008), II.27–62.

66 Heidegger (1962), 185.

67 Heidegger (1962), 38; all emphasis in citations from Heidegger original.

68 Heidegger (1962), 39.

69 Heidegger (1962), 39.

70 Cf. Inwood (2000), 58: 'In extreme depression or anxiety, the closest that we come in our waking state to lacking care, we find it hard to will or to wish for anything, even for release from our condition.'

71 Not forgetting Oedipus – perhaps.

72 Cf. Heidegger (1962), 377: *'Temporality is the primordial "outside-of-itself" in and for itself.* We therefore call the phenomena of the future, the character of having been, and the Present the *"ecstases"* of temporality.' Taylor (2007), 56 suggests, 'In a sense, Augustine may be thought to have foreshadowed the three ekstaseis of Heidegger.' But only in a sense; the language of foreshadowing suggests Taylor's prophetic emplotment of intellectual history as repetition, with Heidegger representing more of the same.

73 See Heidegger (1962), 372 n. 3 for the hyphen in *Zu-kunft*, and for the etymological association he suggests with *zukommen*.

74 We have seen Herennius variously constructed as a Peripatetic philosopher, as a counterfactual historian *avant la lettre*, and now as a Heideggerian-to-be. Within this perspective, texts from the past do not simply determine our interpretation of them, such that we could say definitively who or what Herennius was, but are instead fields of potential read against our current 'care'. More on this shortly.

75 Heidegger (1962), 473–74.

76 Heidegger (1962), 459.

77 Cf. Heidegger (1972), 24: 'a regard for metaphysics still prevails even in the intention to overcome metaphysics. Therefore our task is to cease all overcoming, and leave metaphysics to itself.' Vattimo (2011), 110 puts this Heideggerian outlook well: 'even at the risk of adopting a mistaken position, one must assume the responsibility of a project. And this project will be more authentic the more it surrenders the claim to attain the truth once and for all, which would be to deny its basic objective.' Vattimo glosses 'a mistaken position' as 'Heidegger's Nazi error'.

78 Thus Strawson's metaphysics favours nouns and nominal forms (one *is* an 'Episodic' or a 'Diachronic'), a quasi-Cratylan gesture that would point and name. In contrast, Heidegger's philosophy shifts Being from an abstract noun to a verbal one, a gerund that signifies action over time.

79 Rorty (1978).

80 Rorty (1995), 203.

81 Runciman (2010), 120–21; emphasis original.

82 Runciman (2010), 123.

83 Strawson (2004), 433, also to be found in (2008), 194; emphasis mine.

84 Recall that for Aristotle, the 'now' is not a point in time, without dimension, but a moving boundary which separates past from future. Two such boundaries would demarcate a period of time, or episode. The Episodic still finds himself 'within' time.

CHAPTER 5

1 Barthes (1967), 30; cf. Chapter 1 above.

2 For a recent discussion of the notion of creation out of nothing in the context of Augustine's broader theological thinking, see Harrison (2006), 74–114.

3 See Blumenberg (1981); on Augustine, 48–50.

4 Rorty (1989), 73.

5 In *Poetics* 1450b31, Aristotle describes a 'middle' as when 'one thing comes after another, and then another after that'; the temporality of 'after' gives rise, as we have seen in Chapter 3, to the search for some thing that can be accounted an antecedent cause.

6 For the philosophical problems surrounding creation, time and cause Plato's account throws up, see the concise discussion in Sedley (2007), 98–107.

7 Sedley (2007), 204.

8 See Sedley (2007), 174–81. Thus: what produces the eye and what is it for?

9 In such a work, a methodological statement would say that the study of nature has its approach which begins 'after the manner of poetry' (*kata poiēsin*) first of all from first things; and where the word 'natural' springs to our lips as a shorthand epistemological validation, 'poetical' would take its place.

10 Cf. Kahn (1985).

11 What follows compresses the complex relationship between the early atomists, Aristotle and Epicurus, and skews it towards the latter for the sake of the present argument; for a fuller account see Furley (1989), 1–13 and 103–14.

12 See Kennedy (2002), 70–71, drawing on the discussion of Beer (1983), 53.

13 Cf. Locke (1992), 176–83.

14 For informative analyses of this passage, see Schrijvers (1970), 255–61; Buchheit (1971), English translation (2007); Kenney (1974), excellent on the rhetorical structure.

15 This puns etymologically on *superstition*.

16 See Furley (1989), 2 for a discussion of the imagery, and for the distinction Lucretius draws between the 'world' [*mundus*] that is local to us and the infinite 'universe' [*omne immensum*] that lies beyond.

17 The Latin *terminus*, boundary-stone, is also the word that gives the English word 'term'.

18 For the chief texts cf. Long and Sedley (1987), 1.44–46. In 1.958–83, Lucretius argues that the universe (*omne*, 958) is not limited (*finitum*, 959) along any of its paths, for if so, it ought to have an extremity. Suppose existing space is bounded, then imagine somebody going to what he thinks is the outermost edge and throwing a spear. Either it flies on or hits something; in either case, he is not where he thought he was, the edge.

19 See the discussion of Sedley (2007), 136–39 and 155–66.

20 See Sorabji (1983), 213 for discussion and full references.

21 In addressing his patron in 1.143–45, Lucretius represents himself as working long into the night 'seeking by what words and what poetry [*quo carmine*] I may at last be able to open out [*praepandere*] before your mind clear lights, whereby you may be able to see right into hidden things'. The sense of the rare verb *praepandere* is hard to pin down, as Farrell (2001), 41–42 points out. I wonder whether it metaphorically refers to unrolling a scroll before someone so as to show them something?

22 For instance Furley (1989), 12 has seen the atomist idea of an infinite universe as an important component in thinking about the problem of motion.

23 Lucretius compares these atoms, which do not have an infinite number of shapes, to the letters of the alphabet, which can be combined to form a multiplicity of different words (1.912–14). That the number of letters in the alphabet is limited is crucial to the analogy.

24 See Long and Sedley (1987), 1.41 on the background to the Epicurean doctrine of 'minimal parts', which again arose as a response to the challenges posed by the infinite: 'The atomism of the fifth century B.C. originated at least partly as an answer to certain of Zeno of Elea's paradoxes, which drew absurd consequences from the supposition that a finite magnitude contains an infinite number of parts: the whole magnitude, being the sum of an infinity of parts, must be infinitely large; and motion over any finite distance is impossible because it requires traversing separately each of its infinity of component distances.' For the relevance of Zeno's paradoxes of motion to theories of time, see Sorabji (1983), 321–35.

25 See further Kennedy (2006), 240–42.

26 Schrijvers (1970), 259 suggests that 'breaking through the confining bolts of nature's gates' (1.71) alludes to the Roman practice of opening the gates of the temple of Janus when war is declared.

27 And is so only insofar as the explanation is of something that unfolds in time. Thus explanation takes a narrative form in modern evolutionary biology and in certain versions of cosmology (e.g. the Big Bang), as it does in Lucretius's account of the emergence of life and human society in Book 5; in Epicurean physics, the coming into being and dissolution of atomic compounds partakes of narrative form, though the atom itself, never created and never destroyed and never changing, escapes those bounds.

28 Rouse (1996), 181 suggests that 'the practices of scientific research and the knowledge which results from them acquire their intelligibility and significance from their being situated within a narrative.' Rouse offers a Heideggerian understanding of action, arguing that narrative is not a structure imposed from without on an unnarrativised sequence of events. Rather the intelligibility of action depends on those events already belonging to a field of possible narratives.

29 Lyotard (1984), 31.

30 The subtitle of Lyotard (1984), *A Report on Knowledge*, suggests a similar narrative role for its author!

31 Buchheit (1971), 305 n. 1, English translation (2007), 106 n. 7, compares the phrase *spolia referre*.

32 For the philosophical ramifications of this see Furley (1989), 7–8.

33 See Quint (1993), 31–46, discussed in Chapter 2 above.

34 See Kennedy (1999) for the narrative significance of the triumph ceremony, and the journey more generally, in the conception of Rome as a universal empire.

35 Buchheit (1971), 305–8, English translation (2007), 108–11.
36 Buchheit (1971), 309, English translation (2007), 112–13.
37 And also, subsequently, in Virgil's *Aeneid*, of Augustus Caesar, who, in Anchises's prophecy to Aeneas in Book 6, 'will extend the empire beyond the Garamantes and the Indians, where a land lies outside the stars, outside the paths of the year and the sun, where Atlas, bearer of the heavens, turns on his shoulders the axis studded with fiery stars' (*super et Garamantas et Indos/proferet imperium; iacet extra sidera tellus,/ extra anni solisque uias, ubi caelifer Atlas/axem umero torquet stellis ardentibus aptum*, 6.794–97).
38 Referred to by both Seneca the Elder (*Suasoriae* 1) and Quintilian (3.8.16).
39 Buchheit (1971), 312–14, English translation (2007), 116–19.
40 Hippolytus, *Refutation of all Heresies* 1.13.2; Cicero, *Academica* 2.55 (*ais Democritum dicere innumerabiles esse mundos*); cf. Furley (1987), 139–40; Sedley (2007), 136–38.
41 I have explored this in detail in Kennedy (2002).
42 Shapin and Schaffer (1985), in perhaps the most influential of all books in science studies, explore what they present as the complementary programmes during the English civil wars and their aftermath of the political philosopher Thomas Hobbes as he writes *Leviathan* and the natural philosopher Boyle as he develops the air pump. For an incisive summary of Shapin and Schaffer's approach, see Latour (1993), 15–29.
43 See Latour (1993) and especially (1999), 216–65, which reads Plato's *Gorgias* from a science-studies perspective, and (2004), on the Cave in Plato's *Republic*. For further discussion, see Kennedy (2010).
44 Netz (1999) explores the historical development of deduction in Greek mathematics, and plots Plato's appropriation of it for his ethical discourse. For a witty, perceptive and intellectually engaged review of Netz, see Latour (2008).
45 See Gross and Levitt (1994); Ross (1996); Labinger and Collins (2001).
46 See e.g. Drayton (2000).
47 Murphy (2004).
48 König and Whitmarsh (2007), 3.
49 Schiesaro (2007), 52–53.
50 Barrow (1995), 47; for further comment on this extract see Kennedy (2002), 105–6 and 129–30.
51 Kennedy (2002), 71–72 and 108–10.
52 Kennedy (2002), 68–69.

53 Kennedy (2002), 85–86.

54 Long and Sedley (1987), 1.102–12; also Sedley (2007), 164–65. The imagery of *swerve* (*clinamen*) is associated with that of the 'direct route' associated with determinism, examined in Chapter 4 above.

55 Hawking (1988), 175.

56 Cf. Lucretius 3.1042–44: *ipse Epicurus obit decurso lumine vitae,/qui genus humanum ingenio superavit et omnis/restinxit, stellas exortus ut aetherius sol* ('Epicurus himself died when his life's daylight had run its course, who surpassed the human race with his intellect and extinguished the light of all, as the sun risen in the sky quenches the stars'). The conceit here was used of the deified rulers of the Hellenistic world, and later of Augustus; cf. Doblhofer (1966), 86–91.

57 For the atom's role in ideologies of the individual both in the *De rerum natura* and the modern world see Kennedy (2006), 243–52.

58 Disturbing too for the scholarly orthodoxy which would seek to read off Republican sympathies from Lucretius's poem and are puzzled by the failure of Epicureanism to emerge as a source of opposition to the principate; cf. Kennedy (forthcoming). That role fell to another philosophical school, the Stoics.

59 Cf. Blumenberg (1981), 49.

60 Rheinberger (1997), 22.

61 Nobody nowadays accepts Epicurean atomic theory to be 'true' in the final sense that Lucretius claims for it, and the atom as an *epistemic thing* or *scientific object*, in the terminology of 'applied metaphysics' used by Rheinberger (1997) and Daston (2000) respectively, has undergone significant transformations over time; cf. Kennedy (2002), 61–62. These approaches are inflected by the Heideggerian view on history from within time explored in Chapter 4 above, which assesses texts in terms of unrealised potentialities rather than definitive judgements of right and wrong. But if Lucretius's text, as Runciman (2010) suggests (cf. Chapter 4 above) of Plato, Hobbes and Marx and Engels, is found wanting in the indicative mode (i.e. it no longer unequivocally points to something 'real' that is 'there'), it retains its power to excite in the optative (its aspiration to a final theory that excludes the supernatural; Greenblatt [2011] recounts the intellectual ferment generated by the rediscovery of Lucretius's text in 1417 by Poggio Bracciolini).

62 Bacon (1996), 480; emphasis mine.

63 See Yates (1975), especially 1–28; the device of Charles V mentioned below is reproduced as Plate 3a.

64 See the analysis of Blumenberg (1983), 309–23.

65 Rosenthal (1971), 228.

66 This notion underlies Salomon's House in the *New Atlantis*, which embodies an ideal of a research institute that was to be realised later in the seventeenth century in the foundation of the Royal College of Physicians, where according to a contemporary, Walter Charleton, 'you may behold Salomon's house in reality', and the Royal Society of London.

67 Writing of this verse from Daniel in 1608 in his *Refutation of Philosophies*, Bacon asks, 'What else can the prophet mean … in speaking about the last times? Does he not imply that the passing to and fro or perambulation of the round earth and the increase or multiplication of science were destined to the same age and century?' Rees (in Bacon [2004], lxii suggests that 'Bacon's is a work of Providence, and a fulfilment of the Daniel prophecy … which (as Bacon understands it) means that Providence has ordained that the voyages of exploration and scientific advance are destined to be coeval.' Another part of the *Instauratio Magna* is entitled *Parasceue ad historiam naturalem et experimentalem. Parasceue* means 'preparation', but in the Greek New Testament it refers to the day of preparation for the Sabbath, when all tasks have to be completed so that the Sabbath can be the Day of Rest. Bacon means not the weekly Sabbath, but the ultimate Sabbath of the Day of Judgement. Bacon's own *parasceue* is thus written in expectation of the imminent fulfilment of Daniel's prophecy.

68 Bacon (2004), 11, as translated by Gareth Rees.

69 Bacon (2004), 155; emphasis original.

70 The effectiveness and utility of such interventions were a visible sign of truth, according to the same aphorism: 'Among the signs none is more certain or noble than that derived from fruits. For the discovery of fruits and works as it were guarantees and underwrites the truth of philosophies': Bacon (2004), 117.

71 Bacon (2004), 117.

72 Bacon (2007), 9–11.

73 Cf. Bono (1995), 216.

74 Bacon (2004), 195.

75 For other ancient examples of the analogy of letters see Blumenberg (1981), 36–46. On the metaphor of the genetic 'code' see Doyle (1997), 86–108 and Kay (2000).

76 Derrida (1976), 15.

77 Derrida (1976), 15 n. directs his readers to the classic historical survey in Curtius (1953), 302–47.

78 Derrida (1976), 18.

79 Bono (1995), especially 123–246.

80 Bono (1995), 11.

81 Biagioli (2006), 220.

82 Biagioli (2006), 220.

83 Morson (1994), 55; emphasis original.

84 Shapin and Schaffer (1985), 76.

85 These last three quotations are from Latour (1993), 18.

86 Latour (2000) got himself into hot water, one feels sure quite deliberately, by claiming that the Pharaoh Ramses II did not die of tuberculosis, in spite of the fact that traces of Koch's bacillus were found in his mummy. Koch's bacillus was not isolated until 1882, and such a diagnosis would have meant nothing to the Pharaoh or his physicians or formed the basis of any of their actions. Such retrojection of a causation now taken to be universally true causes a headache for historiography, as Latour suggests, unless it is willing to allow hindsight to override the outlook of the historical actors themselves – which is the imperialist attitude in all its glory: we're right, so just suck it up.

87 As in Pope's epitaph for Sir Isaac Newton: 'Nature and Nature's Laws lay hid in Night./God said, Let Newton be! And all was Light.'

88 Latour (1993).

89 Latour (1993), 40 does not invoke Koselleck, but rather the work of François Furet (1981) on the French Revolution: 'The events of 1789 were no more revolutionary than the modern world has been modern. The actors and chroniclers of 1789 used the notion of revolution to understand what was happening to them, and to influence their own fate.' Cf. Kennedy (2002), 34: '*Revolution* is one of the most potent terms in the rhetoric of scientific, and scientistic, discourses. A term that could invoke a recurrence, a periodically returning cycle, is used of a radical and irreversible reordering, a notion that develops hand in hand with linear, unidirectional conceptions of time. Science marks its "progress" by "discovery" of transcendent entities (Newton's laws, the gene, the theory of relativity) whose miraculous apparition marks the beginning of a new order of time and renders the past archaic at a stroke.' The key work of *Begriffsgeschichte* on the 'Scientific Revolution' is Shapin (1996).

90 So far as I am aware, Latour does not actually refer to the myth; but bear with me.

91 Rheinberger (1997), 28.

92 Eco (1997).

93 Jager (1993), 88.

94 See the analysis of Jager (1993), 91–95; also 134–39.

95 The mortality of the human writers of scripture is for Augustine a crucial part of its authority: 'Indeed, by the very fact of their death the solid authority of your utterances published by them is in a sublime way "stretched out" over everything inferior. While they were alive on earth, it was not stretched out to express this supreme authority' (13.15.16).

96 Jager (1993), 95.

97 Elsewhere also in 1.832 and 3.260; on these passages see the excellent analysis of Farrell (2001), 39–51.

98 See Sedley (1998), 35–61.

99 Farrell (2001), 5. Compare Derrida's preference (2002), 371 for the term *mondialisation* (and sometimes *mondialatinisation*) over *globalisation* to emphasise what he sees as its European, Christian and Roman filiation. Vattimo (2011), 116 makes a similar point at the level of culture rather than language: 'Metaphysics, the rational order in which every entity is fitted securely into the chain of cause and effect, reaches its end at the moment at which it reveals itself to be intolerable – precisely because fully realised. European colonialism and imperialism were the modalities through which metaphysics became the order of the world.'

100 In his famous essay on 'The Task of the Translator', Walter Benjamin (1996), 262 wrote, 'Where the literal quality of the text takes part directly, without any mediating sense, in true language, in the Truth, or in doctrine, this text is unconditionally translatable.'

101 Biagioli (2006), 220.

102 Bono (1995), 193–98 shows how radically this broke with earlier configurations of the Book.

103 Cited in Biagioli (2006), 219.

104 Derrida (1976), 15.

105 Biagioli (2006), 242.

106 This point is alluded to in Biagioli (2006), 247, but is argued explicitly in Biagioli (2003), 576.

107 Biagioli (2006), 252; emphasis mine.

108 Derrida (1976).

109 Penrose (1989), 95.

110 Argued in greater detail in Kennedy (2011).

111 The sense of divine 'giving' or 'granting' of something that is transcendentally there in Manilius's use of *dare* recalls Jupiter's promise in *Aeneid* 1.279: *imperium sine fine **dedi***. Compare the way English 'points to' something in the deictic phrase 'there is' with the German *es gibt*.

112 Though note how Augustine distributes Aristotle's distinction between actual and potential infinity, associating the former with humankind's perspective, the latter with God's.

113 Penrose (1989), 112.

114 *Representation*, with its suggestion of the re-presentation of a prior entity is a tricky word in the anti-realists' vocabulary. Cf. the discussion in Kennedy (2002), 36 and 72, which draws a distinction between the realists' representation *of* (a prior entity) and the anti-realists' representation *as* (a consequent entity).

115 Netz (1999), 6–7; emphasis mine.

116 Netz (1999), 107.

117 Netz (1999), 161.

118 Netz (1999), 32.

119 Netz (1999), 216–35. Netz seeks to distance himself from science studies, but cannot quite resist a pun on Shapin's name in his own title, *The Shaping of Deduction in Greek Mathematics*: (1999), 3 n. 1. Latour (2008), 441 won't let him get way with this coyness, proclaiming Netz's book to be 'without contest, the most important book of science studies to appear since Shapin and Schaffer's *Leviathan and the Air-Pump*' (1985).

120 Netz (1999), 7 n.5.

121 Netz (1999), 292–93. Latour (2008), 443 suggests that what Netz does 'is to transport us back in time to where there was no geometry, no apodeictic reasoning, no deduction, and to when each of those practices had to be devised from scratch without relying on any precedent'.

122 Netz (1999), 214 puts it thus: 'When doing mathematics, one does nothing else'.

123 Netz (1999), 277–92, especially 289–90.

124 Netz (1999), 290.

125 Latour (2008), 445–46.

126 See now Allen (2010) for a searching exploration.

127 Latour (2004), 10–18; the quotation comes from 10–11.

BIBLIOGRAPHY

Ahl, Frederick (1991), *Sophocles' Oedipus: Evidence and Self-Conviction*. Ithaca, NY and London: Cornell University Press

Allen, Danielle S. (2010), *Why Plato Wrote*. Chichester: Wiley-Blackwell

Annas, Julia (1975), 'Aristotle, Number and Time', *The Philosophical Quarterly* 25, 97–113

Auerbach, Erich (1959), *Scenes from the Drama of European Literature: Six Essays*. Translated by Ralph Manheim. Cambridge, MA: Harvard University Press

Austin, J.L. (1962), *How to Do Things with Words*. Oxford: Oxford University Press

Austin, R.G. (1971), *P. Vergili Maronis Aeneidos Liber Primus*. Oxford: Clarendon Press

Bacon, Francis (1996), *The Major Works*. Edited with an Introduction and Notes by Brian Vickers. Oxford: Oxford University Press

— (2004), *The Instauratio Magna Part II; Novum Organum and Associated Texts*. Edited with Introduction, Notes, Commentaries and facing-page translations by Graham Rees with Maria Wakely. Oxford: Clarendon Press

— (2007), *The Instauratio Magna Part III: Historia Naturalis et Experimentalis: Historia Ventorum and Historia Vitae & Mortis*. Edited with Introduction, Notes, Commentaries, and facing-page translations by Graham Rees with Maria Wakely. Oxford: Clarendon Press

Barrow, John (1995), 'Theories of Everything', in Cornwell (1995, ed.), 45–63

Barthes, Roland (1967), *Writing Degree Zero*. Translated by Annette Lavers and Colin Smith. New York: Hill and Wang

— (1986), *The Rustle of Language*. Translated by Richard Howard. Oxford: Basil Blackwell

Beer, Gillian (1983), *Darwin's Plots: Evolutionary Narrative in Darwin, George Eliot and Nineteenth Century Fiction*. London: Routledge and Kegan Paul

— (2002), 'Storytime and its Futures', in Ridderbos (2002, ed.), 126–42

245

Benjamin, Walter (1996), *Selected Writings*, vol. I: *1913–1926*. Cambridge, MA and London: Belknap Press of Harvard University Press

Bennington, Geoffrey (1990), 'Postal Politics: The Institution of the Nation', in Bhabha (1990, ed.), 121–37

Bennington, Geoffrey and Jacques Derrida (1993), *Jacques Derrida*. Translated by Geoffrey Bennington. Chicago and London: University of Chicago Press

Bettini, Maurizio (1991), *Anthropology and Roman Culture: Kinship, Time, Images of the Soul*. Translated by John Van Sickle. Baltimore, MD and London: Johns Hopkins University Press

— (2008), 'Weighty Words, Suspect Speech: *fari* in Roman Culture', *Arethusa* 41, 313–75

Bettinson, H. (2003, trans.), *Saint Augustine: City of God*. London: Penguin Books

Bhabha, Homi K. (1990, ed.), *Nations and Narrations*. London and New York: Routledge

Biagioli, Mario (2003), 'Stress in the Book of Nature: The Supplemental Logic of Galileo's Realism', *Modern Language Notes* 118, 557–85

— (2006), *Galileo's Instruments of Credit: Telescopes, Images, Secrecy*. Chicago and London: University of Chicago Press

Bloomer, W. Martin (2005, ed.), *The Contest of Language: Before and Beyond Nationalism*. Notre Dame, IN: University of Notre Dame Press

Blumenberg, Hans (1981), *Die Lesbarkeit der Welt*. Frankfurt am Main: Suhrkamp Verlag

— (1983), *The Legitimacy of the Modern Age*. Translated by Robert M. Wallace. Cambridge, MA and London: MIT Press

Bono, James J. (1995), *The Word of God and the Languages of Man: Interpreting Nature in Early Modern Science and Medicine*, vol. 1: *Ficino to Descartes*. Madison, WI and London: University of Wisconsin Press

Borges, Jorge Luis (1981), *Labyrinths*. Harmondsworth: Penguin Books

Bostock, David (2006), *Space, Time, Matter, and Form*. Oxford: Clarendon Press

Brooks, Peter (1984), *Reading for the Plot: Design and Intention in Narrative*. Cambridge, MA and London: Harvard University Press

Brown, Peter (2000), *Augustine of Hippo: A Biography*. New Edition. Berkeley, CA and Los Angeles: University of California Press

Buchheit, Vinzenz (1971), 'Epikurs Triumph des Geistes', *Hermes* 99, 303–23

— (2007), 'Epicurus' Triumph of the Mind', in Gale (2007, ed.), 104–31

Burnyeat, Myles F. (1987), 'Wittgenstein and Augustine *de Magistro*', *Proceedings of the Aristotelian Society* supplementary volume 61, 1–24

Cameron, Averil (1989, ed.), *History as Text: The Writing of Ancient History.* London: Duckworth

Caputo, John D. and Michael J. Scanlon (2005, eds), *Augustine and Postmodernism: Confessions and Circumfession.* Bloomington, IN and Indianapolis, IN: Indiana University Press

Carlsen, J., B. Due, O. Due and B. Poulsen (1993, eds), *Alexander the Great: Reality and Myth.* Rome: Analecta Romani Instituti Danici suppl. xx

Carr, David (1986), *Time, Narrative, and History.* Bloomington, IN and Indianapolis, IN: Indiana University Press

— (1987), Review of Reinhart Koselleck, *Futures Past. History and Theory* 26, 197–204

Carroll, Sean (2010), *From Eternity to Here: The Quest for the Ultimate Theory of Time.* New York: Dutton

Cave, Terence (1988), *Recognitions: A Study in Poetics.* Oxford: Clarendon Press

Chadwick, Henry (1991), *Saint Augustine* Confessions. Oxford: Oxford University Press

— (2001), *Augustine: A Very Short Introduction.* Oxford: Oxford University Press

Chatman, Seymour (2009), 'Backwards', *Narrative* 17, 31–55

Commager, Steele (1981), 'Fateful Words: Some Conversations in *Aeneid* 4', *Arethusa* 14, 101–14

Conington, J. (1876), *P. Vergili Maronis Opera.* 3 vols. London: Whittaker and Co.

Conte, Gian Biagio (1986), *The Rhetoric of Imitation: Genre and Poetic Memory in Virgil and Other Latin Poets.* Ithaca, NY and London: Cornell University Press

Coope, Ursula (2005), *Time for Aristotle: Physics IV.10–14.* Oxford: Clarendon Press

Cornwell, John (1995, ed.), *Nature's Imagination: The Frontiers of Scientific Vision.* Oxford: Oxford University Press

Courcelle, Pierre (1950), *Recherches sur les Confessions de Saint Augustin.* Paris: E. de Boccard

— (1963), *Confessions de Saint Augustin dans la Tradition littéraire: Antécédents et Postérité.* Paris: Etudes Augustiniennes

Coward, Harold and Toby Foshay (1992, eds), *Derrida and Negative Theology.* Albany, NY: State University of New York Press

Cowley, Robert (2001, ed.), *What If? Military Historians Imagine What Might Have Been.* Basingstoke and Oxford: Pan Macmillan

— (2002, ed.), *More What If? Eminent Historians Imagine What Might Have Been.* Basingstoke and Oxford: Pan Macmillan

Culler, Jonathan (1981), *The Pursuit of Signs: Semiotics, Literature, Deconstruction*. London and Henley: Routledge and Kegan Paul
— (2007), *The Literary in Theory*. Stanford, CA: Stanford University Press
Currie, Gregory (2010), *Narratives and Narrators: A Philosophy of Stories*. Oxford: Oxford University Press
Currie, Mark (2007), *About Time: Narrative, Fiction and the Philosophy of Time*. Edinburgh: Edinburgh University Press
Curtius, Ernst Robert (1953), *European Literature and the Latin Middle Ages*. Translated by Willard R. Trask. London and Henley: Routledge and Kegan Paul
Danto, Arthur C. (1968), *Analytical Philosophy of History*. Cambridge: Cambridge University Press
— (2007), *Narration and Knowledge*. New York: Columbia University Press
Daston, Lorraine (2000, ed.), *Biographies of Scientific Objects*. Chicago and London: University of Chicago Press
Dawe, R.D. (2006), *Sophocles: Oedipus Rex*. Revised edition. Cambridge: Cambridge University Press
Dawson, John David (2002), *Christian Figural Reading and the Fashioning of Identity*. Berkeley, CA, Los Angeles and London: University of California Press
Dawson, Paul (2009), 'The Return of Omniscience in Contemporary Fiction', *Narrative* 17, 143–61
Depew, Mary and Dirk Obbink (2000, eds), *Matrices of Genre: Authors, Canons, and Society*. Cambridge, MA and London: Harvard University Press
Derrida, Jacques (1976), *Of Grammatology*. Translated by Gayatri Chakravorty Spivak. Baltimore, MD and London: Johns Hopkins University Press
— (1980), 'The Law of Genre', *Critical Inquiry* 7, 55–81
— (1982), *Margins of Philosophy*. Translated by Alan Bass. Brighton: Harvester Press
— (1992), 'Of an Apocalyptic Tone Newly Adopted in Philosophy', in Coward and Foshay (1992, eds), 25–71
— (1995), *Points…Interviews 1974–94*. Translated by Peggy Kamuf. Stanford, CA: Stanford University Press
— (2002), *Negotiations: Interventions and Interviews 1971–2001*. Translated by Elizabeth Rottenberg. Stanford, CA: Stanford University Press
— (2005), *Rogues*. Translated by P.-A. Brault and M. Naas. Stanford, CA: Stanford University Press

— (2008), *Psyche: Inventions of the Other.* Edited by Peggy Kamuf and Elizabeth Rottenberg. 2 vols. Stanford, CA: Stanford University Press

Derrida, Jacques and Maurizio Ferraris (2001), *A Taste for the Secret.* Translated by Giacomo Donis. Cambridge: Polity

Dewald, Carolyn and John Marincola (2006, eds), *The Cambridge Companion to Herodotus.* Cambridge: Cambridge University Press

Dobbin, R.F. (1995), 'Julius Caesar in Jupiter's Prophecy, *Aeneid* Book 1', *Classical Antiquity* 14, 5–40

Doblhofer, Ernst (1966), *Die Augustuspanegyrik des Horaz in formalhistorischer Sicht.* Heidelberg: Georg Olms

Doyle, Richard (1997), *On Beyond Living: Rhetorical Transformations of the Life Sciences.* Stanford, CA: Stanford University Press

Drayton, Richard (2000), *Nature's Government: Science, Imperial Britain, and the 'Improvement' of the World.* Oxford: Oxford University Press

Eagleton, Terry (2003), *Sweet Violence: The Idea of the Tragic.* Malden, MA and Oxford: Blackwell Publishing

Eco, Umberto (1997), *The Search for the Perfect Language.* Translated by James Fentress. London: Fontana Press

Edwards, Catharine (1996), *Writing Rome: Textual Approaches to the City.* Cambridge: Cambridge University Press

— (1999, ed.), *Roman Presences: Receptions of Rome in European Culture, 1789–1945.* Cambridge: Cambridge University Press

Eliot, T.S. (1957), *On Poetry and Poets.* London: Faber and Faber

Farrell, Joseph (2001), *Latin Language and Latin Culture: From Ancient to Modern Times.* Cambridge: Cambridge University Press

Feeney, D.C. (1991), *The Gods in Epic: Poets and Critics of the Classical Tradition.* Oxford: Clarendon Press

— (2007), *Caesar's Calendar: Ancient Time and the Beginnings of History.* Berkeley, CA, Los Angeles and London: University of California Press

Ferguson, Niall (1997), *Virtual History: Alternatives and Counterfactuals.* London, Basingstoke and Oxford: Macmillan

Fludernik, Monika (2005), 'Time in Narrative', in Herman, Jahn and Ryan (2005, eds), 608–12

Forster, E.M. (2005), *Aspects of the Novel.* London: Penguin Books

Fowler, Don (1997), 'Virgilian Narrative: Story-telling', in Martindale (1997, ed.), 259–70

Fowles, John (1971), *The French Lieutenant's Woman.* London: Panther Books

Fredriksen, P. (1986), 'Paul and Augustine: Conversion Narratives, Orthodox Traditions and the Retrospective Self', *Journal of Theological Studies* 37: 3–34

Fukuyama, Francis (1989), 'The End of History?', *The National Interest* 16, 3–18

— (1992), *The End of History and the Last Man*. London: Penguin Books

Furet, François (1981), *Interpreting the French Revolution*. Translated by Elborg Forsher. Cambridge: Cambridge University Press

Furley, David (1987), *The Greek Cosmologists*, vol. I: *The Formation of the Atomic Theory and its Earliest Critics*. Cambridge: Cambridge University Press

— (1989), *Cosmic Problems: Essays on Greek and Roman Philosophy of Nature*. Cambridge: Cambridge University Press

Gale, Monica R. (2007, ed.), *Oxford Readings in Classical Studies: Lucretius*. Oxford: Oxford University Press

Genette, Gérard (1980), *Narrative Discourse*. Translated by Jane E. Lewin. Oxford: Basil Blackwell

Gersh, Stephen (2010), 'Negative Theology and Conversion: Derrida's Neoplatonic Compulsions', in Leonard (2010, ed.), 101–32

Gibbon, Edward (1994), *The History of the Decline and Fall of the Roman Empire*. 3 vols. Edited by David Womersley. London: Allen Lane the Penguin Press

Gillespie, Stuart and Philip Hardie (2007, eds), *The Cambridge Companion to Lucretius*. Cambridge: Cambridge University Press

Goldhill, Simon (1996), 'East Coast Oedipus: Suspicious Readings', *Arion* n.s. 4, 155–71

— (2009), 'Undoing in Sophoclean Drama: *Lusis* and the Analysis of Irony', *Transactions of the American Philological Association* 139, 21–52

Goodhart, Sandor (1978), '*Lēistas ephaske*: Oedipus and Laius' Many Murderers', *Diacritics* 8, 55–71

— (1996), *Sacrificing Commentary: Reading the End of Literature*. Baltimore, MD and London: Johns Hopkins University Press

Gotthelf, A. (1985, ed.), *Aristotle on Nature and Living Things*. Cambridge: Cambridge University Press

Grafton, Anthony (1992), *New Worlds, Ancient Texts: The Power of Tradition and the Shock of Discovery*. With April Shelford and Nancy Siraisi. Cambridge, MA and London: Belknap Press of Harvard University Press

Green, Peter (1978), 'Caesar and Alexander: aemulatio, imitation, comparatio', *American Journal of Ancient History* 3, 1–26

Green, R.P.H. (1997, trans.), *Augustine On Christian Teaching*. Oxford: Oxford University Press

Green, Steven J. and Katharina Volk (2011, eds), *Forgotten Stars: Rediscovering Manilius' Astronomica*. Oxford: Oxford University Press

Greenblatt, Stephen (2011), *The Swerve: How the Renaissance Began*. London: The Bodley Head

Gross, Paul R. and Norman Levitt (1994), *Higher Superstition: The Academic Left and its Quarrels with Science*. Baltimore, MD and London: Johns Hopkins University Press

Halliwell, Stephen (1987), *The Poetics of Aristotle: Translation and Commentary*. Chapel Hill, NC: University of North Carolina Press

Hardt, Michael and Antonio Negri (2000), *Empire*. Cambridge, MA and London: Harvard University Press

Hardwick, Lorna and Carol Gillespie (2007, eds), *Classics in Post-Colonial Worlds*. Oxford: Oxford University Press

Harrison, Carol (2006), *Rethinking Augustine's Early Theology: An Argument for Continuity*. Oxford: Oxford University Press

Hawking, Stephen (1988), *A Brief History of Time*. London: Bantam

Hawthorn, Geoffrey (1991), *Plausible Worlds: Possibility and Understanding in History and the Social Sciences*. Cambridge: Cambridge University Press

Hedjuk, J. (2009), 'Jupiter's *Aeneid*: *Fama* and *Imperium*', *Classical Antiquity* 28, 279–327

Hegel, G.W.F. (1975), *Lectures on the Philosophy of World History*. Translated by H.B. Nisbet. Cambridge: Cambridge University Press

Heidegger, Martin (1962), *Being and Time*. Translated by John Macquarrie and Edward Robinson. Oxford: Blackwell Publishing

— (1972), *Of Time and Being*. Translated by Joan Stambaugh. New York: Harper and Row

— (2000), *Introduction to Metaphysics*. Translated by Gregory Fried and Richard Polt. New Haven, CT and London: Yale University Press

Heinze, Richard (1915), *Virgils epische Technik*. 3rd edition. Leipzig and Berlin: B.G. Teubner

— (1993), *Virgil's Epic Technique*. Translated by Hazel and David Harvey and Fred Robertson. London: Bristol Classical Press

Heise, Ursula K. (1997), *Chronoschisms: Time, Narrative, and Postmodernism*. Cambridge: Cambridge University Press

Henderson, John (1989), 'Livy and the Invention of History', in Cameron (1989, ed.), 64–85

Henry, James (1873), *Aeneidea*. London and Edinburgh: Williams and Norgate

Herman, David, Manfred Jahn and Marie-Laure Ryan (2005, eds), *Routledge Encyclopaedia of Narrative Theory*. London and New York: Routledge

Hinds, Stephen (1998), *Allusion and Intertext: Dynamics of Appropriation in Roman Poetry*. Cambridge: Cambridge University Press

Horky, Philip Sidney (2011), 'Herennius Pontius: The Construction of a Samnite Philosopher', *Classical Antiquity* 30, 119–47

Hösle, Vittorio (2005), 'Philosophy and its Languages: A Philosopher's Reflections on the Rise of English as the Universal Academic Language', in Bloomer (2005, ed.), 245–62

Hussey, Edward (1983), *Aristotle* Physics *Books III and IV*. Oxford: Clarendon Press

Inwood, Michael (2000), *Heidegger: A Very Short Introduction*. Oxford: Oxford University Press

Isager, J. (1993), 'Alexander the Great in Roman Literature from Pompey to Vespasian', in Carlsen, Due, Due and Poulsen (1993, eds), 75–84

Jager, Eric (1993), *The Tempter's Voice: Language and the Fall in Medieval Literature*. Ithaca, NY and London: Cornell University Press

— (2000), *The Book of the Heart*. Chicago and London: University of Chicago Press

Kahn, C.H. (1985), 'The Place of the Prime Mover in Aristotle's Teleology', in Gotthelf (1985, ed.), 183–205

Kay, Lily E. (2000), *Who Wrote the Book of Life? A History of the Genetic Code*. Stanford, CA: Stanford University Press

Kennedy, Duncan F. (1999), 'A Sense of Place: Rome, History and Empire Revisited', in Edwards (1999, ed.), 19–34

— (2002), *Rethinking Reality: Lucretius and the Textualization of Nature*. Ann Arbor, MI: University of Michigan Press

— (2006), 'Atoms, Individuals and Myths', in Zajko and Leonard (2006, eds), 233–52

— (2010), 'Knowledge and the Political: Bruno Latour's Political Epistemology', *Cultural Critique* 74, 83–97

— (2011), 'Sums in Verse or a Mathematical Aesthetic?', in Green and Volk (2011, eds), 165–87

— (forthcoming), 'The Political Epistemology of Infinity', in Lehoux, Morrison and Sharrock (forthcoming, eds)

Kenney, E.J. (1974), '*Viuida uis*: Polemic and Pathos in Lucretius 1.62–101', in Woodman and West (1974, eds), 18–30

Kermode, Frank (1966), *The Sense of an Ending: Studies in the Theory of Fiction*. New York: Oxford University Press

— (1983), *The Classic: Literary Images of Permanence and Change*. Cambridge, MA and London: Harvard University Press

Kern, Stephen (2004), *A Cultural History of Causality: Science, Murder Novels, and Systems of Thought*. Princeton, NJ and Oxford: Princeton University Press

King, Peter (1995, trans.), *Augustine: Against the Academicians and The Teacher*. Indianapolis: Hackett Publishing Company, Inc.

Kirwan, Christopher (1989), *Augustine*. London and New York: Routledge and Kegan Paul

König, Jason and Tim Whitmarsh (2007, eds), *Ordering Knowledge in the Roman Empire*. Cambridge: Cambridge University Press

Koselleck, Reinhart (1979), *Vergangene Zukunft: Zur Semantik geschichtlicher Zeiten*. Frankfurt am Main: Suhrkamp Verlag

— (2002), *The Practice of Conceptual History: Timing History, Spacing Concepts*. Translated by Todd Samuel Presner and others. Stanford, CA: Stanford University Press

— (2004), *Futures Past: On the Semantics of Historical Time*. Translated with an Introduction by Keith Tribe. New York and Chichester, West Sussex: Columbia University Press

Kraggerud, E. (1992), 'Which Julius Caesar? On *Aen.* 1, 286–96', *Symbolae Osloenses* 67, 103–12

Labinger, Jay A. and Collins, Harry (2001, eds), *The One Culture? A Conversation About Science*. Chicago and London: University of Chicago Press

Latour, Bruno (1993), *We Have Never Been Modern*. Translated by Catherine Porter. Cambridge, MA: Harvard University Press

— (1999), *Pandora's Hope: Essays on the Reality of Science Studies*. Cambridge, MA and London: Harvard University Press

— (2000), 'On the Partial Existence of Existing *and* Nonexisting Objects', in Daston (2000, ed.), 247–69

— (2004), *Politics of Nature: How to Bring the Sciences into Democracy*. Translated by Catherine Porter. Cambridge, MA and London: Harvard University Press

— (2008), 'Review Essay: The Netz-Works of Greek Deductions', *Social Studies of Science* 38, 441–59

Lattimore, Richmond (1999, trans.), *The Odyssey of Homer*. New York: HarperCollins

Lehoux, Daryn, Andrew Morrison and Alison Sharrock (forthcoming), *Lucretius: Poetry, Philosophy, and Science*. Oxford: Oxford University Press

Leonard, Miriam (2005), *Athens in Paris: Ancient Greece and the Political in Post-war French Thought*. Oxford: Oxford University Press

— (2010, ed.), *Derrida and Antiquity*. Oxford: Oxford University Press

Liveley, Genevieve (2008), 'Paraquel Lines: Time and Narrative in Ovid's *Heroides*', in Liveley and Salzman-Mitchell (2008, eds), 86–102

Liveley, Genevieve and Patricia Salzman-Mitchell (2008, eds), *Latin Elegy and Narratology: Fragments of Story*. Columbus, OH: Ohio State University Press

Lloyd, Genevieve (1993), *Being in Time: Selves and Narrators in Philosophy and Literature*. London and New York: Routledge

— (2008), *Providence Lost*. Cambridge, MA and London: Harvard University Press

Locke, David (1992), *Science as Writing*. New Haven, CT and London: Yale University Press

Long, A.A. and D.N. Sedley (1987), *The Hellenistic Philosophers*. 2 vols. Cambridge: Cambridge University Press

Lucas, D.W. (1968), *Aristotle: Poetics*. Oxford: Clarendon Press

Lyne, R.O.A.M. (1987), *Further Voices in Vergil's Aeneid*. Oxford: Clarendon Press

Lyotard, Jean-François (1984), *The Postmodern Condition: A Report on Knowledge*. Translated by Geoff Bennington and Brian Massumi. Manchester: Manchester University Press

MacCormack, Sabine (1998), *The Shadows of Poetry: Vergil in the Mind of Augustine*. Berkeley, CA, Los Angeles and London: University of California Press

Mack, Sara (1978), *Patterns of Time in Vergil*. Hamden, CT: Archon Books

Majumdar, Deepa (2007), *Plotinus on the Appearance of Time and the World of Sense*. Aldershot and Burlington, VT: Ashgate

Martin, Dale B. and Patricia Cox Miller (2005, eds), *The Cultural Turn in Late Ancient Studies: Gender, Asceticism, and Historiography*. Durham, NC and London: Duke University Press

Martindale, Charles (1997, ed.), *The Cambridge Companion to Virgil*. Cambridge: Cambridge University Press

Mitchell, Stanley (2008, trans.), *Alexander Pushkin: Eugene Onegin*. London: Penguin Books

Mitchell-Boyask, Robin N. (1996), 'Sine fine: Vergil's Masterplot', *American Journal of Philology* 117, 289–307

Morello, Ruth (2002), 'Livy's Alexander Digression (9.17–19): Counterfactuals and Apologetics', *Journal of Roman Studies* 92, 62–85

Morley, Neville (2000), 'Trajan's Engines', *Greece and Rome* 47, 197–210

Morson, Gary Saul (1994), *Narrative and Freedom: The Shadows of Time*. New Haven, CT and London: Yale University Press

Most, Glenn (2000), 'Generating Genres: The Idea of the Tragic', in Depew and Obbink (2000, eds), 15–35

Murphy, Trevor (2004), *Pliny the Elder's Natural History: The Empire in the Encyclopaedia*. Oxford: Oxford University Press

Nabokov, Vladimir (1964), *Eugene Onegin*. 4 vols. New York: Pantheon Books

Netz, Reviel (1999), *The Shaping of Deduction in Greek Mathematics: A Study in Cognitive History*. Cambridge: Cambridge University Press

Nightingale, Andrea (2011), *Once Out of Nature: Augustine on Time and the Body*. Chicago and London: University of Chicago Press

O'Daly, Gerard (1987), *Augustine's Philosophy of Mind*. London: Duckworth

— (1999), *Augustine's City of God: A Reader's Guide*. Oxford: Oxford University Press

O'Donnell, James J. (n.d.), 'Augustine, *City of God*', http://ccat.sas.upenn.edu/jod/augustine/civ.html. Accessed 14 May 2009 (no longer available)

— (1992), *Augustine* Confessions. 3 vols. Oxford: Clarendon Press

— (2005a), 'Augustine's Unconfessions', in Caputo and Scanlon (2005, eds), 212–21

— (2005b), *Augustine: A New Biography*. New York: HarperCollins

O'Hara, James J. (1990), *Death and the Optimistic Prophecy in Vergil's Aeneid*. Princeton: Princeton University Press

— (1996), *True Names: Vergil and the Alexandrian Tradition of Etymological Wordplay*. Ann Arbor: University of Michigan Press

— (2007), *Inconsistency in Roman Epic: Studies in Catullus, Lucretius, Vergil, Ovid and Lucan*. Cambridge: Cambridge University Press

Oakley, S.P. (2005), *A Commentary on Livy Books VI–X*, vol. III, Book IX. Oxford: Clarendon Press

Ober, Josiah (2001), 'Conquest Denied: The Premature Death of Alexander the Great', in Cowley (2001, ed.), 37–56

Olson, Barbara K. (1997), *Authorial Divinity in the Twentieth Century: Omniscient Narration in Woolf, Hemingway, and Others*. Lewisburg, PA: Bucknell University Press

— (2006), '"Who Thinks This Book?" Or Why the Author/God Analogy Merits Our Continued Attention', *Narrative* 14, 339–46

Orwell, George (1969), *Nineteen Eighty-Four*. Harmondsworth: Penguin Books

Pagden, Anthony (1995), *Lords of All the World: Ideologies of Empire in Spain, Britain and France c. 1500–c. 1800*. New Haven, CT and London: Yale University Press

Paschoud, François (1967), *Roma Aeterna: Etudes sur le patriotisme romain dans l'occident latin à l'époque des grandes invasions*. Rome: Institut Suisse

Pelling, Christopher (2006), 'Speech and Narrative in the *Histories*', in Dewald and Marincola (2006, eds), 103–21

Penrose, Roger (1989), *The Emperor's New Mind*. Oxford: Oxford University Press

Peradotto, John (1992), 'Disauthorizing Prophecy: The Ideological Mapping of *Oedipus Tyrannus*', *Transactions of the American Philological Association* 122, 1–15

Price, Leah (2008), Review of Sherman (2008). *London Review of Books*, 9 October 2008

Prickett, Stephen (2002), *Narrative, Religion and Science: Fundamentalism versus Irony, 1700–1999*. Cambridge: Cambridge University Press

Quint, David (1993), *Epic and Empire: Politics and Generic Form from Virgil to Milton*. Princeton: Princeton University Press

Rheinberger, Hans-Jörg (1997), *Toward a History of Epistemic Things: Synthesizing Proteins in the Test Tube*. Stanford, CA: Stanford University Press

Richardson, John (2009), *The Language of Empire: Rome and the Idea of Empire from the Third Century BC to the Second Century AD*. Cambridge: Cambridge University Press

Ricoeur, Paul (1978), *The Rule of Metaphor: The Creation of Meaning in Language*. Translated by Robert Czerny with Kathleen McLaughlin and John Costello, SJ. London and New York: Routledge

— (1984), *Time and Narrative*, vol. 1. Translated by Kathleen McLaughlin and David Pellauer. Chicago and London: University of Chicago Press

— (1985), *Time and Narrative*, vol. 2. Translated by Kathleen McLaughlin and David Pellauer. Chicago and London: University of Chicago Press

— (1988), *Time and Narrative*, vol. 3. Translated by Kathleen Blamey and David Pellauer. Chicago and London: University of Chicago Press

— (1990), *Oneself as Another*. Translated by Kathleen Blamey. Chicago: University of Chicago Press

Ridderbos, Katinka (2002, ed.), *On Time*. Cambridge: Cambridge University Press

Riffaterre, Michael (1981), 'Interview: Michael Riffaterre', *Diacritics* 11, 12–16

Roark, Tony (2011), *Aristotle on Time: A Study of the* Physics. Cambridge: Cambridge University Press

Roberts, Andrew (2004, ed.), *What Might Have Been: Imaginary History From Twelve Leading Historians*. London: Weidenfeld & Nicolson

Rorty, Richard (1978), 'Philosophy as a Kind of Writing: An Essay on Derrida', *New Literary History* 10, 141–60

— (1989), *Contingency, Irony, and Solidarity*. Cambridge: Cambridge University Press

— (1995), 'Philosophy and the Future', in Saatkamp Jr. (1995, ed.), 197–205

Rosenthal, Earl (1971), '*Plus ultra, non plus ultra*, and the Columnar Device of Emperor Charles V', *Journal of the Warburg and Courtauld Institutes* 34, 204–28

Ross, Andrew (1996, ed.), *Science Wars*. Durham, NC and London: Duke University Press

Rothfield, Lawrence (1981), 'Autobiography and Perspective in the *Confessions* of St. Augustine', *Comparative Literature* 33, 209–23

Rouse, Joseph (1996), *Engaging Science: How to Understand its Practices Philosophically*. Ithaca, NY and London: Cornell University Press

Royle, Nicholas (2003), *Jacques Derrida*. London: Routledge

Rudnytsky, Peter L. (1987), *Freud and Oedipus*. New York: Columbia University Press

Runciman, W.G. (2010), *Great Books, Bad Arguments: Republic, Leviathan, and The Communist Manifesto*. Princeton, NJ and Oxford: Princeton University Press

Saatkamp Jr., Herman J. (1995, ed.), *Rorty and Pragmatism: The Philosopher Responds to His Critics*. Nashville, TN and London: Vanderbilt University Press

Sacks, Oliver (1985), *The Man Who Mistook His Wife For a Hat*. London: Duckworth

Schiesaro, Alessandro (2007), 'Lucretius and Roman Politics and History', in Gillespie and Hardie (2007, eds), 41–58

Schrijvers, P.H. (1970), *Horror ac Divina Voluptas: Etudes sur la Poétique et la Poésie de Lucrèce*. Amsterdam: Adolf M. Hakkert

Sedley, David (1998), *Lucretius and the Transformation of Greek Wisdom*. Cambridge: Cambridge University Press

— (2003), *Plato's* Cratylus. Cambridge: Cambridge University Press
— (2007), *Creationism and its Critics in Antiquity*. Berkeley, CA, Los Angeles and London: University of California Press
Segal, Charles (1995), *Sophocles' Tragic World: Divinity, Nature, Society*. Cambridge, MA and London: Harvard University Press
— (2001), *Oedipus Tyrannus: Tragic Heroism and the Limits of Knowledge*. 2nd edition. New York and Oxford: Oxford University Press
Shapin, Steven (1996), *The Scientific Revolution*. Chicago and London: University of Chicago Press
Shapin, Steven and Simon Schaffer (1985), *Leviathan and the Air-Pump: Hobbes, Boyle, and the Experimental Life*. Princeton, NJ: Princeton University Press
Sherman, William H. (2008), *Used Books: Marking Readers in Renaissance England*. Philadelphia, PA: University of Pennsylvania Press
Sizoo, Alexander (1958), 'Ad August. *Conf.* VIII, XII, 29', *Vigiliae Christianae* 12, 104–6
Sorabji, Richard (1983), *Time, Creation and the Continuum: Theories in Antiquity and the Early Middle Ages*. London: Duckworth
Steiner, George (1986), *Antigones: How the Antigone Legend has Endured in Western Literature, Art, and Thought*. Oxford: Clarendon Press
— (1989), *Real Presences*. London and Boston: Faber and Faber
Sternberg, Meir (1978), *Expositional Modes and Temporal Ordering in Fiction*. Bloomington, IN and Indianapolis, IN: Indiana University Press
Stock, Brian (1996), *Augustine the Reader: Meditation, Self-Knowledge, and the Ethics of Interpretation*. Cambridge, MA and London: Harvard University Press
Strawson, Galen (2004), 'Against Narrativity', *Ratio* 17, 428–52
— (2008), *Real Materialism and Other Essays*. Oxford: Clarendon Press
Stump, Eleonore (2001), 'Augustine on Free Will', in Stump and Kretzmann (2001, eds), 124–47
Stump, Eleonore and Norman Kretzmann (2001, eds), *The Cambridge Companion to Augustine*. Cambridge: Cambridge University Press
Suerbaum, W. (1997), 'Am Scheideweg zur Zukunft: alternative Geschehensverläufe bei römischen Historikern', *Gymnasium* 104, 36–54
Tallis, Raymond (2010), *Michelangelo's Finger: An Exploration of Everyday Transcendence*. London: Atlantic Books
Taylor, Charles (1989), *Sources of the Self: The Making of Modern Identity*. Cambridge: Cambridge University Press

— (2007), *A Secular Age*. Cambridge, MA and London: Belknap Press of Harvard University Press

Thilo, G. and H. Hagen (1923), *Servii Grammatici Qui Feruntur in Vergilii Carmina Commentarii*. 2 vols. Leipzig and Berlin: B.G. Teubner

Thompson, E.P. (1978), *The Poverty of Theory and Other Essays*. London: Merlin Press

Tolstoy, Leo (1957), *War and Peace*. Translated by Rosemary Edmonds. Harmondsworth: Penguin Books

Toynbee, A.J. (1969), *Some Problems of Greek History*. Oxford: Oxford University Press

Vance, E. (1973), 'Augustine's *Confessions* and the Grammar of Selfhood', *Genre* 6, 1–28

— (1984), 'The Functions and Limits of Autobiography in Augustine's *Confessions*', *Poetics Today* 5, 399–409

Vattimo, Giani (2011), *A Farewell to Truth*. Translated by William McCuaig. New York: Columbia University Press

Velleman, J. David (2003), 'Narrative Explanation', *Philosophical Review* 112, 1–25

Vernant, Jean-Pierre and Pierre Vidal-Naquet (1988), *Myth and Tragedy in Ancient Greece*. Translated by Janet Lloyd. New York: Zone Books

Vessey, Mark (2005), 'History, Fiction, and Figuralism in Book 8 of Augustine's *Confessions*', in Martin and Miller (2005, eds), 237–57

Walbank, F.W. (1970), *A Historical Commentary on Polybius*. 3 vols. Oxford: Clarendon Press

Waquet, Françoise (2001), *Latin Or the Empire of a Sign*. Translated by John Howe. London and New York: Verso

Waterfield, Robin (1996, trans.), *Aristotle: Physics*. Oxford: Oxford University Press

Wilcox, Donald J. (1987), *The Measure of Times Past: Pre-Newtonian Chronologies and the Rhetoric of Relative Time*. Chicago and London: University of Chicago Press

Willis, Ika (2007), 'The Empire Never Ended', in Hardwick and Gillespie (2007, eds), 329–48

— (2010), *Now and Rome*. London: Continuum Books

Wills, Garry (2011), *Augustine's Confessions: A Biography*. Princeton, NJ and Oxford: Princeton University Press

Wood, David (2001), *The Deconstruction of Time*. Evanston, IL: Northwestern University Press

Wood, Michael (2003), *The Road to Delphi: The Life and Afterlife of Oracles*. New York: Farrar, Straus and Giroux

Woodman, Tony and David West (1974, eds), *Quality and Pleasure in Latin Poetry*. Cambridge: Cambridge University Press

Yates, Frances A. (1975), *Astraea: The Imperial Theme in the Sixteenth Century*. London: Routledge and Kegan Paul

Zajko, Vanda and Miriam Leonard (2006, eds), *Laughing with Medusa: Classical Myth and Feminist Thought*. Oxford: Oxford University Press

INDEX

www.ingramcontent.com/pod-product-compliance
Lightning Source LLC
Chambersburg PA
CBHW070445030726
47503CB00004B/907